Sheena Iyengar is a professor at the Columbia Business School, with a joint appointment in the Department of Psychology. She is recognised as one of the world's leading experts on choice and has been the recipient of numerous honours, most notably the Presidential Early Career Award in 2002. Her work is regularly cited in the *New York Times*, the *Wall Street Journal*, *Fortune*, and *Time* magazines, the BBC and National Public Radio, as well as in bestselling books such as *Blink* by Malcolm Gladwell. Sheena currently resides in New York City with her husband, Garud, and their son, Ishaan.

THE ART OF CHOOSING

SHEENA IYENGAR

Little, Brown

LITTLE, BROWN

First published in 2010 by Little, Brown
Reprinted 2010

First published in the United States of America in 2010 by Twelve,
an imprint of Grand Central Publishing

Copyright © Sheena Iyengar 2010

A CIP catalogue record for this book
is available from the British Library.

ISBN 978-1-4087-0262-8
ISBN 978-1-4087-0003-7

Printed and bound in Great Britain by
Clays Ltd, St Ives plc

Papers used by Little, Brown are natural, renewable and
recyclable products sourced from well-managed forests and certified
in accordance with the rules of the Forest Stewardship Council.

Mixed Sources
Product group from well-managed
forests and other controlled sources
www.fsc.org Cert no. SGS-COC-004081
© 1996 Forest Stewardship Council

FSC

Little, Brown
An imprint of
Little, Brown Book Group
100 Victoria Embankment
London EC4Y 0DY

An Hachette UK Company
www.hachette.co.uk

www.littlebrown.co.uk

To Dad, who told me anything was possible
To Mom, for being there every step of the way

Contents

Past Is Prologue

Everything begins with a story.
—Joseph Campbell

I was born in Toronto, one month early and during a blizzard that covered the city in snow and silence. The surprise and the low-visibility conditions that accompanied my arrival were portents, though they went unrecognized at the time. My mother, as a recent immigrant from India, was of two worlds, and she would pass that multiple identity on to me. My father was making his way to Canada, but had not yet arrived; his absence at my birth was a sign of the deeper absence yet to come. Looking back, I see all the ways in which my life was set the moment I was born into it. Whether in the stars or in stone, whether by the hand of God or some unnameable force, it was already written, and every action of mine would serve to confirm the text.

That is one story. Here's another.

You never know, do you? It's a jack-in-the-box life: You open it carefully, one parcel at a time, but things keep springing up and out. That's how I came into the world—suddenly—a month before I was due, my father not even able to receive me. He was still in India, where my mother had always imagined she, too, would be. Yet, somehow, she had ended up in Toronto with me in her arms, and through the window she could see the snow whirling. Like those flakes of ice, we were carried to other places: Flushing, Queens, and then Elmwood Park, New Jersey. I grew up in enclaves of Sikh immigrants, who—like my parents—had left India but had also brought it with them. And so I was raised in a country within a country, my parents trying to re-create the life that was familiar to them.

Three days a week, they took me to the *gurudwara*, or temple, where I sat on the right side with the women, while the men clustered on the left. In accordance with the articles of the Sikh faith, I kept my hair long and uncut, a symbol of the perfection of God's creation. I wore a *kara*, a steel bracelet, on my right wrist as a symbol of my resilience and devotion, and as a reminder that whatever I did was done under the watchful eyes of God. At all times, even in the shower, I wore a *kachchha*, an undergarment that resembled boxers and represented control over sexual desire. These were just some of the rules I followed, as do all observant Sikhs, and whatever was not dictated by religion was decided by my parents. Ostensibly, this was for my own good, but life has a way of poking holes in your plans, or in the plans others make for you.

As a toddler, I constantly ran into things, and at first my parents thought I was just very clumsy. But surely a parking meter was a large enough obstacle to avoid? And why did I need to be warned so frequently to watch where I was going? When it became obvious that I was no ordinary klutz, I was taken to a vision specialist at Columbia Presbyterian Hospital. He quickly solved the mystery: I had a rare form of retinitis pigmentosa, an inherited disease of retinal degeneration, which had left me with 20/400 vision. By the time I reached high school, I was fully blind, able to perceive only light.

A surprise today does prepare us, I suppose, for the ones still in store. Coping with blindness must have made me more resilient. (Or was I able to cope well *because* of my innate resilience?) No matter how prepared we are, though, we can still have the wind knocked out of us. I was 13 when my father died. That morning, he dropped my mother off at work in Harlem and promised to see a doctor for the leg pain and breathing problems he'd been having. At the doctor's office, however, there was some confusion about his appointment time, and no one could see him right then. Frustrated by this—and already stressed for other reasons—he stormed out of the office and pounded the pavement, until he collapsed in front of a bar. The bartender pulled him inside and called for an ambulance, and my father was eventually taken to the hospital, but he could not survive the multiple heart attacks he had suffered by the time he got there.

This is not to say that our lives are shaped solely by random and unpleasant events, but they do seem, for better or worse, to move forward along largely unmapped terrain. To what extent can you direct your own life when you can see only so far and the weather changes quicker than you can say "Surprise!"?

———

Wait. I have still another story for you. And though it is mine, once again, I suspect that this time you will see your own in it, too.

In 1971, my parents emigrated from India to America by way of Canada. Like so many before them, when they landed on the shores of this new country and a new life, they sought the American Dream. They soon found out that pursuing it entailed many hardships, but they persevered. I was born into the dream, and I think I understood it better than my parents did, for I was more fluent in American culture. In particular, I realized that the shining thing at its center—so bright you could see it even if you, like me, were blind—was choice.

My parents had chosen to come to this country, but they had also chosen to hold on to as much of India as possible. They lived among other Sikhs, followed closely the tenets of their religion, and taught me the value of obedience. What to eat, wear, study, and later on, where to work and whom to marry—I was to allow these to be determined by the rules of Sikhism and by my family's wishes. But in public school I learned that it was not only natural but desirable that I should make my own decisions. It was not a matter of cultural background or personality or abilities; it was simply what was true and right. For a blind Sikh girl otherwise subject to so many restrictions, this was a very powerful idea. I could have thought of my life as already written, which would have been more in line with my parents' views. Or I could have thought of it as a series of accidents beyond my control, which was one way to account for my blindness and my father's death. However, it seemed much more promising to think of it in terms of choice, in terms of what was still possible and what I could make happen.

Many of us have conceived and told our stories only in the language of choice. It is certainly the lingua franca of America, and its use has risen rapidly in much of the rest of the world. We are more likely to recognize one another's stories when we tell them in this language, and as I hope to show in this book, "speaking choice" has many benefits. But I also hope to reveal other ways in which we live and tell our lives and form narratives that are more complex and nuanced than the simplified alternatives of Destiny and Chance that I have presented here.

———

The informal study of choice that I undertook as a child turned academic when I got to college. At the University of Pennsylvania, I studied different religious groups to find out how religion affects one's outlook on life. This research suggested that ideas about choice vary widely, that my experience as a Sikh and an American had exposed me to only a small set of them. Later, as a doctoral student in social psychology at Stanford University, I compared the construction and practice of choice across cultures. I examined cultural differences and also the everyday factors that affect our choices. This has been the focus of my work for the past 15 years.

"Choice" can mean so many different things and its study can be approached in so many different ways that one book cannot contain its fullness. I aim to explore those aspects of it that I have found to be most thought provoking and most relevant to how we live. This book is firmly grounded in psychology, but I draw on various fields and disciplines, including business, economics, biology, philosophy, cultural studies, public policy, and medicine. In doing so, I hope to present as many perspectives as possible and to challenge received notions about the role and practice of choice in our lives.

Each of the following seven chapters will look at choice from a different vantage point and tackle various questions about the way choice affects our lives. Why is choice powerful, and where does its power come from? Do we all choose in the same way? What is the relationship between how we choose and who we are? Why are we so often disappointed by our choices, and how do we make the most effective use of the tool of choice? How much control do we really have over our everyday choices? How do we choose when our options are practically unlimited? Should we ever let others choose for us, and if yes, who and why? Whether or not you agree with my opinions, suggestions, and conclusions—and I'm sure we won't always see eye to eye—just the process of exploring these questions can help you make more informed decisions. Choice, ranging from the trivial to the life-altering, in both its presence and its absence, is an inextricable part of our life stories. As you read this book, I hope you will gain insight into yourself, your life, how it all began, and where it is headed.

THE ART OF
CHOOSING

What is freedom? Freedom is the right to choose:
the right to create for oneself the alternatives of choice.
Without the possibility of choice a man is not a man
but a member, an instrument, a thing.

—Archibald MacLeish,
     Pulitzer Prize–winning American poet

CHAPTER ONE

The Call of the Wild

I. SURVIVORSHIP

What would you do? If you were stranded at sea in a small inflatable raft, or stuck in the mountains with a broken leg, or just generally up the proverbial creek without a paddle, what do you suppose you would do? How long, say, would you swim before letting yourself drown? How long could you hold out hope? We ask these questions—over dinner, at parties, on lazy Sunday afternoons—not because we're looking for survival tips but because we're fascinated by our limits and our ability to cope with the kinds of extreme conditions for which there is little preparation or precedent. Who among us, we want to know, would live to tell the tale?

Take Steven Callahan, for example. On February 5, 1982, some 800 miles west of the Canary Islands, his boat, the *Napoleon Solo*, capsized in a storm. Callahan, then 30, found himself alone and adrift in a leaky inflatable raft with few resources. He collected rainwater for drinking and fashioned a makeshift spear for fishing. He ate barnacles and sometimes the birds attracted to the remains of those barnacles. To maintain his sanity, he took notes on his experience and did yoga whenever his weak body allowed it. Other than that, he waited and drifted west. Seventy-six days later, on April 21, a boat discovered Callahan off the coast of Guadeloupe. Even today, he is one of the only people to have lasted more than a month at sea on his own.

Callahan—an experienced mariner—possessed seafaring skills that were undoubtedly critical to his survival, but were these alone enough to save him? In his book *Adrift: Seventy-six Days Lost at Sea*, he describes his state of mind not long after the disaster:

> About me lie the remnants of *Solo*. My equipment is properly secured, vital systems are functioning, and daily priorities are set, priorities not to be argued with. I somehow rise above mutinous apprehension, fear, and pain. I am captain of my tiny ship in treacherous waters. I escaped the confused turmoil following *Solo*'s loss, and I have finally gotten food and water. I have overcome almost certain death. I now have a choice: to pilot myself to a new life or to give up and watch myself die. I choose to kick as long as I can.

Callahan framed his situation, dire though it was, in terms of choice. A vast ocean stretched before him on all sides. He saw nothing but its endless blue surface, below which lurked many dangers. However, in the lapping of the waves and the whistle of the wind, he did not hear a verdict of death. Instead, he heard a question: "Do you want to live?" The ability to hear that question and to answer it in the affirmative—to reclaim for himself the choice that the circumstances seemed to have taken away—may be what enabled him to survive. Next time someone asks you, "What would you do?," you might take a page from Callahan's book and reply, "I would choose."

Joe Simpson, another famous survivor, almost died during his descent from a mountain in the icy heights of the Peruvian Andes. After breaking his leg in a fall, he could barely walk, so his climbing partner, Simon Yates, attempted to lower him to safety using ropes.

When Yates, who couldn't see or hear Simpson, unwittingly lowered him over the edge of a cliff, Simpson could no longer steady himself against the face of the mountain or climb back up. Yates now had to support all of Simpson's weight; sooner or later, he would no longer be able to do so, and both of them would plummet to their deaths. Finally, seeing no alternative, Yates cut the rope, believing he was sentencing his friend to death. What happened next was remarkable: Simpson fell onto a ledge in a crevasse, and over the next few days, he crawled five miles across a glacier, reaching base camp just as Yates was preparing to leave. In *Touching the Void*, his account of the incident, Simpson writes:

> The desire to stop abseiling was almost unbearable. I had no idea what lay below me, and I was certain of only two things: Simon had gone and would not return. This meant that to stay on the ice bridge would finish me. There was no escape upwards, and the drop on the other side was nothing more than an invitation to end it all quickly. I had been tempted, but even in my despair I found that I didn't have the courage for suicide. It would be a long time before cold and exhaustion overtook me on the ice bridge, and the idea of waiting alone and maddened for so long had forced me to this choice: abseil until I could find a way out, or die in the process. I would meet it rather than wait for it to come to me. There was no going back now, yet inside I was screaming to stop.

For the willful Callahan and Simpson, survival was a matter of choice. And as presented by Simpson, in particular, the choice was an imperative rather than an opportunity; you might squander the latter, but it's almost impossible to resist the former.

Though most of us will never experience such extreme circumstances (we hope), we are nonetheless faced daily with our own imperatives to choose. Should we act or should we hang back and observe?

Calmly accept whatever comes our way, or doggedly pursue the goals we have set for ourselves? We measure our lives using different markers: years, major events, achievements. We can also measure them by the choices we make, the sum total of which has brought us to wherever and whoever we are today. When we view life through this lens, it becomes clear that choice is an enormously powerful force, an essential determinant of how we live. But from where does the power of choice originate, and how best can we take advantage of it?

II. OF RATS AND MEN

In 1957 Curt Richter, a prolific psychobiology researcher at Johns Hopkins School of Medicine, conducted an experiment that you might find shocking. To study the effect of water temperature on endurance, Richter and his colleagues placed dozens of rats into glass jars—one rodent per jar—and then filled the jars with water. Because the walls of these jars were too high and slick to climb, the rats were left in a literal sink-or-swim situation. Richter even had water jets blasting from above to force the rats below the surface if they tried to float idly instead of swimming for their lives. He then measured how long the rats swam—without food, rest, or chance of escape—before they drowned.

The researchers were surprised to find that even when the water temperatures were identical, rats of equal fitness swam for markedly different lengths of time. Some continued swimming for an average of 60 hours before succumbing to exhaustion, while others sank almost immediately. It was as though, after struggling for 15 minutes, some rats simply gave up, while others were determined to push themselves to the utmost physical limit. The perplexed researchers wondered whether some rats were more convinced than others that if they continued to swim, they would eventually escape. Were rats even capable of having different "convictions"? But what else could account for such a significant disparity in performance, especially when the survival instinct of *all* the rats must have kicked in? Perhaps the rats that showed more resilience had somehow been given reason to expect escape from their terrible predicament.

So in the next round of the experiment, rather than throwing them into the water straightaway, researchers first picked up the rats several times, each time allowing them to wriggle free. After they had become accustomed to such handling, the rats were placed in the jars, blasted with water for several minutes, then removed and returned to their cages. This process was repeated multiple times. Finally, the rats were put into the jars for the sink-or-swim test. This time, none of the rats showed signs of giving up. They swam for an average of more than 60 hours before becoming exhausted and drowning.

We're probably uncomfortable describing rats as having "beliefs," but having previously wriggled away from their captors and having also survived blasts of water, they seemed to believe they could not only withstand unpleasant circumstances but break free of them. Their experience had taught them that they had some control over the outcome and, perhaps, that rescue was just around the corner. In their incredible persistence, they were not unlike Callahan and Simpson, so could we say that these rats made a choice? Did they *choose* to live, at least for as long as their bodies could hold out?

There's a suffering that comes when persistence is unrewarded, and then there's the heartbreak of possible rescue gone unrecognized. In 1965, at Cornell University, psychologist Martin Seligman launched a series of experiments that fundamentally changed the way we think about control. His research team began by leading mongrel dogs—around the same size as beagles or Welsh corgis—into a white cubicle, one by one, and suspending them in rubberized, cloth harnesses. Panels were placed on either side of each dog's head, and a yoke between the panels—across the neck—held the head in place. Every dog was assigned a partner dog located in a different cubicle.

During the experiment each pair of dogs was periodically subjected to physically nondamaging yet painful electrical shocks, but there was a crucial difference between the two dogs' cubicles: One could put an end to the shock simply by pressing the side panels with its head, while the other could not turn it off, no matter how it writhed. The shocks were synchronized, starting at the same moment for each dog in the pair, and ending for both when the dog with the ability to deactivate pressed the side panel. Thus, the amount of shock was identical for the pair, but one dog experienced the pain as controllable, while the other did not. The dogs that could do nothing to end the shocks on their own soon began to cower and whine, signs of anxiety and depression that continued even after the sessions were over. The dogs that could stop the shocks, however, showed some irritation but soon learned to anticipate the pain and avoid it by pressing their panels.

In the second phase of the experiment, both dogs in the pair were exposed to a new situation to see how they would apply what they'd learned from being in—or out of—control. Researchers put each dog in a large black box with two compartments, divided by a low wall that came up to about shoulder height on the animals. On the dog's side, the floor was periodically electrified. On the other side, it was not. The wall was low enough to jump over, and the dogs that had previously been able to stop the shocks quickly figured out how to escape. But of the dogs that had not been able to end the shocks, two-thirds lay passively on the floor and suffered. The shocks continued, and although the dogs whined, they made no attempt to free themselves. Even when they saw other dogs jumping the wall, and even after researchers dragged them to the other side of the box to show them that the shocks were escapable, the dogs still gave up and endured the pain. For them, the freedom from pain just on the other side of the wall—so near and so readily accessible—was invisible.

When we speak of choice, what we mean is the ability to exercise control over ourselves and our environment. In order to choose, we must first perceive that control is possible. The rats kept swimming despite mounting fatigue and no apparent means of escape because they had already tasted freedom, which—as far as they knew—they had attained through their own vigorous wriggling efforts. The dogs, on the other hand, having earlier suffered a complete loss of control, had learned that they were helpless. When control was restored to them later on, their behavior didn't change because they still could not *perceive* the control. For all practical purposes, they remained helpless. In other words, how much choice the animals *technically* had was far less important than how much choice they *felt* they had. And while the rats were doomed because of the design of the experiment, the persistence they exhibited could well have paid off in the real world, as it did for Callahan and Simpson.

III. CHOICE ON THE MIND

When we look in the mirror, we see some of the "instruments" necessary for choice. Our eyes, nose, ears, and mouth gather information from our environment, while our arms and legs enable us to act on it. We depend on these capabilities to effectively negotiate between hunger and satiation, safety and vulnerability, even between life and death. Yet our ability to *choose* involves more than simply reacting to sensory information. Your knee may twitch if hit in the right place by a doctor's rubber mallet, but no one would consider this reflex to be a choice. To be able to truly choose, we must evaluate all available options and select the best one, making the mind as vital to choice as the body.

Thanks to recent advances in technology, such as functional magnetic resonance imaging (fMRI) scans, we can identify the main brain system engaged when making choices: the corticostriatal network. Its first major component, the striatum, is buried deep in the middle of the brain and is relatively consistent in size and function across the animal kingdom, from reptiles to birds to mammals. It is part of a set of structures known as the basal ganglia, which serve as a sort of switchboard connecting the higher and lower mental functions. The striatum receives sensory information from other parts of the brain and has a role in planning movement, which is critical for our choice making. But its main choice-related function has to do with evaluating the reward associated with the experience; it is responsible for alerting us that "sugar = good" and "root canal = bad." Essentially, it provides the mental connection needed for wanting what we want.

Yet the mere knowledge that sweet things are appealing and root canals excruciating is not enough to guide our choices. We must also make the connection that under certain conditions, too much of a sweet thing can eventually lead to a root canal. This is where the other half of the corticostriatal network, the prefrontal cortex, comes into play. Located directly behind our foreheads, the prefrontal cortex acts as the brain's command center, receiving messages from the striatum and other parts of the body and using those messages to determine and execute the best overall course of action. It is involved in making complex cost-benefit analyses of immediate and future consequences. It also enables us to exercise impulse control when we are tempted to give in to something that we know to be detrimental to us in the long run.

The development of the prefrontal cortex is a perfect example of natural selection in action. While humans and animals both possess a prefrontal cortex, the percentage of the brain it occupies in humans is larger than in any other species, granting us an unparalleled ability to choose "rationally," superseding all other competing instincts. This facility improves with age, as our prefrontal cortex continues to develop well past adolescence. While motor abilities are largely developed by childhood, and factual reasoning abilities by adolescence, the prefrontal cortex undergoes a process of growth and consolidation that continues into our mid-20s. This is why young children have more difficulty understanding abstract concepts than adults, and both children and teenagers are especially prone to acting on impulse.

The ability to choose well is arguably the most powerful tool for controlling our environment. After all, it is humans who have dominated the planet, despite a conspicuous absence of sharp claws, thick hides, wings, or other obvious defenses. We are born with the tools to exercise choice, but just as significantly, we're born with the desire to do so. Neurons in the striatum, for example, respond more to rewards that people or animals actively choose than to identical rewards that are passively received. As the song goes, "Fish gotta swim, birds gotta fly," and we all gotta choose.

This desire to choose is so innate that we act on it even before we can express it. In a study of infants as young as four months, researchers attached strings to the infants' hands and let them learn that by tugging the string, they could cause pleasant music to play. When the researchers later broke the association with the string, making the music play at random intervals instead, the children became sad and angry, even though the experiment was designed so that they heard the same amount of music as when they had activated the music themselves. These children didn't *only* want to hear music; they craved the power to choose it.

Ironically, while the power of choice lies in its ability to unearth the best option possible out of all those presented, sometimes the desire to choose is so strong that it can interfere with the pursuit of these very benefits. Even in situations where there is no advantage to having more choice, meaning that it actually raises the cost in time and effort, choice is still instinctively preferred. In one experiment, rats in a maze were given the option of taking a direct path or one that branched into several other paths. The direct and the branched paths eventually led to the same amount of food, so one held no advantage over the other. Nevertheless, over multiple trials, nearly every rat preferred to take the branching path. Similarly, pigeons and monkeys that learned to press buttons to dispense food preferred to have a choice of multiple buttons to press, even though the choice of two buttons as opposed to one didn't result in a greater food reward. And though humans can consciously override this preference, this doesn't necessarily mean we will. In another experiment, people given a casino chip preferred to spend it at a table with two identical roulette-style wheels rather than at a table with a single wheel, even though they could bet on only one of the wheels, and *all three* wheels were identical.

The desire to choose is thus a natural drive, and though it most likely developed because it is a crucial aid to our survival, it often operates independently of any concrete benefits. In such cases, the power of choice is so great that it becomes not merely a means to an end but something intrinsically valuable and necessary. So what happens when we enjoy the benefits that choice is meant to confer but our need for choice itself is not met?

IV. THE PANTHER IN THE GILDED CAGE

Imagine the ultimate luxury hotel. There's gourmet food for breakfast, lunch, and dinner. During the day, you do as you please: lounge by the pool, get a spa treatment, romp in the game room. At night, you sleep in a king-size bed with down pillows and 600-thread-count sheets. The staff is ever present and ever pleasant, happy to fulfill any requests you might have, and the hotel even boasts state-of-the-art medical services. You can bring your whole family and socialize with lots of new people. If you're single, you might find that special someone among all the attractive men and women around. And the best part is that it's free. There's just one small catch: Once you check in, you can never leave.

No, it's not the famous Hotel California. Such luxurious imprisonment is the norm for animals in zoos across the world. Since the

1970s and 1980s, zoos have strived to reproduce the natural habitats of their animals, replacing concrete floors and steel bars with grass, boulders, trees, and pools of water. These environments may simulate the wild, but the animals don't have to worry about finding food, shelter, or safety from predators; all the necessities of life seem to be provided for them. While this may not seem like such a bad deal at first glance, the animals experience numerous complications. The zebras live constantly under the sword of Damocles, smelling the lions in the nearby Great Cats exhibit every day and finding themselves unable to escape. There's no possibility of migrating or of hoarding food for the winter, which must seem to promise equally certain doom to a bird or bear. In fact, the animals have no way of even knowing whether the food that has magically appeared each day thus far will appear again tomorrow, and no power to provide for themselves. In short, zoo life is utterly incompatible with an animal's most deeply ingrained survival instincts.

In spite of the dedication of their human caretakers, animals in zoos may feel caught in a death trap because they exert minimal control over their own lives. Every year, undaunted by the extensive moats, walls, nets, and glass surrounding their habitats, many animals attempt escape, and some of them even succeed. In 2008, Bruno, a 29-year-old orangutan at the Los Angeles Zoo, punched a hole in the mesh surrounding his habitat, only to find himself in a holding pen. No one was hurt, but 3,000 visitors were evacuated before Bruno was sedated by a handler. A year earlier, a four-year-old Siberian tiger known as Tatiana had jumped the 25-foot moat at the San Diego Zoo, killing one person and injuring two others before she was shot dead. And in 2004, at the Berlin Zoo, the Andean bespectacled bear Juan used a log to "surf" his way across the moat surrounding his habitat before climbing a wall to freedom. After he had taken a whirl on the zoo's merry-go-round and a few trips down the slide, he was shot with a tranquilizer dart by zoo officials.

These and countless other stories reveal that the need for control is a powerful motivator, even when it can lead to harm. This isn't only because exercising control feels good, but because being unable to do so is naturally unpleasant and stressful. Under duress, the endocrine system produces stress hormones such as adrenaline that prepare the body for dealing with immediate danger. We've all felt the fight-or-flight response in a dangerous situation or when stressed, frustrated, or panicked. Breathing and heart rates increase and the blood vessels narrow, enabling oxygen-rich blood to be pumped quickly to the extremities. Energy spent on bodily processes such as digestion and maintaining the immune system is temporarily reduced, freeing more energy for sudden action. Pupils dilate, reflexes quicken, and concentration increases. Only when the crisis has passed does the body resume normal function.

Such responses are survival-enhancing for short-term situations in the wild because they motivate an animal to terminate the source of stress and regain control. But when the source of stress is unending—that is, when it can't be fled or fought—the body continues its stressed response until it is exhausted. Animals in a zoo still experience anxiety over basic survival needs and the possibility of predator attacks because they don't know that they're safe. Physically, remaining in a constant state of heightened alert can induce a weakened immune system, ulcers, and even heart problems. Mentally, this stress can cause a variety of repetitive and sometimes self-destructive behaviors known as stereotypies, the animal equivalent of wringing one's hands or biting one's lip, which are considered a sign of depression or anxiety by most biologists.

Gus, the 700-pound polar bear at the Central Park Zoo, exhibited such behavior back in 1994 when, to the dismay of zoo-goers and his keepers, he spent the bulk of his time swimming an endless series of short laps. In order to address his neuroses, Gus—a true New Yorker—was set up with a therapist: animal behaviorist Tim Desmond, known for training the whale in *Free Willy*. Desmond concluded that Gus needed more challenges and opportunities to exercise his instincts. Gus wanted to feel as if he still had the ability to choose where he spent his time and how—he needed to reassume control of his own destiny. Similarly, the frequent grooming that pet hamsters and lab mice engage in isn't due to their fastidious natures; it's a nervous habit that can continue until they completely rub and gnaw away patches of their fur. If administered fluoxetine, the anti-depressant most commonly known as Prozac, the animals reduce or discontinue these behaviors.

Due to these physically and psychologically harmful effects, captivity can often result in lower life expectancies despite objectively improved living conditions. Wild African elephants, for example, have an average life span of 56 years as compared to 17 years for zoo-born elephants. Other deleterious effects include fewer births (a chronic problem with captive pandas) and high infant mortality rates (over 65 percent for polar bears). Though this is bad news for any captive animal, it is especially alarming in the case of endangered species.

For all the material comforts zoos provide and all their attempts to replicate animals' natural habitats as closely as possible, even the most sophisticated zoos cannot match the level of stimulation and exercise of natural instincts that animals experience in the wild. The desperation of a life in captivity is perhaps conveyed best in Rainer Maria Rilke's poem "The Panther": As the animal "paces in cramped circles, over and over," he seems to perform "a ritual dance around a center / in which a mighty will stands paralyzed." Unlike the dogs in the Seligman experiment, the panther displays his paralysis not by lying still, but by constantly moving. Just like the helpless dogs, however, he cannot see past his confinement: "It seems to him there are / a thousand bars; and behind the bars, no world." Whether the bars are real or metaphorical, when one has no control, it is as if nothing exists beyond the pain of this loss.

V. CHOOSING HEALTH, HEALTHY CHOOSING

While we may not face the threat of captivity like our animal counterparts, humans voluntarily create and follow systems that restrict
some of our individual choices to benefit the greater good. We vote
to create laws, enact contracts, and agree to be gainfully employed
because we recognize that the alternative is chaos. But what happens
when our ability to rationally recognize the benefits of these restrictions conflicts with an instinctive aversion to them? The degree to
which we are able to strike a balance of control in our lives has a
significant bearing on our health.

A decades-long research project known as the Whitehall Studies, conducted by Professor Michael Marmot of University College
London, provides a powerful demonstration of how our perceptions
of choice can affect our well-being. Beginning in 1967, researchers
followed more than 10,000 British civil servants aged 20 to 64, comparing the health outcomes of employees from different pay grades.
Contradicting the stereotype of the hard-charging boss who drops
dead of a heart attack at 45, the studies found that although the
higher-paying jobs came with greater pressure, employees in the lowest pay grade, such as doormen, were three times more likely to die
from coronary heart disease than the highest-grade workers were.

In part, this was because lower-grade employees were more likely
to smoke and be overweight, and less likely to exercise regularly,
than their higher-grade counterparts. But when scientists accounted
for the differences in smoking, obesity, and exercise, the lowest-
grade employees were still twice as likely to die from heart disease.
Though the higher income that comes with being at the top of the
ladder obviously enhances the potential for control in one's life, this
isn't the sole explanation for the poorer health of the lower-grade
employees. Even employees from the second-highest grade, including doctors, lawyers, and other professionals considered well-off by
society's standards, were at notably higher risk than their bosses.

As it turned out, the chief reason for these results was that pay grades directly correlated with the degree of control employees had over their work. The boss took home a bigger paycheck, but more importantly, he directed his own tasks as well as those of his assistants. Although a CEO's shouldering of responsibility for his company's profit is certainly stressful, it turns out that his assistant's responsibility for, say, collating an endless number of memos is even more stressful. The less control people had over their work, the higher their blood pressure during work hours. Moreover, blood pressure at home was unrelated to the level of job control, indicating that the spike during work hours was specifically caused by lack of choice on the job. People with little control over their work also experienced more back pain, missed more days of work due to illness in general, and had higher rates of mental illness—the human equivalent of stereotypies, resulting in the decreased quality of life common to animals reared in captivity.

Unfortunately, the news only gets worse. Several studies have found that apart from the stressors at work, we suffer greatly due to elements of the daily grind that are beyond our control, such as interruptions, traffic jams, missing the bus, smog, and noisy or flickering fluorescent lights. The very agitation and muscle tension that enable quick, lifesaving movement in the wild can lead to frustration and backache in the modern world. Fight or flight was never intended to address 6:30 a.m. wake-up calls or the long commute to a dead-end job. Because we can't recover with time, these continuous low-grade stressors can actually deteriorate health to a greater extent than infrequent calamities like getting fired or going through a divorce. When it comes to lack of control, often the devil is indeed in the details.

Is there any hope, then, for those who can't or choose not to climb the corporate ladder? The Whitehall Studies, though disturbing, suggest there is. What affected people's health most in these studies wasn't the actual level of control that people had in their jobs, but the amount of control they perceived themselves as having. True, the lower-ranked employees perceived less control on average than those higher up because their jobs actually offered less control, but within each position there was considerable variation in people's perceptions of their control and their corresponding measures of health. Thus, a well-compensated executive who feels helpless will suffer the same type of negative physiological response as a low-paid mailroom clerk.

Unlike captive animals, people's perceptions of control or help-lessness aren't entirely dictated by outside forces. We have the ability to *create* choice by altering our interpretations of the world. Callahan's choice to live rather than die is an extreme example, but by asserting control in seemingly uncontrollable situations, we can improve our health and happiness. People who perceive the negative experiences in their lives as the result of uncontrollable forces are at a higher risk for depression than those who believe they have control. They are less likely to try to escape damaging situations such as drug addiction or abusive relationships. They are also less likely to survive heart attacks and more likely to suffer weakened immune systems, asthma, arthritis, ulcers, headaches, or backaches. So what does it take to cultivate "learned optimism," adjusting our vision to see that we have control rather than passively suffering the shocks of life?

We can find some clues in a 1976 study at Arden House, a nursing home in Connecticut, where scientists Ellen Langer and Judy Rodin manipulated the perception of control among residents aged 65 to 90. To begin, the nursing home's social coordinator called separate meetings for the residents of two different floors. At the first floor's meeting he handed out a plant to each resident and informed them that the nurses would take care of their plants for them. He also told them that movies were screened on Thursdays and Fridays, and that they would be scheduled to see the movie on one of those days. He assured residents that they were *permitted* to visit with people on other floors and engage in different types of activities, such as reading, listening to the radio, and watching TV. The focus of his message was that the residents were *allowed* to do some things, but the responsibility for their well-being lay in the competent hands of the staff, an approach that was the norm for nursing homes at that time (and still is). As the coordinator said, "We feel it is our responsibility to make this a home you can be proud of and happy in, and we want to do all we can to help you."

Then the coordinator called a meeting for the other floor. This time he let each resident choose which plant he or she wanted, and told them that taking care of the plants would be their responsibility. He likewise allowed them to choose whether to watch the weekly movie screening on Thursday or Friday, and reminded them of the many ways in which they could *choose* to spend their time, such as visiting with other residents, reading, listening to the radio, and watching TV. Overall he emphasized that it was the residents' responsibility to make their new home a happy place. "It's your life," he said. "You can make of it whatever you want."

Despite the differences in these messages, the staff treated the residents of the two floors identically, giving them the same amount of attention. Moreover, the additional choices given to the second group of residents were seemingly trivial, since everyone got a plant and saw the same movie each week, whether on Thursday or Friday. Nevertheless, when examined three weeks later, the residents who had been given more choices were happier and more alert, and they interacted more with other residents and staff than those who hadn't been given the same choices. Even within the short, three-week time frame of the study, the physical health of over 70 percent of the residents from the "choiceless" group deteriorated. By contrast, over 90 percent of the people with choice saw their health improve. Six months later, researchers even found that the residents who'd been given greater choice—or, indeed, the *perception* of it—were less likely to have died.

The nursing home residents benefited from having choices that were largely symbolic. Being able to exercise their innate need to control some of their environment prevented the residents from suffering the stress and anxiety that caged zoo animals and lower-pay-grade employees often experience. The study suggests that minor but frequent choice making can have a disproportionately large and positive impact on our perception of overall control, just as the accumulation of minor stresses is often more harmful over time than the stress caused by a few major events. More profoundly, this suggests that we can give choice to ourselves and to others, along with the benefits that accompany choice. A small change in our actions, such as speaking or thinking in a way that highlights our agency, can have a big effect on our mental and physical state.

According to various studies examining mind-over-matter attitudes in medical patients, even those struggling against the most malignant illnesses such as cancer and HIV, refusing to accept the situation as hopeless can increase chances of survival and reduce the chance of relapse, or at least postpone death. For example, in one study at Royal Marsden Hospital in the United Kingdom—the first hospital in the world to be dedicated solely to the study and treatment of cancer—breast cancer patients who scored higher on helplessness and hopelessness had a significantly increased risk of relapse or death within five years as compared to members of the study who scored lower on those measures. Numerous studies also found this to be the case for patients with HIV in the years before effective treatments were available; those who reported more feelings of helplessness were more likely to progress from HIV to full-blown AIDS, and died more quickly after developing AIDS. Is it really possible that the way someone thinks about their illness can directly affect their physical well-being?

The debate in the medical community rages on, but what's clear is that, whenever possible, people reach for choice—we want to believe that seeing our lives in these terms will make us better off. And even if it doesn't make us better off physically, there is certainly reason to believe that it makes us *feel* better. For example, in one study conducted at UCLA, two-thirds of breast cancer patients reported that they believed they could personally control the course of their illness, and of these, more than a third believed they had *a lot* of control. This perception often led to behavioral changes, for example eating more fruits and vegetables. However, more often than not, the control manifested as purely mental action, such as picturing chemotherapy as a cannon blasting away pieces of the cancer dragon. Patients also told themselves, "I absolutely refuse to have any more cancer." However implausible these beliefs may have been, the greater the control the patients felt they had over their disease, the happier they were. Indeed, the patients' need to believe in their power over their illnesses echoes the craving for control that all people, healthy or sick, young or old, instinctively need to exert over their lives. We wish to see our lives as offering us choice and the potential for control, even in the most dismal of circumstances.

VI. TELLING STORIES

Here's the disclaimer: There is no guarantee that choosing to live will actually help you survive. Stories about "the triumph of the human spirit" often highlight the crucial point at which the hero/ survivor said, "I knew now that I had a choice," or "A difficult choice lay before me." Frequently, what follows is purple prose about the inspirational journey from darkness to light and a platitude-filled explanation of the lessons to be learned. But Richter's rats seemed to "believe" as hard as any creature could that they would reach safety, and we have never heard the stories of the many sailors and moun- taineers and terminally ill people who died even though they, too, had chosen to live. So survivor stories can be misleading, especially if they emphasize the individual's "phenomenal strength of char- acter" above all else. At other times, they can seem too familiar, as though read from the same script handed out to all survivors before they face TV cameras.

Nevertheless, such stories do help people withstand the fear and suffering that accompany serious illness and tragedy. Even beliefs that are unrealistically optimistic according to medical consensus are more beneficial for coping than a realistic outlook. And though one might expect a backlash from patients who suffer a relapse after having fervently believed that they were cured, studies show that this is not the case. If you're healthy, you might reject such optimism as delusion, but if the tables were turned, perhaps you would also reach for anything that could jigger the odds ever so slightly in your favor.

Joan Didion begins her essay "The White Album" with the following phrase: "We tell ourselves stories in order to live." It is a simple but stunning claim. A few sentences later, she writes, "We look for the sermon in the suicide, for the social or moral lesson in the murder of five. We interpret what we see, select the most workable of the multiple choices. We live entirely, especially if we are writers, by the imposition of a narrative line upon disparate images, by the 'ideas' with which we have learned to freeze the shifting phantasmagoria which is our actual experience." The imposed narrative, even if it is trite or sentimental, serves an important function by allowing us to make some sense of our lives. When that narrative is about choice, when it is the idea that we have control, we can tell it to ourselves— quite literally—"in order to live."

One could even argue that we have a duty to create and pass on stories about choice because once a person knows such stories, they can't be taken away from him. He may lose his possessions, his home, his loved ones, but if he holds on to a story about choice, he retains the ability to practice choice. The Stoic philosopher Seneca the Younger wrote, "It is a mistake to imagine that slavery pervades a man's whole being; the better part of him is exempt from it: the body indeed is subjected and in the power of a master, but the mind is independent, and indeed is so free and wild, that it cannot be restrained even by this prison of the body, wherein it is confined." For animals, the confinement of the body is the confinement of the whole being, but a person can *choose* freedom even when he has no physical autonomy. In order to do so, he must know what choice is, and he must believe that he deserves it. By sharing stories, we keep choice alive in the imagination and in language. We give each other the strength to perform choice in the mind even when we cannot perform it with the body.

It is no wonder, then, that the narrative of choice keeps growing, spreading, and acquiring more power. In America, it fuels the American Dream founded upon the "unalienable Rights" of "Life, Liberty and the pursuit of Happiness" promised in the Declaration of Independence. Its origins extend much further back since it is implicit in any discussion of freedom or self-determination. Indeed, we can sense its comforting presence even when the word "choice" is absent. When we act out this narrative, often by following scripts written by others, we claim control no matter what our circumstances. And though our scripts and performances vary, as we will see next, the desire and need for choice is universal. Whatever our differences—in temperament, culture, language—choice connects us and allows us to speak to one another about freedom and hope.

CHAPTER TWO

A Stranger in Strange Lands

I. A BLESSED UNION

On an August morning over 40 years ago, Kanwar Jit Singh Sethi woke at dawn to prepare for the day. He began with a ceremonial bath; wearing only his *kachchha*, the traditional Sikh undergarment of white drawstring shorts, he walked into the bathing room of his family's Delhi home. In the small space lit by a single window, he sat on a short wooden stool, the stone floor cold beneath his bare feet. His mother and grandmother entered the bathing room and anointed him with *vatna*, a fragrant paste of turmeric, sandalwood, milk, and rosewater. Then they filled a bucket with water and poured cupfuls over his head and shoulders.

Kanwar Jit's mother washed his hair, which fell to the middle of his back, and his beard, which reached to his breastbone; in accordance with Sikh tradition, they had never been cut. After his hair was clean, she vigorously massaged it with fragrant oil and rolled it into tight knots, tying his hair atop his head and his beard beneath his chin. After donning his best suit, Kanwar Jit cut an impressive figure: 28 years old, 160 pounds, six feet tall in his bright red turban. One could not help but be drawn to his appearance and jolly demeanor, his soft eyes and easy way. He walked through the doors into the courtyard, where nearly a hundred friends and relatives had gathered, to begin the celebrations.

Several blocks away, 23-year-old Kuldeep Kaur Anand started her morning in much the same way, though she was, in many respects, Kanwar Jit's opposite. At a diminutive five foot one and 85 pounds, and as shy as Kanwar Jit was outgoing, she didn't call attention to herself, instead focusing her keen eyes on others. After the ceremonial bath, she dressed in an orange sari that matched the one worn by Mumtaz, her favorite actress, in that year's hit film *Brahmachari*. She welcomed the many guests now arriving at the house, all of them smiling and wishing her the best for the future.

In both homes, the festivities continued throughout the day with platters of cheese and vegetable *pakoras* providing sustenance for all the meeting and greeting. At dusk, each household began to prepare for the *Milni*, the ceremony in which the two families would come together. At Kanwar Jit's home, a band arrived, playing a traditional song on the *shehnai*, a reed instrument thought to bring good luck. A white horse covered with a brown embroidered rug came too; Kanwar Jit would ride it to Kuldeep's home. But before he set off, his sister covered his face with a *sehra*, several tassels of gold entwined with flowers that hung from his turban. Then Kanwar Jit mounted the horse and, flanked by his family, rode to his destination, the band leading the way.

At her home, Kuldeep stood at the front door singing hymns with her family. Her face was covered by an ornately embroidered veil given to her by Kanwar Jit's mother. When the procession arrived, *shehnai* blaring and *tabla* beating, Kanwar Jit and Kuldeep exchanged garlands of roses and jasmine. At the same time, each member of one family specially greeted his or her counterpart in the other family. Mother greeted mother, sister greeted sister, and so on. These familial "couples" also exchanged garlands. The families then celebrated by singing and dancing until it was time for Kanwar Jit's family to depart.

The next day at dawn, Kuldeep's and Kanwar Jit's families traveled to a nearby temple for the ceremony of *Anand Karaj*, or Blessed Union. Kanwar Jit, again wearing a red turban and dark suit, knelt in front of the wooden altar that held the Guru Granth Sahib, the Sikh holy book. Kuldeep, wearing a pink *salwar kameez*, an outfit of loose pants and a long tunic, knelt beside him, an opaque veil with gold tassels covering her almost to the waist. After singing hymns and saying prayers, Kanwar Jit's grandfather tied one end of a long

scarf to his grandson's hand and the other end to Kuldeep's hand. Connected in this way, the couple circled the Guru Granth Sahib four times. They paused after each circuit to hear the *Sant*, or holy man, read a prayer related to their union: karma, dharma, trust, and blessings. Afterward, in celebration, both families tossed money and garlands at the couple's feet. Then Kanwar Jit lifted the veil and, for the first time, saw his wife's face.

This is how my parents were married. Every detail of the ceremony was decided for them, from whom to marry to what to wear to what to eat. It was all part of a closely followed cultural script that had evolved over time into the Sikh traditions that they and their families adhered to on that day. Whenever I mention to people that

my parents met for the first time on their wedding day, the most common reaction is shock: "Their families decided on the match? How could your parents let that happen to them?" Simply explaining to people that this is the way marriages were decided upon in my family—in most Indian families—does not seem to satisfy their curiosity or diminish their incredulity. On the surface, people understand that there are cultural differences in the way marriages come about. But the part that really doesn't sit well, the part that they simply can't wrap their heads around, is that my parents allowed such an important choice to be taken out of their hands. How could they do such a thing, and why?

II. A MATTER OF FAITH

Remember Martin Seligman, the psychologist who ran those unsettling experiments with dogs? His compelling studies with both humans and animals, as well as the other studies we learned about in the previous chapter, demonstrate just how much we need to feel in control of what happens to us. When we can't maintain control, we're left feeling helpless, bereft, unable to function. I first learned about these experiments when taking a course with Seligman as an undergraduate at the University of Pennsylvania. The findings from such research made me start to question whether my own Sikh tradition, rather than empowering or uplifting its followers, could actually engender a sense of helplessness. As a member of the Sikh faith, I was constantly keeping track of so many rules: what to wear, what to eat, forbidden behaviors, and my duties to family. When I added it all up, there wasn't much left for me to decide—so many of my decisions had been made for me. This was true not only for Sikhism but for many other religions. I brought my questions to Seligman, hoping he could help shed some light on whether members of religious faiths were likely to experience greater helplessness in their lives.

But he, too, was unsure, as there were no scientific investigations into this subject. So we decided to embark on a study examining the effects of religious adherence on people's health and happiness.

For the next two years, anyone glancing at my social calendar might have assumed I was trying to atone for a lifetime of sin. Each week my research began at sundown on Friday with a visit to a mosque, immediately followed by a visit to a synagogue. On Saturdays I visited more synagogues and mosques, and on Sundays I went church-hopping. In total, I interviewed over 600 people from nine different religions. These faiths were categorized as fundamentalist (Calvinism, Islam, and Orthodox Judaism), which imposed many day-to-day regulations on their followers; conservative (Catholicism, Lutheranism, Methodism, and Conservative Judaism); or liberal (Unitarianism and Reform Judaism), which imposed the fewest restrictions. In fact, some branches of the liberal religions don't even require their practicing members to believe in God, and the largest percentage of Unitarian Universalists described themselves as secular humanists, followed by those with an earth- or nature-centered spirituality.

The worshippers were asked to fill out three surveys. The first contained questions regarding the impact of religion in their lives, including the extent to which it affected what they ate, drank, wore, whom they would associate with, and whom they would marry. Members of the fundamentalist faiths indeed scored the highest on these questions and members of the liberal faiths scored the lowest. The survey also asked about religious involvement (how often they attended services or prayed) and religious hope ("Do you believe there is a heaven?" and "Do you believe your suffering will be rewarded?"). A second survey measured each individual's level of optimism by examining their reactions to a series of hypothetical good and bad life events. When asked how they would react to being fired, optimists gave answers like, "If I was fired from my job it would be for something specific that would be easy to fix," while pessimists said things like, "If I was fired from my job it would be because there's something wrong with me that I'll never be able to fix." In essence, they were describing how much control they believed they had over their lives. Last, they filled out a commonly used mental health questionnaire to determine if they had any symptoms of depression, such as weight loss or lack of sleep. To my surprise, it turned out that members of more fundamentalist faiths experienced greater hope, were more optimistic when faced with adversity, and were less likely to be depressed than their counterparts. Indeed, the people most susceptible to pessimism and depression were the Unitarians, especially those who were atheists. The presence of so many rules didn't debilitate people; instead, it seemed to empower them. Many of their choices were taken away, and yet they experienced a sense of control over their lives.

This study was an eye-opener: Restrictions do not necessarily diminish a sense of control, and freedom to think and do as you please does not necessarily increase it. The resolution of this seeming paradox lies in the different narratives about the nature of the world—and our role within it—that are passed down from generation to generation. We all want and need to be in control of our lives, but how we understand control depends on the stories we are told and the beliefs we come to hold. Some of us come to believe that control comes solely through the exercise of personal choice. We must find our own path to happiness because no one will (or can) find it for us. Others believe that it is God who is in control, and only by understanding His ways and behaving accordingly will we be able to find happiness in our own lives. We are all exposed to different narratives about life and choice as a function of where we're born, who our parents are, and numerous other factors. In moving from culture to culture and country to country, then, we encounter remarkable variations in people's beliefs about who should make choices, what to expect from them, and how to judge the consequences.

Since beginning my formal study of choice as an undergraduate,

I have interviewed, surveyed, and run experiments with people from all walks of life: old and young, secular and religiously observant, members of Asian cultures, veterans of the communist system, and people whose families have been in the United States for generations. In the rest of this chapter, I'll share with you my own research and also the observations of a growing number of researchers who have been looking at the ways in which geography, religion, political systems, and demographics can fundamentally shape how people perceive themselves and their roles. The stories of our lives, told differently in every culture and every home, have profound implications for what and why we choose, and it is only by learning how to understand these stories that we can begin to account for the wonderful and baffling differences among us.

III. THE INDIVIDUAL AND THE COLLECTIVE

In 1995, I spent several months in Kyoto, Japan, living with a local family while I did research for my PhD dissertation with Shinobu Kitayama, one of the founders of the field of cultural social psychology. I knew I would experience cultural differences, even misunderstandings, but they often popped up where I least expected them. The most surprising might have been when I ordered green tea with sugar at a restaurant. After a pause, the waiter politely explained that one does not drink green tea with sugar. I responded that yes, I was aware of this custom, but I liked my tea sweet. My request was met with an even more courteous version of the same explanation: One does not drink green tea with sugar. While I understood, I told him, that the Japanese do not put sugar in *their* green tea, I would still like to put some in *my* green tea. Thus thwarted, the waiter took up the issue with the manager, and the two of them began a lengthy conversation. Finally, the manager came over to me and said, "I am very sorry. We do not have sugar." Since I couldn't have the green tea as I liked it, I changed my order to a cup of coffee, which the waiter soon brought over. Resting on the saucer were two packets of sugar.

My failed campaign for a cup of sweet green tea makes for an amusing story, but it also serves as shorthand for how views on choice vary by culture. From the American perspective, when a paying customer makes a reasonable request based on her personal preferences, she has every right to have those preferences met. From the perspective of the Japanese, however, the way I liked my tea was terribly inappropriate according to accepted cultural standards, and the waitstaff was simply trying to prevent me from making such an awful faux pas. Looking beyond the trappings of the situation, similar patterns of personal choice or social influence can be seen in family life, at work, and in potentially every other aspect of life when comparing American and Japanese cultures. While there are numerous differences between these two cultures, or indeed any two cultures, one particular cultural feature has proved especially useful for understanding how the ideas and practice of choice vary across the globe: the degree of individualism or collectivism.

Ask yourself: When making a choice, do you first and foremost consider what you want, what will make you happy, or do you consider what is best for you *and* the people around you? This seemingly simple question lies at the heart of major differences between cultures and individuals, both within and between nations. Certainly, most of us would not be so egocentric as to say that we would ignore all others or so selfless as to say that we would ignore our own needs and wants entirely—but setting aside the extremes, there can still be a great deal of variation. Where we fall on this continuum is very much a product of our cultural upbringing and the script we are given for how to choose—in making decisions, are we told to focus primarily on the "I" or on the "we"? Whichever set of assumptions we're given, these cultural scripts are intended not only to help us successfully navigate our own lives but also to perpetuate a set of values regarding the way in which society as a whole functions best.

Those of us raised in more individualist societies, such as the United States, are taught to focus primarily on the "I" when choosing. In his book *Individualism and Collectivism*, cultural psychologist Harry Triandis notes that individualists "are primarily motivated by their own preferences, needs, rights, and the contracts they have established with others" and "give priority to their personal goals over the goals of others." Not only do people choose based on their own preferences, which is itself significant given the number of choices in life and their importance; they also come to see themselves as defined by their individual interests, personality traits, and actions; for example, "I am a film buff" or "I am environmentally conscious." In this worldview, it's critical that one be able to determine one's own path in life in order to be a complete person, and any obstacle to doing so is seen as patently unjust.

Modern individualism has its most direct roots in the Enlightenment of seventeenth- and eighteenth-century Europe, which itself drew on a variety of influences: the works of Greek philosophers, especially Socrates, Plato, and Aristotle; René Descartes' attempt to derive all knowledge from the maxim "I think, therefore I am"; the Protestant Reformation's challenge to the central authority of the Catholic Church with the idea that every individual had a direct line to God; and scientific advances by such figures as Galileo and Isaac Newton that provided ways to understand the world without recourse to religion. These led to a new worldview, one that rejected the traditions that had long ruled society in favor of the power of reason. Each person possessed the ability to discover for himself what was right and best instead of depending on external sources like kings and clergy.

The founding fathers of the United States were heavily influenced by Enlightenment philosophy, in particular John Locke's arguments for the existence of universal individual rights, and in turn incorporated these ideas into the U.S. Constitution and Bill of Rights. The signing of the Declaration of Independence coincided with another milestone in the history of individualism: Adam Smith's *The Wealth of Nations*, published in 1776, which argued that if each person pursued his own economic self-interest, society as a whole would benefit as if guided by an "invisible hand." Central to individualist ideology is the conceiving of choice in terms of opportunity—promoting an individual's ability to be or to do whatever he or she desires. The cumulative effect of these events on people's expectations about the role choice should play in life and its implications for the structure of society was eloquently expressed by the nineteenth-century philosopher and economist John Stuart Mill, who wrote, "The only freedom deserving the name is that of pursuing our own good in our own way, long as we do not attempt to deprive others of theirs, or impede their efforts to obtain it.... Mankind are greater gainers by suffering each other to live as seems good to themselves, than by compelling each to live as seems good to the rest."

This way of thinking has become so ingrained that we rarely pause to consider that it may not be a universally shared ideal—that we may not always want to make choices, or that some people prefer to have their choices prescribed by another. But in fact the construct of individualism is a relatively new one that guides the thinking of only a small percentage of the world's population. Let's now turn to the equally rich tradition of collectivism and how it impacts people's notions of choice across much of the globe.

Members of collectivist societies, including Japan, are taught to privilege the "we" in choosing, and they see themselves primarily in terms of the groups to which they belong, such as family, coworkers, village, or nation. In the words of Harry Triandis, they are "primarily motivated by the norms of, and duties imposed by, those collectives" and "are willing to give priority to the goals of these collectives over their own personal goals," emphasizing above all else "their connectedness to members of these collectives." Rather than everyone looking out for number one, it's believed that individuals can be happy only when the needs of the group as a whole are met.

For example, the Japanese saying *makeru ga kachi* (literally "to lose is to win") expresses the idea that getting one's way is less desirable than maintaining peace and harmony. The effects of a collectivist worldview go beyond determining who should choose. Rather than defining themselves solely by their personal traits, collectivists understand their identities through their relationships to certain groups. People in such societies, then, strive to fit in and to maintain harmony with their social in-groups.

Collectivism has, if anything, been the more pervasive way of life throughout history. The earliest hunter-gatherer societies were highly collectivist by necessity, as looking out for one another increased everyone's chances of survival, and the value placed on the collective grew after humans shifted to agriculture as a means of sustenance. As populations increased and the formerly unifying familial and tribal forces became less powerful, other forces such as religion filled the gap, providing people with a sense of belongingness and common purpose.

Whereas value for individualism solidified mainly in the Enlightenment, multiple manifestations of collectivism have emerged over time. The first can be traced directly back to the cultural emphasis on duty and fate that gradually developed in Asia—essentially independent of the West—thousands of years ago and is still influential today. Hinduism and those religions that succeeded it, including Buddhism, Sikhism, and Jainism, place a strong emphasis on some form of dharma, which defines each person's duties as a function of his caste or religion, as well as on karma, the universal law of cause and effect that transcends even death. Another significant influence is Confucianism, a codification of preexisting cultural practices that originated in China but later also spread to Southeast Asia and Japan. In *The Analects*, Confucius wrote, "In the world, there are two great decrees: one is fate and the other is duty. That a son should love his parents is fate—you cannot erase this from his heart. That a subject should serve his ruler is duty—there is no place he can go and be without his ruler, no place he can escape to between heaven and earth." The ultimate goal was to make these inevitable relationships as harmonious as possible. This form of collectivism remains foremost in the East today; in these cultures, individuals tend to understand their lives relatively more in terms of their duties and less in terms of personal preferences.

A second major strain of collectivism emerged in nineteenth-century Europe, in many ways as a response to individualism. Political theorists like Karl Marx criticized the era's capitalist institutions, arguing that the focus on individual self-interest perpetuated a system in which a small upper class benefited at the expense of the larger working class. They called for people to develop "class consciousness," to identify with their fellow workers and rise up to establish a new social order in which all people were equal in practice as well as in principle, and this rallying cry often received considerable support. In contrast to individualism, this more populist ideology focused on guaranteeing each and every person's access to a certain amount of resources rather than on maximizing the overall number of opportunities available. This philosophy's most significant effect on the world occurred when the communist Bolshevik faction came to power in Russia as a result of the October Revolution in 1917, which led to the eventual formation of the Soviet Union and offered an alternative model of government to emerging nations around the world.

So where do the borders between individualism and collectivism lie in the modern world? Geert Hofstede, one of the most well-known researchers in this field, has created perhaps the most comprehensive ranking system for a country's level of individualism based on the results of his work with the employees of IBM branches across the globe. Not surprisingly, the United States consistently ranks as the most individualist country, scoring 91 out of 100. Australia (90) and the United Kingdom (89) are close behind, while Western European countries primarily fall in the 60 to 80 range. Moving across the map to Eastern Europe, rankings begin to fall more on the collectivist end, with Russia at 39. Asia as a whole also tends to be more collectivist, with a number of countries hovering around 20, including China, though Japan and India are somewhat higher with scores of 46 and 48, respectively. Central and South American countries tend to rank quite high in collectivism, generally between 10 and 40, with Ecuador rated the most collectivist country of all, with a 6 out of 100 on the scale. Africa is understudied, though a handful of countries in East and West Africa are estimated to score between 20 and 30. Subsequent studies have consistently found a similar pattern of results around the world, with individualists tending to endorse statements like, "I often 'do my own thing,'" or "One should live one's life independently of others," while collectivists endorse, "It is important to maintain harmony within my group," or "Children should be taught to place duty before pleasure."

It's important to note that a country's score on scales like these is nothing more than the average of its citizens' scores, which aren't solely dependent on the prevailing culture and can cover a significant range. Many of the same factors that affect the culture of a nation or a community can have an effect on the individual as well. Greater wealth is associated with greater individualism at all levels, whether we compare nations by GDP, or blue-collar and upper-middle-class Americans by annual income. Higher population density is associated with collectivism, as living in close proximity to others requires more restrictions on behavior in order to keep the peace. On the other hand, greater exposure to other cultures and higher levels of education are both associated with individualism, so cities aren't necessarily more collectivist than rural areas. People become slightly more collectivist with age as they develop more numerous and stronger relationships with others, and just as important, they become more set in their views over time, meaning they will be less affected than the younger generations by broad cultural changes. All these factors, not to mention personality and incidental experiences in life, combine and interact to determine each person's position on the individualism-collectivism spectrum.

IV. A TALE OF TWO WEDDINGS

So why did my parents let others decide whom they would be spending the rest of their lives with? Perhaps we can find an answer to this question by using the concepts of individualism and collectivism. If you look at the narratives of love and arranged marriage, it seems clear that a love marriage is a fundamentally individualist endeavor, while an arranged marriage is quintessentially collectivist. Let's examine how these narratives unfold and the different messages that they convey.

Consider the fairy tale of Cinderella, the kind and lovely young maiden forced to work as a servant by the evil stepmother and the two ugly stepsisters. Aided by a magical fairy godmother, she manages to attend the royal ball despite her stepmother's forbidding her to do so, and steals the spotlight when she arrives in a carriage, wearing a beautiful gown and stunning glass slippers. She also manages to steal the heart of the prince himself—he falls in love with her at first sight—but she must leave before the spell that transformed her from a servant girl into a lovely maiden wears off at midnight. In spite of her stepfamily's attempts to sabotage her love, she finally succeeds in proving herself the wearer of the glass slipper and marries the prince, and the story ends with the declaration that they "lived happily ever after."

Now let me share with you a very different story, about a real princess who lived long, long ago. In the fifteenth century, a beautiful 14-year-old girl was chosen to become the third wife of the powerful Mughal emperor Shah Jahan. They were said to have fallen in love at first sight but had to wait five years for their marriage to be consecrated. The real story begins after their lives were joined as one, as Mumtaz Mahal (meaning "Chosen One of the Palace") accompanied her husband everywhere he went on his travels and military campaigns throughout the Mughal Empire, bearing 13 children along the way.

Court chroniclers dutifully documented their intimate and loving marriage, in which Mumtaz acted not only as a wife and companion but also frequently as a trusted adviser and a benevolent influence upon her powerful husband. She was widely considered to be the perfect wife and was celebrated by poets even during her lifetime for her wisdom, beauty, and kindness. When she died while bearing her fourteenth child, it was rumored that the emperor had made a promise to her on her deathbed that he would build a monument to their loving life together. After her death and a period of deep grief and mourning, Shah Jahan set about designing the mausoleum and gardens that would do justice to the beauty and incredible life of his late spouse. The result, the Taj Mahal, remains standing in Agra, India, as one of the Seven Wonders of the World and as a testament to a legendary marriage.

Each of these tales represents the basic human practice of matrimony at its most idealized, and yet the values celebrated in each represent two completely different cultural narratives regarding choice. The Cinderella story is all about the protagonist and her lover pursuing their choice against all odds, defying the restrictions of class and the opposition of family. The implicit message is that the hero and heroine should fight for the triumph of their own hearts' desire, and the tale ends when their choice prevails: on the day of their wedding. The focus is on who makes the choice and how the choice is made. We're not told how the two get to "happily ever after," just that it happens—everything will work out because Cinderella and the prince chose each other out of love. The tale of Mumtaz Mahal and Shah Jahan, however, takes the opposite tack. At the outset, the respective authorities have already made the decision that the two will wed. The story instead unfolds the consequences of that decision and celebrates the development of a great love following the arranged match. The assumption is that it's not only possible for someone else to pick the "perfect" person for you, but that the two characters would not have had the ability to pick such a person even if they had so desired. Ultimate happiness comes not from making the choice but in the fulfillment of one's duties. Each story carries a distinct message about what one should expect of marriage, but how is it that we came to tell such different tales?

My own parents' marriage was an ordinary arranged marriage with little fanfare, yet it followed much the same script. The process began when my two grandmothers, who were the wives of first cousins, met over tea one day to discuss the possibility of creating an alliance between their two families. Among the criteria discussed for a good match were various factors of compatibility, not only between the prospective bride and groom but between their respective families as well. All the practical matters were in order: They were both from the same caste and lived near each other. My father was believed to be financially capable of providing for my mother, his family would treat her well, and he might get along well with her brothers. My mother, in turn, was deemed suitably well educated, and the fact that she had a brother living in America could only count as a bonus. The idea that they might emigrate after marriage was viewed as a very favorable sign not only for their financial future but also for the rest of the family remaining in India. Thus, after many discussions among various family members, it was agreed that Kanwar Jit Singh Sethi would marry Kuldeep Kaur Anand. It was a match that seemed in every respect to be in alignment with the odds rather than in defiance of them, and it was this assessment of common ground that led to my parents' union.

As you already know, they met for the first time on their wedding day, and they did indeed wind up in America. They were no Shah Jahan and Mumtaz Mahal, but they did successfully fulfill their spousal duties to each other, had two children, and generally got along. It was in the everyday living of habitual life rather than in the highly ritualized day of their wedding that their union truly revealed itself: in the way my father drove my mother to work every day or kept her company as she cooked meals in the kitchen, sharing his thoughts or telling her about his day. It wasn't a marriage that would result in any fascinating court histories or grand monuments, but it was a more quotidian incarnation of the ideal of arranged marriage that the tale of Mumtaz Mahal and Shah Jahan epitomizes.

And though the concept of an arranged marriage may seem unthinkable to many modern readers, the planning of my parents' marriage was not some anomalous event or a custom specific to India, but part and parcel of a way of life that was prevalent across the world for 5,000 years. From ancient China to classical Greece to the tribes of Israel, marriage has quite normatively been a family affair. A man and a woman were wed to forge and maintain bonds between families (anything from turning the strangers in the nearby tribe into in-laws to cementing a political alliance between two nations), for the economic benefits of distributing labor among the two people and their children, and to ensure the continuity of one's bloodline and of one's way of life. In other words, the union was based on shared goals. The spouses were bound by duties not only to each other but also to the rest of their kin. The notion of familial duty could be so strong as to extend even beyond life; the book of Deuteronomy in the Hebrew Bible states that if a man's brother dies, he is required to marry and provide for his brother's widow, and a similar version of this tradition is practiced in India even today. This emphasis on duty in and through marriage was due largely to the fact that every family member needed to pitch in to make a living.

That does not mean that people were drawn together only by the need for survival. Romantic love is one of the most universal human experiences, and practically every civilization for which records exist has acknowledged its power. Some of the earliest known examples of language, Sumerian cuneiform carved into clay tablets, are love poems; in one the speaker addresses his beloved as "my darling, my fruitful vine, my honey sweet." The Song of Songs in the Hebrew Bible begins with "You have stolen my heart with one glance of your eyes," before progressing to language that is not only ardent but erotic. The mythologies, or sacred narratives, of all the great ancient civilizations are filled with gods and goddesses embodying love, like the Greek love goddess Aphrodite, and divine couples like the Egyptian Osiris and Isis, and the Hindu Shiva and Parvati. In classical epics, love impels people to wage wars, journey to the underworld, and overcome all manner of obstacles.

So many verses penned, so much blood shed in the name of love! Yet so often the love that spurred heroes to their greatest deeds existed outside marriage. When Andreas Capellanus, the twelfth-century author of a treatise known as *The Art of Courtly Love*, wrote "Marriage is no real excuse for not loving," he *was* advocating romance between husbands and wives—just not between those who were married to one another. His suggestion, in other words, was to love your neighbor's husband or wife as you did not love your own. The tradition he inspired encouraged members of the European nobility to conduct emotionally intense—albeit usually chaste—affairs with other lords and ladies in order to experience the passion that their politically motivated marriages rarely provided. Elsewhere in the world it was even believed that love within a marriage could be an obstacle to its success. In China, for example, it wasn't unheard of for parents to forcibly dissolve a marriage if the newlyweds' love for each other began to interfere with their obligations to family.

So when and how did love and marriage become, well, hitched? There's no precise moment when society flipped the switch from duty fulfillment to love, but one of the earliest expressions of love in the context of marriage is found in one of the phrases still most commonly used: "To have and to hold from this day forward, for better for worse, for richer for poorer, in sickness and in health, to love and to cherish 'til death us do part." You likely recognize this from almost any Christian wedding or civil ceremony you've attended or seen in film or television. It comes from the Book of Common Prayer, the first version of which was published in 1549 by the Church of England—nearly half a century before the lovers in Shakespeare's masterpiece *Romeo and Juliet* lived out the concept "'til death us do part." There's still nothing quite like a good story about star-crossed lovers pursuing love against all odds to stir the heart and lubricate the eyes.

The idea of love marriage went hand in hand with the rise of individualism in Western society: The Book of Common Prayer was itself a product of the English Reformation. It contained the prayers for various common religious services, including the core wedding vows, written in English for the first time, representing the break from the Catholic Church in Rome and the advent of the radical concept that one's destiny and relationship with God could, in fact, be individually determined. The Reformation was but one of many vast social upheavals to occur in Europe in the centuries between the first utterance of "to have and to hold" and the present day. The consideration of collective family needs became less and less compulsory with urbanization and the growth of the middle class. Instead of relying on the support of relatives, people were able to manage their own households immediately after marriage. Personal happiness could now find a place within the bonds of matrimony, and love was no longer at odds with having a successful marriage. Thus, in 1955, when Frank Sinatra sang, "Love and marriage, love and marriage, go together like a horse and carriage / This, I tell you, brother, you can't have one without the other," he was promoting a rather new outlook, one that had been around for very few of the past 5,000 years of human civilization. So on the one hand, we have the historical norm of marriages arranged for the purpose of fulfilling the interests of the collective, and on the other hand, the modern version in which two people are supposed to be bound for life based on mutual affection. In comparing the two, should we ask if one is better than the other?

Usha Gupta and Pushpa Singh of the University of Rajasthan decided that this was a question worth exploring. They recruited 50 couples in the city of Jaipur, half of whom had had arranged marriages. The other half had married based on love. The couples had been together for varying lengths of time, ranging from 1 to 20 years. Was one set of couples enjoying greater marital bliss than the other? Each person separately completed the Rubin Love Scale, which measured how much he or she agreed with statements like "I feel that I can confide in my husband/wife about virtually everything" and "If I could never be with my [loved one], I would feel miserable." The researchers then compared the responses, not only on the dimension of love versus arranged marriage, but also by the length of time that the couples had been married. The couples who had married for love and been together less than a year averaged a score of 70 points out of a possible 91 on the love scale, but these numbers steadily fell over time. The love couples who had been married ten years or longer had an average score of only 40 points. In contrast, the couples in arranged marriages were less in love at the outset, averaging 58 points, but their feelings increased over time to an average score of 68 at the ten or more years mark.

Is it possible that love marriages start out hot and grow cold, while arranged marriages start cold and grow hot...or at least warm? This would make sense, wouldn't it? In an arranged marriage, two people are brought together based on shared values and goals, with the assumption that they will grow to like each other over time, much in the same way that a bond develops between roommates or business partners or close friends. On the other hand, love marriage is based primarily on affection: People often speak of the immediate chemistry that drew them together, the spark that they took as a sign they were meant to be. But in the words of George Bernard

Shaw, marriage inspired by love brings two people together "under the influence of the most violent, most insane, most delusive, and most transient of passions. They are required to swear that they will remain in that excited, abnormal, and exhausting condition continuously until death do them part." Indeed, both surveys and direct measurements of brain activity show that by the time couples have been together for 20 years, 90 percent have lost that all-consuming passion they initially felt.

So why not hand over the reins to your family members, maybe your friends, and trust them to lead you to the right partner? Unless you were raised in a culture in which arranged marriage is still the norm, this probably sounds crazy. Even if you were to sign up for eHarmony and allow a computer to pair you with "a highly select group of compatible singles—singles who have been prescreened on 29 Dimensions™ of personality: scientific predictors of long-term relationship success," you would never allow the computer to make your first date a binding contract. No matter how well your family and friends know you, it seems reckless to make a life-changing decision by proxy. And yet, that's exactly what so many people around the world do. They believe in the value of family-approved arrangements, even that it is a mark of good character to marry in this way. If you were such a person, and I came along and said, "The rules have changed: Go forth and find your own spouse, without direction or assistance," you might consider me an agitator. After all, who am I to challenge tradition, to sow seeds of doubt and, most likely, discontent? Who am I to urge you to break your parents' hearts, to humiliate them with your transgression? Even if familial harmony and honor were not at stake, you might still prefer the guidance of your wise and experienced elders, especially of those who have maintained their own marriages for decades.

In fact, the question "Which kind of marriage will lead to greater happiness?" can probably be answered only tautologically: "The happy kind." While the results of Gupta and Singh's study do give pause, they don't necessarily offer any answers to potential couples in Rajasthan, let alone in the rest of the world. Cultural scripts for the performance of marriage are so powerful and so deeply internalized that even a small deviation from your particular script might be enough—for both personal and social reasons—to upset the apple cart. If arranged marriage is not part of your script, my parents' wedding may seem, at best, a curiosity, and at worst, an affront to their individual rights and dignity. In India, however, over 90 percent of the marriages are arranged, and most people do not consider this a tragedy. That being said, as collectivist cultures like India's become more individualist, we're seeing the practice of arranged marriage take on elements of individualism, so that today's version of arranged marriage looks more like arranged courtship. It's more common now for a young person to have one or two high-powered "interviews" with a potential spouse before the choice is made. Still, more than 75 percent of Indian college students—as compared to only 14 percent of their American counterparts—say they'd marry someone they didn't love but who had all the other right qualities.

The daily rituals of setting up a home, raising children, and caring for each other may look the same whether two people were drawn together by love or arrangement. And of course, in both cases, there are some who would say they are happy and others who would say they are not. They might even use similar language to describe their feelings and experiences, but their definitions of happiness and the criteria by which they judge the success of their marriages are based on the scripts they were handed by their parents and culture. In arranged partnerships, marital bliss is primarily gauged by the fulfillment of duties, while for love marriages the major criterion is the intensity and duration of the emotional connection between two people. Whether people are consciously aware of this or not, their feelings and the consequences of those feelings follow from the assumptions they have about how married life must unfold. Each narrative of wedded bliss comes with its own set of expectations and its own measures of fulfillment. In the end, these narratives don't just set us on the path we're supposed to take to get to marriage, but give us an entire script for a performance that may last one month or a year or 50 years. Some of us improvise, some of us rip out half the pages, but the show must and does go on.

V. MINE, YOURS, AND OURS

Our cultural backgrounds influence not only how we marry but how we make choices in nearly every area of our lives. From early on, members of individualist societies are taught the special importance of personal choice. Even a walk through the local grocery store becomes an opportunity to teach lessons about choosing, particularly in the United States, where stores routinely offer hundreds of options. As soon as children can talk, or perhaps as soon as they can accurately point, they are asked, "Which one of these would you like?" A parent would probably narrow down the number of choices and explain the differences between this cereal and that one, or that toy and this one, but the child would be encouraged to express a preference. After a while, the child would graduate to making tougher choices, and by the ripe old age of four, he may well be expected to both understand and respond to the daunting question, "What do you want to be when you grow up?" From this children learn that they should be able to figure out what they like and dislike, what will make them happy and what won't. Because their happiness is on the line, their own opinions truly matter, and they must figure out how to judge the outcomes of their choices.

By contrast, members of collectivist societies place greater emphasis on duty. Children are often told, "If you're a good child, you'll do what your parents tell you," and the parents need not explain themselves. From what you eat to what you wear, the toys you play with to what you study, it is what you're *supposed* to do that's most important. As you grow older, instead of being asked what you want, you may be asked, "How will you take care of your parents' needs and wants? How will you make them proud?" The assumption is that your parents, and elders in general, will show you the right way to live your life so that you will be protected from making a costly mistake. There are "right" choices and "wrong" ones, and by following your elders, you will learn to choose correctly, even relinquish choice when appropriate.

We've already seen how these different approaches can affect our ideas about marriage. Let's try an exercise to explore how else they might shape our daily lives. Get a piece of paper, and on the front write down all the aspects of your life in which you like having choice. On the back, list all the aspects in which you would prefer not to have choice, or to have someone else choose for you. Take a few extra minutes to make sure you haven't left anything out. Satisfied? Okay, now compare the two sides. Do you notice any patterns in the kinds of things you put in each list? For what types of decisions do you feel most adamantly that you wouldn't want someone else to choose for you? And which choices would you strongly prefer to pass on to others?

When I had 100 American and Japanese college students do this exercise during my time in Kyoto, the front sides of the Americans' pages were often completely filled with answers such as "my job," "where I live," and "who I vote for." In fact, many people's lists were so long that they were forced to squeeze answers into the margins of the page. In contrast, the backs, without exception, were either completely blank or contained only a single item, most commonly "when I die" or "when my loved ones die." The Americans, in other words, expressed a nearly limitless desire for choice in every dimension of their lives. The Japanese showed a very different pattern of results, with not a single one wishing to have choice all or nearly all of the time. In fact, on average they listed twice as many domains in which they did not want choice as compared to domains in which they did. They often wanted someone else to decide, for example, what they ate, what they wore, when they woke up in the morning, or what they did at their job. Comparing responses between the two, Americans desired personal choice in four times as many domains of life as did the Japanese.

These were college students, but it is evident from an early age that we absorb different ideas about choice from the world around us and behave accordingly. As a graduate student at Stanford University, I collaborated with my adviser Mark Lepper on a set of studies that demonstrated these differences. The first study took place at an elementary school in Japantown, San Francisco. A small classroom was set up with a table and two chairs. In one chair sat the experimenter; let's call her Ms. Smith. On the table lay six markers, each a different color, and six piles of anagrams, each of which was labeled with a different category (family, animals, San Francisco, food, party, or house) and consisted of a series of jumbled letters that could be rearranged to form a word related to that category. For example, one card labeled "animal" contained the letters R-I-B-D, which could be rearranged to form the word "bird." One by one, seven- to nine-year-old students, half of whom were Asian American—children of Japanese and Chinese immigrants who spoke their parents' native language at home—and half of whom were Anglo American, entered the room and sat across from Ms. Smith.

Each child had been previously assigned, at random, to one of three groups. The first group of children was shown the anagrams and colored markers and told by Ms. Smith, "Here are six piles of word puzzles you can choose from. Which one would you like to do? It's your choice." After choosing a category of anagrams (let's say animals), each child also chose a colored marker with which to write the answers (let's say blue). The second group of children also saw all six anagrams and all six markers, but as each child perused the options, Ms. Smith said, "I would like you to work on the animal anagrams and write your answers with a blue marker." The third group of children was also interrupted while they looked through the anagrams and markers, but this time, Ms. Smith flipped through a stack of papers and announced, "We asked your mom to fill out a form earlier. It says here that your mother wants you to work on the animal anagrams and write your answers with the blue marker." In reality, none of their mothers were asked about their preferences. Instead, when Ms. Smith chose for the children, she picked the same anagram and marker that the previous child from the first group had freely chosen. This procedure ensured that children in all three groups worked on the same task so that their performance and reactions were easily comparable. After the children completed the anagram task, they were left alone in the room for several minutes, during which time they could continue working on the anagrams or choose to explore the other word games in the room, such as crosswords and word search puzzles. While the children played, their behavior was discreetly observed and recorded by another experimenter.

Such small differences in the way the task was administered yielded striking differences in how well the children performed on the anagram task. Anglo American children who were allowed to choose their own anagrams and markers solved four times as many anagrams as when Ms. Smith made their choices for them, and two and a half times more than when their mothers supposedly chose for them. These children also spent three times as long working on anagrams during their free play compared to the other two groups of children. In other words, Anglo American children did better and worked longer when they were able to exercise personal choice. The moment anyone else told them what to do, their performance and subsequent motivation dropped dramatically.

By comparison, the Asian American children performed best and were most motivated when they believed their mothers had chosen for them. These children solved 30 percent more anagrams than those who were allowed to choose their materials themselves, and twice as many anagrams as children who were assigned materials by Ms. Smith. When Asian American children were allowed to play freely after solving their puzzles, those who believed their mothers had chosen for them spent 50 percent more time playing with anagrams than those children who chose for themselves, and three times longer than those for whom Ms. Smith had selected the materials.

Indeed, a number of the Anglo American children expressed visible embarrassment at the thought that their mothers had been consulted in the experiment. Mary had an especially memorable reaction. After being read her instructions, she reacted with a horror that only seven-year-olds freely express: "You asked my *mother*?" Contrast this with the reaction of Natsumi, a young Japanese American girl who thought that her mother had chosen for her. As Ms. Smith was leaving the room, Natsumi approached her, tugged on her skirt, and asked, "Could you please tell my mommy that I did it just like she said?"

It was particularly motivating for the Asian American children when the choice was made by their mothers—even more so than when they made it on their own—because their relationships with their mothers represented a large part of their identities. Letting their mothers choose the anagrams didn't threaten their sense of control because their mothers' preferences were such an important factor in determining their own preferences: They were practically one and the same. In contrast, the Anglo American children saw themselves as much more autonomous—though they didn't love their mothers any less—and wanted to assert their own separate set of preferences, which created a conflict when the selections were dictated for them. When the choices were made by Ms. Smith, a stranger, both groups of children felt the imposition and reacted negatively.

The process of incorporating others into one's own identity isn't limited to only mothers or family members in general, but can occur for any group with which people perceive a sense of shared goals and characteristics, as demonstrated in another of my studies with Mark

Lepper. We asked both Anglo and Asian American fifth-graders to complete a math test, then returned to their classrooms a week later and taught them how to play a computer game called *Space Quest*, which is designed to enhance mathematical learning by engaging players in a mission to save Earth from attack by a computer-controlled alien ship.

Before playing the game, each student was shown a screen on which to select a name and image for his spaceship and the alien spaceship, and the class as a whole was polled about which names and images would be best. Just as in the previous study, the selection process varied for students assigned to different groups. The students in the first group were allowed to choose any spaceship they wanted from the options on the screen. The second group of students saw one set of options highlighted, and a message on the screen told them they would be assigned these choices because these had been most popular in their class poll. The final group of students again saw preselected options, but this time the message said they had been chosen by a poll of the third-graders at another school. As in the previous study, students in the second and third groups actually received the same options that the students from the first group had freely chosen.

One week after the students played *Space Quest*, we returned to the classroom and gave them a follow-up math test to find out how much they had learned since the previous test. Even though the choices of name and image for both their spaceship and the alien ship were purely cosmetic and had no impact on the actual gameplay, they still had significant effects. As in the previous study, Anglo Americans benefited from personally making choices, jumping 18 percent (almost two full letter grades) from the first to the second test, and in fact showing zero improvement in their math scores when anyone else chose for them. The Asian Americans, on the other hand, scored highest when their choice was in the hands of their fellow classmates (matching the Anglo Americans' 18 percent gain), performed

11 percent better when they made their own choices, and showed zero improvement when their choices were determined by strangers. We also observed comparable effects on the students' liking of math more generally.

These two groups of children had two different conceptions of choice and the role that it plays in their lives. The Anglo American students looked at the situation and thought, "I'm playing the game, so I should get to choose what ship to play with, not anybody else." The Asian Americans, on the other hand, preferred the sense of solidarity and common purpose provided by knowing their spaceship name was the same as that of the rest of their classmates: "We're all in the same class, so of course we should have the same ship." Such conceptions are initially learned through family and culture, but as we draw upon them constantly and consistently, they become second nature. So deeply do they take root that we regularly fail to recognize the degree to which our own worldviews differ from those of others and how these differences can affect our interactions. These beliefs play a powerful role in shaping not only our attitudes but also real-world outcomes—in this case, school performance. What happens, then, when people with considerably different narratives about choice are assembled under one roof and told that their fortunes will rise and fall based on how seamlessly they work together?

More and more, we're creating global organizations that link diverse groups of employees in locations around the world, and at the same time strive to implement standardized policies and practices in order to ensure the highest degree of efficiency. In the process, though, such organizations may inadvertently run afoul of cultural differences in workers' expectations. Consider the struggles faced by the Sealed Air Corporation, best known as the innovators of Bubble Wrap, as it restructured the setup of its manufacturing plants in the 1980s, moving from a traditional assembly-line structure to organizing workers in small teams. Instead of being told what to do by a supervisor, the teams were given the responsibility of setting and meeting production goals on their own. The results from the first plant at which the team-creation process was pilot tested were highly encouraging. Not only were the employees happier, they were setting records for both the quality and quantity of materials produced.

Delighted, Sealed Air executives implemented the new structure at a second plant, hoping to reproduce the nearly magical result of happier employees and higher productivity. At this plant, however, many of the employees were Cambodian and Laotian immigrants, and they found the brand-new freedom in their jobs more disconcerting than liberating. "There were a lot of the group who looked at me like I must be the worst production manager in the world," the plant manager recalled, because in his attempts to empower the employees, whenever they came to him with a question about what to do at work, he would turn it around and ask, "What do you think is the best way to do this?" While the Anglo American employees at the first plant had welcomed the chance to express their opinions, the Asian employees at the second plant wondered why their manager wasn't doing *his* job of managing.

In response to this outcome, Sealed Air started from scratch at the new plant and took very gradual steps toward implementing the team-based model. By progressing slowly, managers hoped that the workers would gradually become accustomed to making their own decisions, and that it would become clear that doing so wouldn't thwart collective harmony. Supervisors also believed that when the workers saw that their decisions effected positive, rather than negative, change, they would continue to make more of them. Finally, managers encouraged informal meetings among coworkers so that they could get comfortable sharing their ideas with one another, thereby laying the groundwork for future teamwork. That plant was able to convert to a team-based system only after significantly more time and effort had been spent finding culturally acceptable ways for its employees to function autonomously. No doubt it became clear to the Sealed Air management that culture can profoundly affect the way that we understand our position in the world. As I'll show next, it can even affect the way we *see* the world itself.

VI. IN THE EYE OF THE BEHOLDER

Study the picture below for no more than five seconds.

Then describe it out loud without looking at it. Go ahead, I'll wait.

What did you see, and what did you say? Did you focus on the three large fish, the most prominent individual creatures in view? Or did you attempt to describe the scene more broadly, paying as much or greater attention to the vegetation, rocks, bubbles, and small creatures in the background? It turns out that your answers to even this simple and straightforward task depend on whether you have an individualist or collectivist worldview.

When American and Japanese participants performed this task, as part of a study by psychologists Richard Nisbett and Takahiko Masuda, the Americans paid more attention to the large fish, the "main characters" of the scene, while the Japanese described the scene more holistically. Their varying descriptions were indicative of other differences in perception, particularly of who they believed to be the powerful agents. From the American viewpoint, the large fish were the crucial actors in the scene, influencing everything else around them. For the Japanese, though, it was the environment that dominated, interacting with and influencing the characters.

This difference was further borne out when the participants were subsequently shown several variations of the initial scene in which some of the elements were changed, then asked which things they still recognized and which had changed. When it came to noticing disparities in the background elements, the Japanese outperformed the Americans. On the other hand, although the Americans tended not to notice changes that didn't involve the large fish, they proved especially adept at recognizing these large fish wherever they appeared, while the Japanese had difficulty recognizing them if they were removed from the original environment and placed in a different context. These results suggest that culture is an important factor in shaping our ideas about who or what exercises control in a specific situation. When these different frameworks are applied to real-life situations rather than abstract aquarium scenes, they can result in objectively identical or similar circumstances being understood quite differently by members of different cultures, and this can in turn affect how people choose.

Perhaps you remember reading *The Little Engine That Could* as a child, or maybe you've read it to your own children. The little engine saves the day with his insistent mantra of "I-think-I-can-I-think-I-can," proving that even the smallest engine can reach the highest mountaintops if only it has the will and determination to do so. From Benjamin Franklin's aphorism "God helps those who help themselves" to Barack Obama's iconic slogan "Yes we can!" to the numerous stories of self-made men and women who are held up as inspirations, individualist cultures naturally create and promote a strong narrative about the power of individual action to change the world: If people so choose, they can take control of their own lives and achieve anything. We're told to direct our focus not to the question of *whether* we can overcome the obstacles or barriers before us, but *how* we will do so.

Collectivist cultures, by contrast, encourage people to think about control in a more holistic way. In perhaps the most famous passage of the Hindu scripture the Bhagavad Gita, the god Krishna tells the hero Arjuna, "You have control only over your actions, never over the fruit of your actions. You should never act for the sake of reward, nor should you succumb to inaction." Because the world is affected by not just an individual's goals, but also by the social context and the dictates of fate, people should ensure that their actions are righteous without fixating on obtaining a particular result. Similar acknowledgments of the limits on one's ability to affect the world can be seen in the Arabic phrase *in sha' Allah* (God willing), which Muslims regularly append to statements about the future; for example, "I'll see you tomorrow, God willing," and in the Japanese *shikata ga nai* (it can't be helped), which is widely used by people coping with adverse circumstances or unpleasant duties. The individual is by no means powerless, but he is just one player in the drama of life.

One way to observe the consequences of these different narratives is to look at how we understand success and failure. What stories do we tell about our heroes and villains? An analysis of the 2000 and 2002 Olympic winners' acceptance speeches conducted by researchers including Shinobu Kitayama and Hazel Markus found that Americans tended to explain their success in terms of their personal abilities and efforts; for example, "I think I just stayed focused. It was time to show the world what I could do. . . . I just said, 'No, this is my night.'" The Japanese athletes were more likely to attribute their success to the people who supported them, saying things like, "Here is the best coach in the world, the best manager in the world, and all of the people who support me—all of these things were getting together and became a gold medal. . . . I didn't get it alone." At the other end of the spectrum, a study by my colleague Michael Morris and his collaborators compared U.S. and Japanese newspapers' coverage of financial scandals, like that of "rogue trader" Nick Leeson, whose unauthorized trades eventually created a $1.4 billion debt that caused the collapse of Barings Bank in 1995, or Toshihide Iguchi, whose own unauthorized trades cost Daiwa Bank $1.1 billion the same year. The researchers found that the American papers were more likely to explain the scandals by referring to the individual actions of the rogue traders, while the Japanese papers referred more to institutional factors, such as poor oversight by managers. Whether considering outcomes worthy of praise or of blame, those from the individualist society assigned responsibility to one individual, whereas the collectivists saw the outcomes as inextricably linked to systems and context.

These ideas about individual control are directly related to the way in which we perceive our everyday choices. During my time in Japan, I asked Japanese and American students residing there to list all the choices they had made on the previous day—everything from the moment they woke up in the morning to the moment they went to bed. These students took the same classes together, so they had virtually the same schedule, and the Americans had been there for only a month, so presumably they weren't as aware of the full range of activities and options available to them. One might expect, then, that the Japanese students said they had made more choices, but it was the Americans who perceived themselves as having nearly 50 percent more choices. Unlike the Japanese, Americans listed such things as brushing their teeth and putting the alarm on snooze as choices. What's more, even though the Americans listed more of these minor choices, they still rated their choices as being more important overall when compared to the Japanese.

What you see determines how you interpret the world, which in turn influences what you expect of the world and how you expect the story of your life to unfold. Consistent with my own findings, other studies have found that Asians in general not only believe they are less able to influence other people, they also see fate as playing a greater role in their lives compared to Westerners. What might be the consequences of these different perceptions of choice? Do people benefit from seeing choice at every turn, or could less be more? One insight into the answer comes from an unexpected source: the world of international banking.

In 1998, I persuaded John Reed, inventor of the ATM and CEO of Citicorp at that time, to allow me to examine how people from different cultural backgrounds perceived their work environment, and how this in turn related to their performance and satisfaction with their jobs. Citicorp was already a prominent global bank at the time, with operations spread out over 93 countries on every continent except Antarctica. With Reed's support, a fleet of research assistants and I conducted a survey with more than 2,000 Citicorp bank tellers and sales representatives in Argentina, Australia, Brazil, Mexico, the Philippines, Singapore, Taiwan, and the United States. Since we also wanted our survey to reflect the high level of diversity within the United States, we went to banks in New York, Chicago, and Los Angeles, where we enlisted a range of participants from different demographics and ethnic backgrounds, including Anglo Americans, Hispanic Americans, African Americans, and Asian Americans.

We first asked employees to rate on a scale of 1 ("not at all") to 9 ("very much") how much choice they had in their jobs, both in specific areas like "the way in which I resolve problems at work" or "when to take vacations" and, in general, "the overall amount of freedom I have to make decisions entirely on my own during a typical day at the bank." Their perceptions of choice were also measured by the extent to which they agreed with the statement "At work, my supervisor makes the majority of the decisions about what I do." One would expect the employees' answers to be quite similar; they were, after all, doing the same job. Take the bank tellers, for example: While their duties aren't as structured as an assembly-line worker's, they are usually confined to specific tasks such as cashing checks, accepting deposits and loan payments, and processing withdrawals. Because Citicorp strove to keep its operating practices standardized both domestically and internationally, bank employees in all the various branches followed routines and incentives that were essentially the same.

When the results came in, however, they clearly revealed that the ethnicity of the employees (closely linked here to their cultural background) significantly affected the degree of choice they felt was available. Employees in Asia, along with the Asian Americans, were less likely than Anglo American, Hispanic American, or African American employees to think of their day-to-day activities at work in terms of choice, and Latin Americans' perceptions of choice fell in between these two groups. The less personal choice they thought they had, the higher the level of supervisor control over their actions they perceived. Even those working at the same bank and for the same manager—who reported giving the same levels of choice to all the employees—perceived different degrees of choice available to them, depending on their culture.

Next, we questioned employees about their personal levels of motivation, how fair they thought their work environments were, how satisfied they were with their jobs, and how happy they were overall. We also asked their managers to rate the employees' current and overall performance at the company. It turned out that for all the American employees except Asian Americans, the more choice they thought they had, the higher they scored on all measures of motivation, satisfaction, and performance. Conversely, the more they felt their jobs were dictated by their managers, the worse they did on all of these measures. In contrast, Asian participants, whether from Asia or the United States, scored higher when they thought their day-to-day tasks were determined primarily by their managers, while greater personal choice had no effect in some areas and even a moderately negative one in others. Latin American employees once again fell somewhere in the middle, slightly benefiting from both greater personal choice and greater control by their managers.

What's interesting about these results is not only that people have different ideas, based on cultural background, about what constitutes "choice," but also that they see more of whatever choice condition they prefer. On average, the employees who benefited from greater personal choice saw themselves as having more of it, while those who preferred choice to be in the hands of others also saw this to be the case. Policy changes that make the presence or absence of choice more explicit could have remarkably different consequences for employees from different cultures, as seen in the case of Sealed Air and even in the students who played *Space Quest*. When left to their own devices, though, people are likely to perceive choice at the level that is optimal for them.

But this isn't the end of the story. The effects of culture go beyond individuals' own perceptions of choice and their desire to choose. They shape the way people *actually* choose (when they do choose), which in turn impacts society as a whole. Let's just consider the office environment for the moment, whether at Citibank or at any other multinational corporation. The American narrative of the workplace doesn't just say that more choice is better; it says more choice is better because more choice creates more opportunity to demonstrate competence. The path to success lies in distinguishing oneself from others, and being micromanaged by one's boss can be stifling both personally and professionally. The Asian narrative, on the other hand, focuses on the benefits to the organization as a whole, which may include leaving choices to the people most qualified to make them: those who are wiser, more experienced, or higher in rank. Though both approaches have benefits, they also have drawbacks: The first can encourage selfishness, while the second can lead to stagnation. This is why companies like Citicorp spend considerable effort on creating a unified corporate culture that tries to capture the best of both worlds from the outset, and they're still never completely successful. Now, consider the world outside the workplace. How do these differing perceptions of choice and, by extension, control, affect how we envision that world at its most ideal?

VII. FEEL FREE

On November 9, 1989, the news that East Germany would open its borders for the first time in decades sent shock waves throughout the entire world. Suddenly, East Berlin and West Berlin were reunited, with free passage between the two, as though the Iron Curtain had never descended upon the city in the form of the Berlin Wall. At the time, I was a college student studying in Madrid, and as soon as I heard the news I hopped on the next available train to join in the festivities at the Wall. Crowds poured through the gates in both directions, with East Berliners rushing to set foot in the West and West Berliners stepping through into the East. A massive celebration ensued. It seemed that the entire world had gathered there to cheer, embrace strangers, cry effusively with joy, chisel off souvenir chunks of the wall, and be a part of the euphoric moment when the Iron Curtain was torn down.

ABC News anchor Peter Jennings declared: "Suddenly today, the Berlin Wall has been rendered meaningless as an obstacle to freedom." As he crossed from East Berlin to West Berlin for the first time, one young man exclaimed to a reporter, "I don't feel like I'm in prison anymore!" Another East Berliner commented, "After this, there can be no turning back. This is the turning point everyone has been talking about." People saw this moment as a triumph for freedom, not just in Germany but in the world at large. In the frenzied celebration and rhetoric that ensued, it became clear that the fall of the Berlin Wall ultimately signaled both the end of communism as a political and economic system and the triumph of democracy and capitalism.

I was drawn back to Berlin several times over the next two decades, often in the name of research, but also because I was curious to observe the change from one system to another. By 1991, most of the Berlin Wall had been demolished, gradually replaced by signs of the new order and of the expansion of choice that came along with it. Where a section of the wall once stood, there was now a shopping mall. There were ever more things to buy in East Berlin and more restaurants in which to dine. Capitalism was steadily and surely taking hold. But despite the sense that everything would be wonderful following the introduction of capitalism and democracy, people were not as uniformly happy with this newfound freedom as one might have expected.

Even 20 years after its reunification, in many ways Berlin still feels like two cities, divided by a barrier of ideas as powerful as the Wall itself. In my conversations with people from East Berlin, I've observed that rather than being grateful for the increasing number of opportunities, choices, and options that they have available to them in the marketplace, they are suspicious of this new way of life, which they increasingly perceive as unfair. A survey in 2007 showed that more than one in five Germans would like to see the Berlin Wall put back up. A remarkable 97 percent of East Germans reported being dissatisfied with German democracy and more than 90 percent believed socialism was a good idea in principle, one that had just been poorly implemented in the past. This longing for the Communist era is so widespread that there's a German word for it: *Ostalgie*, a portmanteau of *Ost* (east) and *Nostalgie* (nostalgia). How is it possible that Berliners went from that wild celebration of November 1989 to wanting to return to the very system they had longed to dismantle?

Consider the economic system adopted by the Soviet Union and its satellites, including East Berlin. The government planned out how much of everything—cars, vegetables, tables, chairs—each family might need, and projected from that to set production goals for the nation as a whole. Each citizen was assigned to a particular career depending upon the skills and abilities he had demonstrated in school, and the careers that were available were also based on the projected needs of the nation. Since rent and health care were free, consumer goods were all that people could spend their wages on, but centrally controlled production ensured that everyone had the same things as everyone else, down to the same television sets, furniture, and types of living space.

History proved that this system could not last. While the salaries of workers were raised over time, prices for goods were kept artificially low to forestall any civilian discontent. This led to people having more money to spend than things to spend it on. While a limited black market of illicit goods sprang up in response, people's money mostly lay idle in the banks, meaning that although the government paid the people, it wasn't getting enough money back to fund its own activities. Combined with rampant internal corruption and the resource-draining arms race with the United States, the Soviet economy eventually collapsed under its own weight.

Though undone by its fatal flaws, the communist system freed people from most concerns about money by virtue of the simple fact that the average person had enough to buy the majority of the goods that were available. There was no option to buy luxury goods or engage in other forms of conspicuous consumption, but the basic necessities of life were affordable for all. Under a capitalist system, there are no such guarantees, as many Eastern Europeans found out the hard way during their countries' economic transitions. People lost their state-controlled jobs overnight, causing particular hardships for members of older generations who were less adept at fighting for a spot in the new marketplace of employment. And since prices had been held constant since the 1950s, inflation now ran rampant. This made consumer goods, especially foreign ones, extremely expensive, and it destroyed the value of people's life savings. Though some people who were in the right place at the right time benefited enormously from the switch to capitalism, they achieved this mostly through profiteering. One man I spoke with summed up the shift quite succinctly: "In the Soviet Union you had money but couldn't buy anything. Now you can buy anything but don't have any money."

His statement nicely illustrates an important distinction, elegantly made by psychologist and social theorist Erich Fromm in his 1941 book *Escape from Freedom*, about the nature of one of our culture's most cherished values. Fromm argues that freedom is composed of two complementary parts. A common view of freedom is that it means "freedom from the political, economic, and spiritual shackles that have bound men," which defines it as the absence of others forcibly interfering with the pursuit of our goals. In contrast to this "freedom from," Fromm identifies an alternate sense of freedom as an *ability*: the "freedom to" attain certain outcomes and realize our full potential. "Freedom from" and "freedom to" don't always go together, but one must be free in both senses to obtain full benefit from choice. A child may be *allowed* to have a cookie, but he won't get it if he can't reach the cookie jar high on the shelf.

The idealized capitalist system first and foremost emphasizes "freedom from" external restrictions on one's ability to rise in society's ranks. At least in theory, people are given equal opportunity to succeed or fail based on their own merits. But a world without restrictions is a competitive one, and people who are more talented, harder working, or simply luckier will have an advantage. As a result, a wide variety of goods and services will exist, but not everyone will have access to the full range of choice available; some people may even be unable to afford basic necessities such as food, housing, and health care. The idealized communist/socialist system, by contrast, aims for equality of outcomes rather than of opportunities, guaranteeing all its members the "freedom to" obtain an adequate standard of living. The rub is that the additional resources given to those in need have to come from somewhere, or more specifically some*one*, which means reducing others' "freedom from" and having the state commandeer their property and dictate their economic activities.

True choice requires that a person have the ability *to* choose an option and not be prevented *from* choosing it by any external force, meaning that a system tending too far toward either extreme will limit people's opportunities. Also, both extremes can produce additional problems in practice. Aside from the fact that a lack of "freedom to" can lead to privation, suffering, and death for those who can't provide for themselves, it can also lead to a de facto plutocracy. The extremely wealthy can come to wield disproportionate power, enabling them to avoid punishment for illegal practices or to change the law itself in ways that perpetuate their advantages at the cost of others, a charge often levied against the "robber baron" industrialists of the late nineteenth century. A lack of "freedom from," on the other hand, can encourage people to do less work than they're capable of since they know their needs will be met, and it may stifle innovation and entrepreneurship because people receive few or no additional material benefits for exerting additional effort. Moreover, a government must have extensive power over its people to implement such a system, and as can be seen in the actions of the majority of communist governments in the past, power corrupts.

Fortunately, although it's impossible to maximize both types of freedom simultaneously, the game isn't zero-sum. It's possible to get the best of both worlds to some extent, for example by levying taxes to create a social safety net—a relatively minor imposition on "freedom from" in exchange for significant benefits to many people's "freedom to." (Of course, a tax rate that one person sees as woefully inadequate to provide for the needy may seem criminally high to another.) While most people will favor some balance between the two extremes, we all make assumptions about the world—based on individual experience and cultural background—that affect our judgment of how that balance should look.

Those who live in formerly communist countries have been handed the challenging task of transitioning from a society on one end of the spectrum to a democratic and capitalist society that lies much closer to the opposite end. As I spoke with a variety of people in Berlin, it became clear that one hurdle in this transition has been that people's long-held assumptions about fairness can't simply be swapped for another set of beliefs. I consistently found that West Berliners, like Westerners in general, understood the world through the lens of "freedom from." On the other hand, East Berliners, and in particular the older people, focused on "freedom to," even though communism was now only a memory for them. For instance, Klaus lamented, "In the old days, the only place I could vacation was Hungary, but at least I knew I had a vacation. Now I could go anywhere, but I can afford to go nowhere." Hermann expressed a similar longing for the old days: "Back then, there were but two TV channels, but everyone had those channels. It wasn't like today, where some have hundreds and others have none." Katja was most dissatisfied with the way the new system affected health care: "Before, I only had one doctor that I could go to. Today, there are many to choose from, but the doctors don't care. The good ones cost money. I don't feel like there's anyone to look out for me when I get sick." The younger East Berliners voiced the same sentiments, although not as strongly as the older generation did, perhaps due to the fact that the older generation had experienced the greatest economic fallout from the transition.

As I expanded the scope of my interviews to countries like Ukraine, Russia, and Poland, again and again I observed similar beliefs regarding the fairest distribution of choice, even among students at the very top universities in these nations, who could expect to enjoy a high level of future success due to their education. During the course of our discussion, I offered the students a hypothetical choice between two worlds: one in which there are fewer choices but everyone has the same access to them, and another in which there are a greater number of choices but some people have more than others. One woman in Poland, Urzula, responded, "Probably, I would like to live in the first world. I think so. I am this kind of person that doesn't like splendor. I am not jealous because everyone works for their status, but I don't like people who boast about it. It turns me off and I wouldn't like that kind of world." Another Polish interviewee, Jozef, echoed the same idea: "Theoretically, the first world is better." In Ukraine, Illya remarked, "If only some people have access to lots of choices but the others do not, there will be many social and interpersonal conflicts. Therefore, it is better when everybody has the same choices." A Polish business student named Henryk responded, "I'm better off in the second system, but I think the first way is more fair." Even if they felt that "freedom from" might offer them greater opportunity on the individual level than "freedom to," the younger interviewees did not believe that this was the best model for society as a whole.

Not only did the respondents find the idea of more choice for fewer people to be unfair, many of the Eastern European interview subjects did not welcome the proliferation of choice. When asked what words or images he associated with choice, Grzegorz from Warsaw responded, "Oh, for me it's fear. There are some dilemmas. I'm used to having no choice. Everything was always done for me.

And when I have to make my own choice about my life I am afraid."
Bohdan from Kiev said of the variety of consumer products available, "It's too much. We do not need everything that is there." As a
sociologist at the Warsaw Survey Agency explained to me, the older
generation didn't have the experience of consumerism that we're
used to in American culture, and they "jumped from nothing to a
world of choice all around them. They didn't have a chance to learn
how to react." As a result, they regard the newfound opportunities
with some amount of ambivalence or suspicion.

One of the most interesting revelations came not from any question we asked during our interview but from a simple gesture of hospitality. When the participants arrived, we offered them something
to drink from a selection of seven popular sodas like Coke, Diet
Coke, Pepsi, and Sprite. When I presented this selection to one of our
first participants and waited for him to respond with his choice, he
caught me off guard with his reply: "Well, but it doesn't matter. It's
all just soda. That's just one choice." I was so struck by his remark
that from then on, I showed the same selection to everyone I interviewed and asked them, "How many choices are there?" I began to
observe a pattern in their responses. Again and again, rather than
viewing the seven sodas as seven separate choices, they saw only one
choice: soda or no soda. When we put out water and juice to accompany the selection of sodas, they saw this as three choices: soda,
water, or juice. For these interviewees, the different types of soda
didn't represent different choices.

We tend to take it for granted in the United States that the
moment a new product enters the marketplace, it will be viewed as
another option. A new flavor of soda expands your choice set. But
with the perspective that such additional options do not represent
more choice, it's no wonder that the citizens of formerly communist
countries reacted to the proliferation of such "choices" with skepticism. As one Polish man, Tomasz, commented, "I do not need ten
types of chewing gum. I don't mean there should be no choice, but

I think some choices are quite artificial. In reality, many choices are between things that are not much different." True choice was instead seen as having "freedom to." For example, Anastasia, a professor in Kiev, said that with the move to capitalism, "I think that we lost the privilege of equal opportunities. And because everybody had equal opportunities, I have an impression that I had more choices in the Soviet Union than what I have now."

These differences in perspective regarding "freedom from" and "freedom to" are not limited to those exposed to competing capitalist and communist ideologies. In general, the more people or cultures emphasize collectivism over individualism, the more they favor systems that guarantee basic necessities to everyone over ones that facilitate individual success. Even Western Europeans, who are quite individualist in an absolute sense but relatively less so than Americans, are more likely to support government policies consistent with "freedom to" rather than "freedom from." For example, the income tax rate for the wealthiest individuals in the United States was 35 percent in 2009, 12 percentage points lower than the average in the European Union. In 1998, the United States spent 11 percent of its Gross Domestic Product (GDP) on subsidies and transfers like Social Security, Medicaid, and welfare benefits, compared to the 21 percent average in the European Union nations.

Our beliefs about how much personal control people have over their lives, which are shaped in part by the level of individualism to which we have been exposed, also play an important role in our preferences for allocating choice. People who see themselves and others as having high personal control tend to favor "freedom from," not only because it provides more opportunities to attain their personal goals but also on grounds of justice—those who put in the most effort will be rewarded, while those who slack off won't be able to ride anyone else's coattails. On the other hand, people who believe that success is primarily determined by fate, including the circumstances of a person's birth, tend to consider systems that prioritize "freedom to" as being more just. After all, if no amount of effort can guarantee success, some deserving people would otherwise be unable to obtain the necessities of life on their own.

The consequences of these differing worldviews can be seen in the fact that beliefs about control are strongly related to political ideology. Conservative political parties typically favor laissez-faire economic policies while liberals favor larger government and social programs, and data from the World Values Survey show that, within both the United States and the states of the European Union, self-described liberals are less likely to endorse statements such as "The poor are lazy" and more likely to endorse ones such as "Luck determines income" than conservatives are. In Europe, where many countries possess strong democratic socialist parties that are further to the left than any mainstream U.S. political party, 54 percent of people believe that one's income is determined by luck, compared to only 30 percent of Americans. And as people vote in accordance with their beliefs, they collectively shift their societies toward one concept of freedom or the other.

At this point, an obvious question would be "Which approach is better overall?" Such questions are effectively impossible to answer, though, because the differences in people's concepts of freedom influence not only the policies they support but also the measures they use for judging the welfare of people affected by them. Those who believe in "freedom from" are more likely to look to measures such as GDP per capita, which gives a rough sense of the potential opportunities available. For example, one might highlight that the United States had a 2008 per capita GDP of $47,000 compared to the $33,400 average of the European Union. America is also home to over six times as many billionaires as any other nation, including three of the five richest people on the planet. Those who believe more strongly in "freedom to" might instead look to measures such as the Gini coefficient, which assesses the equality of income distribution in a given country. Out of the 133 countries for which the

Gini coefficient is measured, Sweden has the most equitable distribution of wealth and resources among its inhabitants, and many of the former members of the Soviet Union and its satellite states fall in the top 30 despite having low per capita GDPs. The United States is ninety-fourth, right below Cameroon and the Ivory Coast. While the great experiment of American democracy has led to unprecedented national wealth, it has also created a society rife with inequality.

Americans as a whole arguably believe more wholeheartedly in the primacy of "freedom from" than any other nation. This ideal is often expressed as the "American Dream," a term coined by historian James Truslow Adams in 1931: "The American Dream is that dream of a land in which life should be better and richer and fuller for everyone, with opportunity for each according to ability or achievement.... [A] dream of social order in which each man and each woman shall be able to attain to the fullest stature of which they are innately capable, and be recognized by others for what they are, regardless of the fortuitous circumstances of birth or position." The basic premise is that no one can stand in the way of your highest aspirations, provided that you have the ambition and the skills to realize them. If you have a dream and a work ethic, there is an international consensus that this is *the* country for making it big.

While the American Dream has undoubtedly inspired many people to achieve great things, it has also remained nothing more than a dream for countless others. The United States was long considered the land of opportunity the world over, and perhaps for a time it was. Today, for the majority of the population, it's on a par with most other postindustrial nations. Recent studies have even found a stronger correlation between parents' income and their children's income in the United States than in Western European countries such as Sweden and Germany, showing that success in the United States is based slightly less on effort and more on the circumstances of one's birth. Whether you interpret these findings as evidence that Americans are too optimistic about their nation's unique status or that citizens of other nations are too pessimistic about their own opportunities, it demonstrates the power and persistence of people's values and beliefs.

In the end, whether the American Dream is achievable in practice may not be what's most important. Like any worldview, it is very real as a force that has shaped the ideals of an entire nation. In the United States, the narrative of the American Dream serves as a foundation for everyone's life story, and when we truly acknowledge its power, maybe we can also begin to understand why other nations and cultures with other dreams have very different ideas about choice, opportunity, and freedom.

VIII. THE END OF TOLERANCE

I hope I successfully answered some of the questions I raised about different approaches to choice, and I hope these answers were both surprising and thought provoking. What I hope most of all, though, is that some of what I have presented here will help to move us past mere tolerance. Today, many of us are taught that learning about other cultures is fun! People are different, and that's okay! Grab a pair of chopsticks, or forgo utensils altogether! There's nothing wrong with this sort of excitement. In fact, it is a very good thing that we are no longer as distrustful of cultural strangers as we used to be. But it's simply not enough to eat sushi, wear a sari, and sing "It's a Small World After All." It is certainly a more *connected* world, but it is also more bewildering and chaotic. What was once contained within cultural and national boundaries now spills over due to powerful forces that blur borders: physical migration (the Census Bureau estimates that fewer than half of Americans will be of European ancestry by 2042), the flood of international media (e.g., BBC, CNN, Al-Jazeera, and other foreign TV and film), and the wide-open forum of the Internet. These developments have led to more and more personal and cultural narratives, and an increasing number of people now assemble their life stories from narratives so disparate that the mind reels from trying to contain all that contradiction. Everything is touching or overlapping with everything else, and while this fosters cultural hybridization, it also leads to conflict.

In the past, the most frequent outcome when different cultures encountered one another was a clash. Each side attempted to demonstrate its superiority, whether rhetorically, economically, or militarily, thereby convincing—or forcing—the other side to assimilate. This isn't surprising since, according to each culture's narrative, it is the best culture with the best values, and the proof is that it has survived when so many others have not. Many people think that we are now in the midst of "the clash of civilizations" so famously predicted by political scientist Samuel P. Huntington in the early 1990s. Even if this is true, the conflict cannot end the way such conflicts did in the past. One civilization can no longer fully consume another, and it also cannot set up a giant barrier to keep the other out. Tolerance and respect don't cut the mustard, either, especially not when deeply held beliefs and lives are at stake. So we seem to be at an impasse, thinking we have little to share and no clear way to move forward.

But there is common ground, though it may sometimes seem to be no-man's-land. At the broadest level, it's unquestionable that the basic values of life, liberty, and the pursuit of happiness truly are common to people around the globe. Indeed, as we saw in the previous chapter, we have a biological need for choice and control. It follows from these universal needs that people have rights—such as equal protection under the law, participation in the political process, education—as was affirmed by 171 nations from all parts of the world at the 1993 World Conference on Human Rights in Vienna. However, it doesn't follow that, when given the freedom to choose for themselves, the social structures that people from other parts of the world create will—or should—closely resemble the Western model. They may decide to choose independently or incorporate others' viewpoints, change the environment or change themselves to better adapt to it, leave each individual responsible for her own well-being or take steps to prevent anyone from falling through the cracks.

So, beyond the level of basic human rights, how best can we observe, evaluate, and learn from cultural differences? While tolerance is certainly better than judging every other culture from the fixed point of one's own, tolerance has severe limitations. Rather than promoting conversation and encouraging critical self-reflection, it often leads to disengagement: "You think your way, I'll think mine, and we won't interfere with one another." Members of different cultures try to segregate themselves, but values-based conflicts flare up when circumstances force them to interact. We cannot tolerate one another by shutting the doors because our spaces, real or virtual, intersect as never before. We can choose to turn these areas of intersection into battlegrounds or into meeting places.

I can't offer a 3-step plan, or even a 30-step plan, for how to reach whatever it is that comes after tolerance. But I know we cannot live solely by our own stories or assume that the stories we live by are the only ones that exist. Since other stories are often told in other languages, we must strive for a metaphorical multilingualism, if not for a literal one. One way to explain what I mean by this is to use a humble example from my own life. Though I am blind, I regularly use the language of the sighted to better communicate in this visually driven world. I "see," I "watch," I "look." With the help of descriptions provided by family, friends, and colleagues, I am able to make my way through the world of the sighted. I am able to write this book and, I hope, make vivid what I have never seen. As I am in a small minority, you might say I have little choice in the matter, but my life is both easier and richer as a result of my fluency in "visual speak." I have access to the dominant language and experience of the sighted, and because I have this access, I can better convey my own experience. There's no easy way to scale up my method and make fluency in multiple cultures a snap, but learning how our narratives of choice differ is a good first step. And for now, all I'm asking is that you take that step into strange lands and strange languages.

CHAPTER THREE

Song of Myself

I. HELP YOURSELF

You are walking down the aisle on this, the first day of the rest of your life. It isn't your wedding day (you'll find your soul mate soon enough), but nonetheless, you're stepping over a threshold: You are getting Self-Help. Like millions of others who have sought growth and knowledge in this row of books, you have a dream. All you want is to have it all—fame, riches, a long life, a doting family—and you hear Self-Help is where you can get it. See this? It says if you can focus and control your mind, you can control the physical world. Control is *exactly* what you need! First, make a list of all your goals. Um, scratch that: a list of all your *habits*. Or was it a list of all the places you want to visit before you die? (Which won't be for years yet—that shelf over there has a great selection of fountain-of-youth books.) In any case, it all begins with loving yourself and being true to who you are. But there's the rub. You're not quite sure who you are because, well, you still need to "find yourself," and isn't Self-Help supposed to tell you where to look? How are you supposed to practice Self-Help if one of its goals is also a prerequisite?

So perhaps you keep on going past the Self-Help aisle to the Travel section, which entices you with glossy cover photographs on guidebooks that promise the trip of a lifetime. Perhaps backpacking through Southeast Asia, skydiving in Australia, or volunteering in Africa will help you figure out who you are. Can you afford to go on the expensive retreat that offers meditation classes to get you in touch with your inner self? Then again, can you afford *not* to?

The great artist Michelangelo claimed that his sculptures were already present in the stone, and all he had to do was carve away everything else. Our understanding of identity is often similar: Beneath the many layers of shoulds and shouldn'ts that cover us, there lies a constant, single, true self that is just waiting to be discovered. We think of the process of finding ourselves as a personal excavation. We dig deep, getting under the surface, throwing away the extraneous, to reveal our everlasting self. And the tool with which we unearth the pièce de résistance is none other than choice. Your choices of which clothes to wear or which soda to drink, where you live, which school to attend and what to study, and of course your profession all say something about you, and it's your job to make sure that they are an accurate reflection of who you really are.

But who are you, really? The imperative "Just be yourself!" seems straightforward enough. (What could be easier than being who you already are?) Yet we often end up blinking in its headlights, perhaps frozen in place by the concomitant notion that we might, if we are not careful, turn into someone else. It's difficult to move forward when each step could move us further away from the "authentic" self, and so we dither. No longer do young adults embark upon a long-term career, get married, and have children shortly after completing their education. Instead, the years from about 18 to 25 are now characterized by the search for identity. Whereas the median age for first marriage in the United States held relatively steady at 21 for women and 23 for men until as recently as 1970, it has since risen sharply to 25 for women and 27 for men.

As *Time* magazine proclaimed in 2005, there's a new breed of "twixters" who seem trapped betwixt and between adolescence and adulthood. The cover describes them as "young adults who live off their parents, bounce from job to job, and hop from mate to mate. They're not lazy...they just won't grow up." And while the term "twixter" was coined to refer specifically to Americans in search of their identities, the phenomenon itself is global. In Europe they're known as NEETs (Not in Education, Employment, or Training), in Japan as "parasite singles," and in Italy as *bamboccioni* ("grown-up babies"). Even in more collectivist countries the pressure to discover one's true self, and the uncertainty and hesitation that often accompany this lofty goal, has become increasingly apparent.

By traditional standards these groups may appear stagnant, but there's no particular reason to measure growth or progress by how early one marries and reproduces. The past decades have seen numerous social changes that have created greater opportunities for people who previously had few options. Is it any surprise that they should wish to explore and take advantage of their newfound freedom to be themselves? Indeed, wouldn't we think less of them if they didn't? And in some ways, standing in the Self-Help aisle, we are after the same thing. But what are we really looking for when we look for ourselves? And why is it so important for us to find it?

II. DO YOUR THING

The search for a meaningful answer to the question "Who am I?" has driven people throughout history. As we saw in the last chapter, for members of traditional collectivist cultures, the answer was often close at hand: Identity was inextricably linked to group affiliation. With the rise and spread of individualism, whether as a culture's dominant paradigm or merely as a contrast to the way things have always been done, identity has become a more personal matter.

At the heart of individualist societies is the idea that what you are in terms of race, class, religion, and nationality cannot fully determine *who* you are—a core self or essence exists independent of external influence. But as we'll see next, the process of defining who we are has itself undergone quite a change.

Since the United States has long touted itself as "the land of the free," and attracted many immigrants for this very reason, looking into its history is a good way of charting how our concept of identity has changed over time. One of the first and most influential conceptions of individualism was the set of beliefs that Max Weber dubbed the "Protestant work ethic," endorsed by many of the American colonists. An exemplary icon of this ethic was founding father Benjamin Franklin, who—in eighteenth-century popular culture—played the roles of Oprah, Dr. Phil, and Warren Buffett all at once. He was widely popular and trusted as a business leader, politician, and journalist, and his *Poor Richard's Almanack* gave America many aphorisms to fuel the striving of farmers, artisans, and entrepreneurs through the nineteenth century and up to the present day. Franklin was practical above all: Do your job well, pinch your pennies, provide for your family, and all will be well in the end. With these standards of character met, there would be opportunity enough for any man to succeed in the world. To be an individual was to find one's own livelihood and then enjoy the resulting success and wealth. A large house, a well-tended garden, and fattened livestock denoted God's favor and attracted the respect of the world.

Though this system allowed people to choose their livelihood, it was not a free pass to do whatever they wanted. While people *could* potentially adopt a far wider range of identities than in previous centuries, there was still a strong social consensus on who they *ought* to be. A person of "good character" was one who acted in accordance with the expectations of his community. If he deviated by being idle or ostentatious, holding unconventional political or religious views, or violating sexual mores by cohabitating or having a child outside of wedlock, then he was judged to be—tsk-tsk—of poor character. The only socially acceptable way to stand out was to fit in, demonstrating excellence by being more industrious and pious, or by otherwise conforming to the prevailing norms more perfectly than the people around you.

The consequences of one's "character" went well beyond social approval or censure. For example, when the Ford Motor Company began offering a $5-a-day wage in 1916 (double the average daily wage at the time), it came with a few strings attached. Workers qualified only if they adhered to Ford's definition of the "American way," which included refraining from drinking or gambling, being able to speak English (recent immigrants were required to attend "Americanization" classes), and maintaining traditional family roles. Women were not eligible for bonuses unless they were single and supporting their family on their own, and if a married woman worked outside the home, even for the Ford Company itself, her husband became ineligible for the bonus as well. These rules were enforced by a committee known as the Socialization Organization, which visited employees' homes to ensure they were behaving properly. Though we would now consider this discriminatory and a violation of privacy, in its day the policy was accepted and even praised by many.

Just as people had to hew to stringent social standards, they had to follow new standards of efficiency and conformity at work. The Ford Company is most famous today for another of its innovations: the assembly line. It was the latest development in a process that had begun with the industrial revolution in eighteenth-century England: a shift from individual farming and craftsmanship to working for wages in factories, where each worker was little more than a replaceable part of the complex machinery. This ethos was boiled down to a science by Frederick Winslow Taylor in his highly influential 1911 monograph *The Principles of Scientific Management*, which advocated the use of precise, rigidly defined procedures in every aspect of a worker's job in order to ensure maximum efficiency. Here's Taylor's account of his conversation with Mr. Schmidt, a pig-iron handler at a steel mill:

> "What I want to find out is whether you are a high-priced man or one of these cheap fellows here. What I want to find out is whether you want to earn $1.85 a day or whether you are satisfied with $1.15, just the same as all those cheap fellows are getting."
>
> "Did I vant $1.85 a day? Vas dot a high-priced man? Vell, yes, I was a high-priced man."
>
> "Well, if you are high-priced man, you will do exactly as this man tells you tomorrow, from morning till night. When he tells you to pick up a pig and walk, you pick it up and you walk, and when he tells you to sit down and rest, you sit down. You do that right straight through the day. And what's more, no back talk....Now you come on to work here tomorrow morning and I'll know before night whether you are really a high-priced man or not."

Taylor goes on to report proudly that Schmidt followed his instructions to the letter, and in doing so increased his efficiency, and therefore his wages, by 60 percent. He makes no mention of how Schmidt felt about this new routine; that was irrelevant to the efficient operation of the mill.

However, even before Ford and Taylor made such standardization the norm, voices were raised in protest against the tendency to squeeze square pegs into round holes. One early and influential critic was essayist and philosopher Ralph Waldo Emerson, who described the society of the mid-nineteenth century as "a joint-stock company, in which the members agree for the better securing of his bread to each shareholder, to surrender the liberty and culture of the eater." "The virtue in most request," he wrote, "is conformity." Emerson

advocated instead a philosophy—radical for its time—of independence and self-reliance, refusing to bow to the dictates of society.
Only in this way could one discover and express one's true self.
"Under all these screens I have difficulty to detect the precise man
you are," he wrote, "but do your thing, and I shall know you." The
"screens" Emerson mentions not only hide us from the full view of
others, they hide us from ourselves, and one could argue that when
we make "authentic" choices, we begin to tear down those screens.

It is no surprise that some trace the beginnings of the self-help
movement to Emerson. "Do your thing!" is certainly the type of
phrase that self-help thrives on. But unlike many of today's "gurus,"
Emerson was not engaging in showmanship or trying to make a
quick buck. He was one of the leading intellectual figures of his day,
and his views provided a powerful counterpoint to the prevailing
social order; one contemporary described his works as America's
"Intellectual Declaration of Independence."

The idea that one should choose all aspects of one's life struck a
chord. It found increasing expression in popular culture, for example in the work of Sinclair Lewis, the first American to receive the
Nobel Prize for Literature. Lewis painted a scathing portrait of the
conformity and hollowness of small-town life during the 1920s in
books like *Main Street*. The novel's protagonist, Carol Kennicott,
is convinced by her husband to relocate from metropolitan St. Paul
to the tiny village of Gopher Prairie, Minnesota, where he grew up.
The free-spirited, deep-thinking Carol finds rural life suffocating in
its embrace of convention and conformity, and believes this is why
so many others like her flee small towns, never to return.

> The reason, Carol insisted, is not a whiskered rusticity. It is
> nothing so amusing!
>
> It's an unimaginatively standardized background, a slug-
> gishness of speech and manners, a rigid ruling of the spirit
> by the desire to appear respectable. It is contentment...the

contentment of the quiet dead, who are scornful of the living for their restless walking. It is negation canonized as the one positive virtue. It is the prohibition of happiness. It is slavery self-sought and self-defended. It is dullness made God.

A savorless people, gulping tasteless food and sitting afterward, coatless and thoughtless, in rocking chairs prickly with inane decorations, listening to mechanical music, saying mechanical things about the excellence of Ford automobiles, and viewing themselves as the greatest race in the world.

In describing Carol's trials and tribulations in Gopher Prairie—meant to represent any and all of the countless small towns across America—Lewis highlighted the struggle that lay ahead for anyone who chose to assert personal independence in a cultural climate that preferred to stifle expressions of individuality. It is true that Carol takes a condescending approach to the village folk, but that doesn't make her observations any less true. Today, Carol and Lewis might be accused by certain parties of being representatives of the "East Coast liberal media elite," which only goes to show that even as the words we use change, many of the same tensions persist.

The "mechanical" quality of life that industrialization fostered was proving to be a source of dissatisfaction for many, which made it ripe for its satirization by Charlie Chaplin in his 1936 film *Modern Times*. Chaplin's legendary character the Little Tramp goes to work in a factory that has taken the spirit of Taylorism to its extreme. He is instructed to stand at a particular spot on a fast-paced assembly line and screw bolts onto the pieces of machinery that pass him at an ever-increasing rate. His hands become so accustomed to the prescribed movement that even after he has left the assembly line, he continues to compulsively twist anything that remotely resembles a screw, much to the consternation of anyone nearby who happens to have a nose or be wearing buttons. While in the factory, the Tramp is not even allowed to eat unsupervised; in the name of efficiency, he is fed at a "feeding machine" station with forkfuls of steak and a corn on the cob that is rotated for him. In the film's most famous scene, he becomes so overwhelmed by his work that he simply lies down on the conveyor belt and allows himself to be pulled into the factory's mechanical belly. His body slides along through the rotating gears and wheels, and he becomes a literal cog in the machine.

Ironically, industrialization played an important role in shaping the landscape of choice that we now take for granted. The Protestant work ethic's emphasis on thriftiness had made practical sense in the nineteenth century, when credit was tight, as well as during the Great Depression, but in the post–World War II era it became increasingly incompatible with the average worker's greater prosperity. What's more, manufacturers could produce more goods than people needed, so they strove to push up demand by adopting innovations in style and advertising, thereby transforming the act of purchasing from a purely practical one to a self-expressive one. When you bought a car, for example, you were not only meeting your need for transportation but making a statement about who you were and what was important to you. The parallel expansion of mass media furthered the trend. People could now participate vicariously in the lives of glamorous movie stars and entertainers like the rebellious James Dean and the provocative Elvis Presley. After the white-picket-fence, Stepford-y early '50s, a bright new vision of success was developing, one that jettisoned blending in and dutifully playing your role in favor of standing out from the crowd by expressing your unique personality.

These economic and cultural forces combined in the late '50s and '60s to create a widespread shift in society's conception of individual identity. An entire generation grew up in an era of prosperity with no great cause to unify them in the way World War II had done for the previous generation: the perfect environment for the rise of an ethos of independence. Beat poets like Allen Ginsberg and Jack Kerouac challenged the mainstream culture of the '50s, and the road they were on led straight to the hippie countercultural movement of the '60s. In 1964, the Beatles made their first live appearance on *The Ed Sullivan Show*, sparking controversy with their unusual mop-tops. Hundreds of thousands of Beatlemaniacs and other young people began to push against the boundaries through music, long hair, soft drug use, and explorations of alternative spirituality. Though the more extreme manifestations of this paradigm shift in the concept of self subsided by the end of the '70s, the message endured: independence over conformity, (almost) always! And thanks to the globalizing forces of mass media technology and increasing international integration in the economic sphere, the individualist values were readily exported to the rest of the world, along with products like Coca-Cola and Levi's jeans, which came to symbolize these values.

Where does this whirlwind tour through history drop us off? In a rather curious place, actually. Here, in Choiceland, I can select among options that didn't exist or weren't available to people like me until quite recently. Variations on the traditional family structure (double income, no kids, stay-at-home fathers, single parenting, adoption, same-sex marriage, and so on) are becoming increasingly acceptable across the globe, and where these families reside is more and more a matter of choice. By 1970, two-thirds of the inhabitants of major U.S. cities had been born elsewhere, as had nearly half the inhabitants of Asian cities. The most recent U.S. census shows that 39 million Americans, or 13 percent of the population, relocated just within the past year.

Even religion, which was once considered as absolute a marker as eye color, now comes in a variety pack; more than half of Americans have changed their faith at least once, according to a 2009 Pew poll. The fastest-growing category consists of those with no religious affiliation at all. For that matter, eye color itself can now be altered, thanks to tinted contact lenses, and with full-blown cosmetic surgery we can literally change the face we present to the world. From baristas with hair colors that don't exist in nature to CEOs in jeans, people are increasingly permitted, even expected, to express their individual styles in the workplace as well as in their personal lives. Online communities like MySpace, Facebook, and Second Life give us full control over the personas we present to others. There are no signs that these trends of increasing choice of identity are temporary; if anything they seem poised to grow in the future.

While this unparalleled freedom of choice can be liberating, it also carries with it certain demands. As Nikolas Rose, professor of sociology at the London School of Economics, writes in his book *Powers of Freedom*, "Modern individuals are not merely 'free to choose,' but *obliged* to be free, to understand and enact their lives in terms of choice. They must interpret their past and dream their future as outcomes of choices made or choices still to make. Their choices are, in their turn, seen as realizations of the attributes of the choosing person—expressions of personality—and reflect back upon the person who has made them." So to be oneself is to make the choices that best reflect the self, and these choices—taken cumulatively—are the expression and enactment of that most treasured value: freedom. As citizens of Choiceland we live in the ultimate democracy, and we are obliged to make choices not only for ourselves, but also in order to affirm our commitment to the very notion of liberty. Our personal decisions have a political dimension.

When the locus of power shifts to the choosing individual, the question of who that individual is—what his goals and motivations are—becomes very important. It necessitates self-scrutiny at a level that is confusing and, frankly, a bit scary. And as our horizons widen, the number of possible selves also multiplies. The block of marble surrounding our sculpture keeps getting bigger, with more and more to chip away before we can uncover the essential form within. In other words, the process of self-discovery becomes more challenging at the very moment it is most imperative. If no single path in life has a privileged claim to being right, there are no easy answers for any of us; it becomes exponentially more difficult to know ourselves, to be ourselves, to do our thing. How are we to go about finding our identity and choosing in accordance with it? Let's explore the three major challenges we face in this process, and perhaps we'll arrive at a different understanding of the relationship between who we are and what we choose.

III. I AM UNIQUE, JUST LIKE EVERYONE ELSE

They say that when one of your senses is compromised, your other senses become sharper. In my case, a rather astonishing sixth sense has developed: I can "read" you and give you a personality assessment without ever having met you. Allow me to demonstrate.

> You are a hardworking person. Others don't always appreciate that about you because you're not able to meet everyone's expectations. But when something really matters to you, you put forth your best effort. No, you're not *always* successful by conventional measures, but that's okay because you're not someone who sets too much store by what the average person thinks. You believe certain rules and standards exist for good reason, so you don't go out of your way to defy them, but what you really rely on to guide you is your strong inner compass. This strength isn't necessarily visible to others, and they may underestimate your resourcefulness, but sometimes you surprise even yourself with your abilities. You enjoy learning new things, but you don't think all education has to take place in a formal environment or have a specific purpose. You would like to be able to do more for the less fortunate, but even when you can't, you are caring and considerate in your own way. Life has dealt you a few harsh blows, but you've pulled through and you intend to keep up your spirits. You know that if you stay focused and confident, your efforts will bear

fruit. In fact, a special opportunity is about to present itself in either your personal or your professional life. If you watch out for it and pursue it fully, you will achieve your goal!

Now be honest. That was a good profile, right? Maybe not entirely accurate, but still pretty amazing considering I wrote it without knowing you and well before you had even picked up this book. If you tell your friends and family members to each get a copy, they can also benefit from my talent. No? You're not going to rush out and proclaim me a seer to your loved ones? Why not?

My not-so-clever ruse is just a less sophisticated form of the tricks that "psychics" and other prognosticators use frequently with great success. As long as the clientele is not too skeptical, and the foreteller has some theatrical flair, the reading is likely to go quite well. Here's what my "sixth sense" actually comes down to:

1. People are more alike than they think.
2. What people believe about themselves, or what they would like to believe, doesn't vary much from person to person.
3. Each person is convinced that he or she is unique.

Betting on these three things, the soothsayer makes a gamble that usually pays off. Because one can speak in generalities that apply to just about anyone, and because nobody thinks that there is anything "general" about them, one doesn't require any magic powers to give a reading that feels detailed, precise, and true to the willing recipient.

Consider the results of a study by Geoffrey Leonardelli and Marilyn Brewer that asked participants to estimate the number of dots on a series of video screens, supposedly as a measure of their unconscious perceptual style. Afterward, they were told that the majority of people (about 75 to 80 percent) tend to habitually over-estimate the number of dots on the screen, while the remaining 20 to 25 percent of people were instead habitual underestimators.

Regardless of their answers, half of the participants were randomly told they had underestimated the true number of dots and the other half were told they had overestimated the true number. At no point were they told the broader implications of being a dot underestimator or overestimator; all they knew was whether they were naturally part of a majority or a minority group. Nonetheless, those who were told they were among the majority suffered a significant blow to their self-esteem. It seems that being lumped in with a crowd, no matter what the crowd stands for, can be harmful. No wonder we find ways to see ourselves as special, distinct individuals; it's a self-protective mechanism. So we would rather believe that the woman in the velvet robe and silk turban has some supernatural ability to see into our minds and souls and future than believe that we are enough like her other clients that she can give us all the same spiel.

That's how heavily invested we are in being singular and in being seen for who we truly are (or think we are). It shouldn't come as a surprise because you've probably repeatedly received the message that people who are one of a kind, or at least one of a few, are simply better people. Why else does every other high school valedictorian speech or college application essay quote from Robert Frost's "The Road Not Taken": "I took the one less traveled by / And that has made all the difference"? Being too much like others, making the choices most others make, is at best a character flaw, a form of laziness and lack of ambition, but more often than not, it is a sign that the person had no character to begin with. Such people are derogatorily referred to as zombies, drones, lemmings, sheep—terms all implying that they lack some fundamental human component. They might eventually turn into the brainwashed conformists of George Orwell's terrifying *1984* or of Pixar's charming hit movie *Wall-E*, in which the docile people of the future do exactly as they're told, switching in unison from the indistinguishable blue outfits they were all wearing a moment ago to new but equally indistinguishable red ones the minute they are told "Red is in!" In fact, in the latter, it is robots that shake the affable but dim humans out of their stupor and show them how to take control. These dystopias illustrate the fear that following the crowd may ultimately destroy the authentic self that lies deep within you.

We try and try again to convince ourselves and others around us that we're clearly different from the rest. The aptly named "better-than-average effect" describes the tendency of most people to judge themselves to be harder workers, smarter investors, better lovers, cleverer storytellers, kinder friends, and more competent parents. A wide variety of studies have shown that across the board, no matter what the ability in question, only the most minute fraction of people are willing to describe themselves as "below average." Ninety percent of us believe ourselves to be in the top 10 percent in terms of overall intelligence and ability. At the very least, we have to congratulate ourselves on our creative statistics. This phenomenon is also sometimes known as the "Lake Wobegon effect," after the fictional town described by radio show host Garrison Keillor as a place where "all the women are strong, all the men are good-looking, and all the children are above average." In our minds, it seems, we are all proud citizens of Lake Wobegon.

Even when we do follow the crowd, we believe we are still exceptional because our decisions are driven by independent thought rather than conformity. In other words, we perceive our own actions as less susceptible to common influence or routine; we are *conscious*. For example, consider two everyday illustrations of this phenomenon revealed by researchers Jonah Berger, Emily Pronin, and Sarah Moulouki, who refer to it as believing ourselves to be "alone in a crowd of sheep." In one study, students were asked to vote on several proposed legislative measures and were given information—to take into consideration—about the Republican and Democratic parties' purported positions. Perhaps unsurprisingly, most of the students voted in accordance with their own party affiliations, but with one twist: Individual voters assessed themselves as being more swayed by the merits of the proposed measures, but they believed their fellow voters had merely toed the party line. In a second study, owners of the ubiquitous iPod were asked about the factors that influenced their purchase. Sure enough, they rated themselves as having been less socially influenced in their purchasing decision than their iPod-toting peers, asserting that their own choices were instead informed by utilitarian reasons, such as small size or large memory capacity, as well as appreciation for the sleekness of the design.

Other studies have consistently revealed the same pattern. Ask

Americans "How similar are you to others?" and on average they will answer "Not very." Ask the same question in reverse—"How similar are others to you?"—and their judgment of similarity increases noticeably. The two answers should be exactly the same because the questions are, in essence, identical, but we manage to delude ourselves, just as we all claim to be above average or wholly unsusceptible to social influence. Time and time again, each one of us assumes that he or she stands out. What is it that makes us believe we're more unique than everyone else?

In part, it is our self-intimacy: I know myself in excruciating detail. I know what I think, feel, do every second I'm awake, and on the basis of this knowledge, I can confidently say that nobody else could possibly think, feel, do exactly the same. But from what I observe of other people? Well, they don't seem to be all that different from one another, do they? They shop at the same stores, watch the same TV shows, listen to the same music. It's easy to assume people are conforming when we witness them all choosing the same option, but when we choose that very option ourselves, we have no short-age of perfectly good reasons for why we just happen to be doing the same thing as those other people; they mindlessly conform, but we mindfully choose. This doesn't mean that we're all conformists in denial. It means that we regularly fail to recognize that others' thoughts and behaviors are just as complex and varied as our own. Rather than being alone in a crowd of sheep, we're all individuals in sheep's clothing.

Actually, what we want is something a little less extreme than true uniqueness. Too much of a unique thing turns us off. The dot estimator researchers ran a variation of the experiment in which some participants were told they were in the overestimating major-ity, others were told they were in the underestimating minority, and each of the rest were told that their scores were so unique, the researchers "were unable to classify you as an overestimator or an underestimator." The overestimators again experienced a decrease in self-esteem, while the underestimators experienced an increase, but the self-esteem of the people who were told they were too unique to classify also took a dive. We feel our best when we're "just right," part of a group that is specialized enough to set us apart from the masses but still definable.

My colleague Daniel Ames and I have examined what people consider to be the optimum level of uniqueness when confronting more concrete, everyday choices. We conducted a study in which some participants were given a list of 40 children's names, while others were shown 30 neckties, pairs of shoes, or sunglasses. These items were selected such that each person saw some that were considered ordinary, some that were moderately unique, and others that were very unique (as previously determined by expert judges). The first list, for example, ranged from names such as Michael or Kate, to Aiden or Addison, and on to the most unique selections, such as Maddux or Nehemiah. And the neckties started out in standard red or navy, acquired more unique characteristics with patterns like stripes or paisley, and then got really wild with neon orange leopard print and shiny panels reminiscent of disco balls.

After reviewing the lists of names or items, participants were asked to rate how unique they thought each item was, how much they liked it, and how much they thought others would like it. In line with the previously mentioned studies, they all believed themselves to be more unique than others and professed a greater tolerance for the unique. In reality, their responses were remarkably similar. Across all four categories, people rated the somewhat unique items more positively, but when it came to those that were extremely unique, they reacted negatively. It turns out that for all the positive associations Western consumer culture attaches to "uniqueness," people had clear personal limits on the amount of uniqueness that made an object appealing. "I think giving a kid a different-sounding name can be okay, as long as it's easy to pronounce and can easily turn into a nickname…but some of these are just bizarre," one participant explained. A fashion-savvy subject who had seen the list of neckties held forth: "When you're wearing a suit, your tie is the one piece that can show off your taste and personality—but with some of these I think there's just too much personality and not enough taste. It doesn't look right for a tie to be too avant-garde."

We may appreciate and aspire to a certain level of uniqueness, but we believe it's also important that our choices be understood. After all, the line between having an inimitable flair for neckwear and making a fashion faux pas is a fine one, and the fact is that most of us would rather play it a little bit safe than challenge people's notions of what constitutes an acceptable tie. We want to stand out from the majority, but usually not in a way that makes us part of a glaring and lonely minority. Sometimes, we may not choose the tie we would really like to wear for fear of where that would put us in relation to others.

"When you lie about yourself, is it to appear closer to or farther away from the middle of the bell curve?"

We are all trying to find the place on the bell curve where we feel most comfortable. If we have to bend the truth to get there, so be it. As John Donne observed 400 years ago: "No man is an island, entire of itself; every man is a piece of the continent, a part of the main." We need a good spot on the landscape of human society, which is to say, we have to work out where we want to stand in relation to the people around us, where to belong. Which groups do we want to be a part of, and how big do we want those groups to be? We may have to do some traveling to get to the place that suits us, but as they say, traveling is a great way to find yourself.

IV. THE RIGHT CONSISTENCY

Dianne was born to a wealthy, conservative family in 1916 and raised in relative comfort, removed from the historical turmoil of her time. Her father was a corporate lawyer and her mother was the daughter of a distinguished banker, so although Dianne came of age at the height of the Great Depression, her family still had the financial cushion necessary to provide her with a good education. Her parents chose for her the newly established and well-regarded Bennington College, a women's college located in rural Vermont. They saw this education as a way to improve further upon her upbringing and to help her fulfill her destiny as a respectable and well-bred young woman, one who had knowledge of the classics, was capable of speaking about them with graceful ease, and who conducted and carried herself in a manner appropriate to her background. But when Dianne entered as a freshman in 1934, she could not have found a formal education—social as well as academic—that was more different from what she had been taught in her childhood.

Bennington College had been founded based on an experimental philosophy of education that heavily emphasized Emerson's ideas of self-reliance. The college community was designed to be self-sufficient and tight-knit. The faculty was young (when the college was founded in 1932, there were no teachers over 50), uniformly liberal, and their relations with students tended to be congenial and informal rather than hierarchical. Open dialogue was encouraged, and constant two-way feedback between students and professors was maintained through consultations. Students even shared in the governance of the college community, as it was called, through participation in student-faculty governing committees in which majority vote ruled even though the faculty was outnumbered. Within this novel mode of education, so different from more traditionally structured schools like Vassar, the most admired student leaders were often described as exemplifying liberal political philosophies.

Though this environment bewildered her at first, Dianne came to feel an exhilarating freedom from the constraints of her upbringing. She began to question much of her received wisdom about the world and acquired a new circle of friends who did the same. Her junior year was an election year, and the campus was abuzz with constant heated discussion over the New Deal and other political issues of the day. The students generally found in favor of Roosevelt, the Democratic candidate, and Dianne was gradually convinced by the passionate arguments for more liberal social policy. Needless to say, her parents were nonplussed when she brought up such ideas at the family dinner table. Her father, who firmly intended to vote for Republican candidate Alf Landon and considered anyone who held liberal views "absolutely insane," accused her of being naive. To everyone's surprise, even her own, Dianne shot right back that it was his life experience that was "severely limited." For the first time in her life, she had cast tension over the household, and she began to feel that her parents were looking at her with concern and maybe even distrust. Her closest friends from high school—who had returned from Vassar and Sarah Lawrence with the expected poise—seemed suspicious of her. Why were things so different now from the way they had once been? She decided there was only one good explanation: She had come into her own, not in the way her parents had envisioned but through a path she had carved for herself. The results were bittersweet, but she was still proud of her accomplishment.

Dianne was not the only student to undergo such a marked and permanent shift in ideology during her college years. Theodore Newcomb extensively interviewed nearly 400 women who were enrolled at Bennington College from 1936 to 1939. Like Dianne, these students were generally from wealthy, conservative, "well-bred" families, and many of them experienced shifts in political views during their time at Bennington. For instance, though the 1936 presidential election was one of the most lopsided in history—Roosevelt won the popular vote by a 60 percent landslide and gained all but eight electoral votes—a full 66 percent of the Bennington parents had voted for Landon. First-year students from that year followed a similar voting pattern, with 62 percent casting the ballot for Landon as well. However, the longer a student had been at Bennington, the less likely she was to vote Republican; 43 percent of sophomores and a mere 15 percent of juniors and seniors voted for Landon.

What's more, the new political identities the students formed at college remained stable for the rest of their lives, as shown by two follow-up studies 25 and 50 years later. The Bennington grads continued to be more favorable than their peers toward liberal causes like the women's rights and civil rights movements, and less favorable toward conservative ones like the Vietnam War. They tended to surround themselves with husbands and friends who shared their political views, which they went on to impart to their own children.

There are two different ways in which the Bennington women's shift in political beliefs and the subsequent stability of their new liberal attitudes can be understood. According to the first, it is a perfect example of acting authentically, with the women moving beyond the values they received from their families and communities in order to find their true place in the world. Even today, college is considered an excellent means by which to find or become one's true self, because it offers freedom from parental influence and a fresh start with one's new classmates. Alternatively, one might say that their attitudes changed merely because they shifted to having their identities determined by a different set of forces: those exerted by the Bennington community, in this case. After all, it's unlikely to be a coincidence that their new attitudes resembled the college's existing norms so closely.

There's an element of truth to both versions, as can be seen in the Bennington alumnae's own words. As one put it, "Becoming radical meant thinking for myself and, figuratively, thumbing my nose at my family. It also meant intellectual identification with the faculty and students that I most wanted to be like." Another observed, "It didn't take me long to see that liberal attitudes had prestige value.... I became liberal at first because of its prestige value; I remain so because the problems around which my liberalism centers are important." What is most noteworthy, however, is the enduring force of their new beliefs. Beyond the question of how they initially arrived at their beliefs, what caused these beliefs to persist and even strengthen over time?

When we're young, we begin the process of sorting out the world around us in terms of our preferences: "I like ice cream. I don't like brussels sprouts. I like football. I don't like homework. I like pirates, and I want to be one when I grow up." The process becomes more sophisticated over time, but the same basic premise remains: "I tend to be an introvert. I'm a risk-taker. I love traveling but I'm impatient and can't stand the hassle of airport security." What we're getting at is the ability to say to ourselves and to the world, "I am a _____ kind of person," and to be met with agreement that we have made an accurate assessment. Ultimately, we want to make sense of ourselves and create a coherent picture of who we are.

But given that we are complicated beings who undergo a great deal of development and change in our lifetimes, making sense of our accumulated past can be quite the challenge. We must wade through the wide pool of our memories, actions, and behaviors, and some-how select whatever represents our core. In doing so, we'll naturally observe contradictions. Certainly there are many times we do things we want to do, but there are many other times when we do things because they are required by the circumstances. For example, our behavior at work—the way we dress, the way we talk to our boss—is often much more formal and conservative than the way we behave at home or with our friends. We must sift through that mixture of conflict and ambiguity to become aware of why we chose the way we did, and then determine how we should act in the future.

In the poem "Song of Myself," Emerson's disciple Walt Whitman captures this dilemma and offers a decidedly poetic retort: "Do I contradict myself? Very well then I contradict myself. (I am large. I contain multitudes.)" For most of us, though, it's not so easy to reconcile the multitudes within us. In particular, problems arise when we experience contradictions between different aspects of our selves, or between our beliefs and our actions, as in the case of the Bennington student who considers herself conservative but finds herself increasingly agreeing with her liberal peers in discussions of political matters. What can she conclude from this state of affairs? Is she acting irrationally and incomprehensibly, or perhaps bowing to social pressure and espousing opinions she doesn't actually believe? Admitting to either alternative will threaten some of the most central elements of her sense of identity as a reasonable and authentic person. This unpleasant experience of being caught between two contradictory forces is known as *cognitive dissonance*, and it can lead to anxiety, guilt, and embarrassment.

In order to function successfully, it's necessary to resolve the dissonance. Recall Aesop's fable of the fox and the grapes. After trying in vain to reach the grapes, the fox gives up and wanders away, muttering, "They were probably sour anyway." The fox's change of heart is a perfect example of a common strategy we instinctively use to reduce dissonance. When we experience a conflict between our beliefs and our actions, we can't rewind time and take back what we've already done, so we adjust our beliefs to bring them in line with our actions. If the story had gone differently, and the fox had managed to get the grapes, only to discover they were sour, he would have told himself that he liked sour grapes in order to avoid feeling that his effort had been a waste.

The need to avoid cognitive dissonance and create a consistent story about who we are can lead people to internalize values and attitudes that they initially adopted for other reasons. Numerous studies have found, for example, that asking people to write an essay that disagrees with their personal beliefs—say, in support of a tax increase that they oppose—causes them to later become more favorable to the position they argued for. For the Bennington students, reducing dissonance might have meant deciding that the prevailing liberal attitudes indeed centered on worthy problems, or even that they had always personally held such attitudes and only now had a chance to express them. By altering how we conceive our identity, external influences can have a lasting impact.

Similarly, once we have developed a coherent identity for ourselves, we preemptively avoid dissonance by choosing in ways that reinforce it. The Bennington women, for example, married liberal husbands and associated with liberal friends, but the same pattern can be seen among the members of any group: conservative, religious, eco-friendly, and so on. Of course, we don't do so purely to avoid dissonance; we also satisfy our need to belong when we seek out and associate with others who are similar to us. The end result of these freely chosen interactions is that our identity tends to become set over time and more easily definable for those around us.

The need for consistency can lead to a dilemma when we try to determine how best to lead our lives. On the one hand, we certainly don't want to be inconsistent, either in our own minds or in the eyes of others. When someone tells us, "I don't even know you anymore," the negative implications are clear: To behave in a way not in keeping with the identity that others have grown to recognize and love is to become unknowable or untrustworthy. On the other hand, the world is an ever-changing place, and in being too consistent we risk becoming inflexible and out of touch. One high-profile example of this tension popped up in the 2004 presidential campaign. John Kerry's candidacy was damaged by accusations of flip-floppery, whereas George W. Bush was admired by many for sticking to his guns. Once in office, though, Bush was criticized for parroting certain mantras with little regard for "the realities on the ground." In his roast of the president at the 2006 White House Correspondents Dinner, comedian Stephen Colbert "praised" Bush by saying, "The greatest thing about this man is he's steady. You know where he stands. He believes the same thing Wednesday that he believed on Monday—no matter what happened Tuesday." It seems that you're damned if you do change, and damned if you don't. That's what makes it so difficult to find the proper balance between consistency and flexibility.

One common, if perhaps not ideal, response to this dilemma can be seen in a study I conducted in collaboration with Rachel Wells, one of my doctoral students. We tracked hundreds of graduating college seniors as they went about looking for their first serious job, a major choice that would significantly affect their subsequent experiences and identity. As part of that study, we asked them to describe what they were looking for in their ideal job on three separate occasions over the six- to nine-month period it took them to go from initial search to successful employment. Each time, we asked them to rank the same 13 attributes of a job, including "high income," "opportunity for advancement," "job security," "opportunity for creativity," and "freedom to make decisions," from most to least important. We looked only at new graduates, but all people, no matter where they are in their career, have to make trade-offs by considering these very attributes. Is it more important to have a job that's personally fulfilling or one that lets you better provide for your family? Is it worth sacrificing job security for the chance to strike it rich? The answers to these questions are strongly influenced by who we are, and our choices, in turn, affect who we will become.

At the beginning stages of the job search process, the students tended to highly value attributes like "opportunity for creativity" and "freedom to make decisions"—in other words, more idealistic attributes that had more to do with individual fulfillment than with earning a living. The months went by, and the new graduates went from scoping out the market and sending out résumés to scheduling interviews and trying to ascertain which positions were actually open to them. Their options narrowed, and as they were forced to compare the pros and cons of real jobs, their ranking of priorities shifted: They began to value practical aspects like "potential for advancement" more highly. "I've just finished investing a lot of time and money in a great degree, and it's obvious that some positions will get me further than others," one participant said. "I want to make the most of that investment." In the third round of rankings, after they had made the final decision of which job to take, the students considered income the top priority.

When we asked the students how they had ranked the various attributes on previous occasions, rather than recognizing that their preferences had changed over time, they mistakenly said that they had always felt the same way about the job criteria. It wasn't just that they couldn't remember their original preferences but that they actively reimagined their past. "No," said one newly employed participant, "I always had job security on my mind, and with the student loans I'm dealing with now, accepting the job offer with the higher salary just made a lot more sense."

The job searchers' willingness to alter their priorities allowed them to adjust their expectations in response to their realistic options, but it also created a conflict between their initial priorities and their later ones. The more successfully they were able to resolve this conflict, by creating a false but consistent story about their values in the life-defining category of "career," the better off they were.

Those who recalled their past preferences less accurately were happier with the jobs they accepted. These protective illusions prevented them from recognizing their inconsistency, allowing them to choose in accordance with their latest priorities rather than feeling obligated to the ones they had outlined earlier in the process.

Another way to resolve the conflict, which is more practical and sustainable in the long term, is to strive for consistency at a higher level, such as the search for truth, a moral code, or a commitment to certain ideals. If our actions contradict themselves, very well then, they contradict themselves. As Stephen Colbert will tell you, it's not inconsistent to say one thing on Monday and another on Wednesday if you gained new knowledge on Tuesday or if the situation itself changed. In fact, to insist on the same thing would be to practice what Emerson called "a foolish consistency," that "hobgoblin of little minds." Keeping the bigger picture in mind allows us to reconcile the multitudes we contain, as long as we are also careful to clearly communicate to the world our broader guiding principles. To be ourselves while remaining adaptable, we must either justify a decision to change as being consistent with our identity, or we must acknowledge that our identity itself is malleable but no less authentic for it. The challenge is to feel that although we have not always been exactly who we are now, we will nevertheless always recognize ourselves.

V. DO YOU SEE WHAT I SEE?

On July 28, 2008, I woke up before the crack of dawn (4 a.m., to be exact), hailed a cab, and headed down to the Apple retail store on Fifth Avenue in Manhattan. I joined the crowds in line to buy my husband the birthday present he coveted: the new iPhone 3G. He had spent days examining the iPhone in the store and online to determine exactly what he wanted, and he had me memorize the specifications in case I made it through the line before he arrived. As I waited for hours, I went over the details: 8GB, unlimited nights and weekends, black, 8GB, unlimited nights and weekends, black. I was nearing the front, when my husband arrived. At the counter, he said, much to my surprise, "I changed my mind. I'll have the white."

"I thought you told me that white would get dirty more easily, and that black was sleeker," I responded.

He replied, "Everyone is getting the black, though. I can't carry around the same thing that everyone else has." He knew which one he wanted, the reasons why he wanted what he wanted, and he knew that he had arrived at the decision by himself. Yet, at that final moment, he changed his preference because, simply put, he did not want to be a copycat.

The "not a copycat" impulse is, in fact, well researched and documented. My favorite example is a study conducted by Dan Ariely and Jonathan Levav at a popular small-town bar and restaurant. They had a server visit each table of two or more people with a menu that gave a short description of four different beers from a local microbrewery. Each customer could choose to try one free four-ounce sample. For half the tables, the server took customer orders sequentially, as is the norm at restaurants, while for the other half he requested that each person mark his or her choice on a card without discussing it with anyone else at the table. While it was common for two or more people at the same table to order the same beer when they filled out the cards, there was much less overlap when people heard what others at their table were ordering. That is to say, the sequentially ordering customers selected a variety, often choosing all the available brews, with no single beer commanding a majority of the orders. This seems like the ultimate customization, no? Everyone gets exactly what they asked for, and no one feels pressured to try the same drink.

But when asked afterward to rate their free samples, it turned out that regardless of which beer they had chosen, people who chose in sequence were less satisfied with their choice; instead, they reported wishing that they had chosen a different beer. On the other hand, when people ordered privately they reported being happier with their sample, even though they were much more likely to be drinking the same beer as everyone else at the table. Most tellingly, only one person at each of the sequential-order tables was as satisfied as the people who had ordered independently: the person who had ordered first.

The first person to order had no other obligation than to be true to himself, but each subsequent customer who had been planning to order the same beer was faced with a dilemma. They could have simply said, "Funny, that's just what I want, too!" or pushed aside their self-consciousness about ordering the same thing, but the desire to assert their independence led them to settle for beer choice B. Once someone else had claimed their first choice, ordering the beer they wanted most became subordinate to showing that they could choose a beer on their own, thank you very much.

This study demonstrates that as we form and express our identity, we need others to see us as we see ourselves. We want to find common ground, but not be a copycat. The need is so powerful that we may even behave in ways inconsistent with our true desires in order to avoid creating the "wrong" impression. When around other people, we want to come off as entertaining but not overly attention-seeking, intelligent but not pretentious, and agreeable but not submissive. We all likely think of ourselves as embodying only the best of these attributes, but how do we go about projecting that socially?

We can't avoid the fact that any choice we make may be considered a statement about who we are, but some choices speak more loudly than others. The music we choose to play on our stereos will probably say more about us than the brand of stereo we play it on, as music choice is supposed to be determined purely by personal taste. The less a choice serves some utilitarian function, the more it implies about identity, which is why we pay special attention to categories such as music and fashion that serve no practical purpose.

To rip playlists directly off a trendy music blog or an in-the-know friend, or to exactly copy outfits from a movie or magazine, is to announce to the world that we have no mind of our own. On the other hand, using the same brand of toothpaste that a favorite actor uses could easily be attributed to the superior tartar-control abilities of the product.

Whether we do it consciously or subconsciously, we tend to organize our lives to display our identity as accurately as possible. Our lifestyle choices often reveal our values, or at least what we'd like people to perceive as our values. Someone who takes the time to volunteer at soup kitchens or clothing drives will be seen as altruistic, someone who runs marathons as highly disciplined and self-motivated, and someone who paints her own living room and reupholsters antique furniture as handy and creative. As we make our everyday choices, we continuously calculate not just which choices best match who we are and what we want but also how those choices will be interpreted by others. We look for cues in our social environment to figure out what others think of this or that, which can require being sensitive to the most localized and up-to-date details of what a particular choice means.

To observe this in action, let's consider a study conducted with Stanford University undergraduates by Jonah Berger and Chip Heath. They had experimenters go door-to-door in several of the dorms at Stanford, asking students to make a small donation to the anticancer efforts of the Lance Armstrong Foundation and to wear a yellow wristband to show their support. A week later they did another round of wristband sales, this time at a "geeky" dorm that was known on campus for its residents' strong focus on academics. A week after that, they took note of how many people were still wearing their wristbands. They found that 32 percent of students from the dorm next door to the geeky dorm, who shared a dining hall with its residents, had abandoned their wristbands in the time since the geeks had started wearing them, compared with just 6 percent of students from the dorms that were farther away. Suddenly, wearing the bracelets had gone from signaling "I'm against cancer and/or for Lance Armstrong" to "I'm against social interaction and/or for learning Klingon for recreational purposes." Those same yellow bands are worn by Lance Armstrong Foundation supporters of all stripes all over the world, and to the casual outside observer would not carry any geeky connotations, but to the students living next to the geeks, wearing the band became a suspect choice almost overnight.

Changing our behavior purely for the sake of appearances may seem to conflict with the need to be authentic and consistent, but in many ways it is actually a result of those needs. After all, resolving the tension between standing out from the crowd and becoming isolated requires finding our niche in the world. But what would happen if we weren't accepted in the place where we felt we belonged? For others to see us as a "poseur" or as "delusional" would be painful. Even worse, what if they were right? The social consequences and self-doubt that follow when our self-perceptions conflict with how others see us can be just as destabilizing to our identity as conflicts between our own self-perceptions and actions.

Because of the importance we place on aligning our self-perception with others' perceptions of us, we're constantly reading others' behavior for clues as to what they really think of us. But in spite of all the time and energy you might dedicate to speculating about what X, Y, and Z think of you, chances are you'll have a more accurate sense of what X, Y, and Z think of one another. This is not surprising since X will much more readily tell you what he thinks of Y and Z than what he thinks of you. Also, we tend to be better at reading the body language and facial expressions of people when those cues are directed not at us but at a third party.

We're pretty good at knowing what people think of us in the aggregate—for example, whether we're seen by most as shy or outgoing, rude or considerate—but to know what any *one* person thinks of us? Well, we might as well roll the dice. Women can usually tell if a man is interested (but not the other way around), and we can all tell if people actually find our jokes funny. Beyond that, numerous studies have found that there are often wide discrepancies between how we see ourselves and how others see us. If we do eventually learn what they thought of us all along, it can come as a rude awakening. The final challenge of establishing an identity lies in dealing with these discrepancies without having to make choices we don't actually want to make, merely to keep up appearances.

To understand how the process of aligning ourselves with the world works, let's look at one of the most widespread, comprehensive, and explicit sources of information on what others think about us. Over the past 20 years or so, an employment performance review system known as 360-degree or multirater feedback—so called because it generally consists of four to eight anonymous evaluations completed by supervisors as well as reporting staff, and by coworkers and customers alike—has been adopted in some form or other by an estimated 90 percent of Fortune 500 companies. The system measures different skills, such as leadership and conflict resolution, as well as broader personality traits, and it often includes a self-assessment to determine how closely one's self-perception matches up with behavior as observed by others. Such assessment tools are used for deciding bonuses and promotions, but they are best used to help us learn some of what the world really thinks of us.

Due to its growing use in the corporate world, in 2000 I led the design and implementation of a new permanent feature of the MBA program at the Columbia Business School, in which all entering students would receive 360-degree feedback from previous coworkers and/or customers, as well as from their current classmates. Every year the results have been the same: Over 90 percent of the students found significant discrepancies between how they saw themselves and how others interpreted their actions, a fact they were usually surprised to learn. Many who thought they were popular and valuable team players learned that they were actually seen as average or difficult to work with. Those who thought they were leaders learned that though people considered them intelligent, few considered them management material. Those who were prone to passionate out-bursts (which they believed to be justified) were quite upset to learn that they had been pegged by others as emotionally unstable. What's more, they were often further surprised by how widely others' per-ceptions of them varied for both positive and negative traits. In other words, though there might have been overall agreement about the fact that someone fell on the "difficult to work with" end of the spec-trum, there was still some variability in the degree to which people perceived and rated this attribute.

Why is there such a disconnect? I tell my distraught students that although they are aware of the intentions behind their own actions and so feel justified in what they do, people react only to what they see. It's like tapping out the rhythm of a well-known song on a table and having someone else try to name the tune. We can hear the music in our heads, so it seems clear as day that we're tapping out "Happy Birthday," but the other person only hears dum-dum-dum-dum-dum-dum, which could just as easily sound like the opening bars of "The Star-Spangled Banner." What's more, others don't judge your actions in a vacuum but interpret them through the lens of their own experience or, failing that, through general stereotypes about the kind of person you appear to be.

The lesson of 360-degree evaluations is not that other people's judgments are too various to be taken seriously. Every day, the way that we behave is subject to interpretation and, consequently, misinterpretation as well. And unless we want to give up on human society and retreat to the woods, we need to align, as much as possible, our self-perception with that of our friends, colleagues, and the hundreds of strangers with whom we interact on a daily basis.

The opinions others have of us can serve as a useful reality check; as we saw earlier, we tend to exhibit the "Lake Wobegon effect." Even without a formal 360-degree feedback process, we can still obtain the same benefits through self-awareness. We need to pay close atten-tion to how people react to our actions and, if possible, talk to them directly about how we come across. (The ability to receive diverse direct feedback is what makes 360-degree evaluations so powerful.) Once we know what others think about us, then we can choose how to respond.

If we learn we're not as great as we thought we were, we can decide to change our behavior so that it aligns more with how we want to be perceived. The manager who discovers that his colleagues see him as arrogant and inconsiderate might influence their opinions positively if he stops interrupting at meetings—even if he thinks he is only doing what's necessary for productivity's sake. Alternatively, he might not change his behavior but instead seek to explain the reasoning behind his interruptions. It may be impossible ever to completely resolve the discrepancies between who we think we are and what others think of us, but we can certainly do much to close the gap.

We should be careful, however, not to give in to the temptation to influence others to see us as better than we actually are. A study by Daniel Ames and colleagues found that in the workplace, the people who attempted to overtly enhance their position and reputa-tion were seen as disruptive to the group and eventually ended up performing poorly. If you're familiar with the American version of the television series *The Office*, you might immediately think of the character Andy Bernard—with his attempts to influence others through "neurolinguistic programming" and constant reminders that he attended Cornell—as the unfortunate exemplar of this type of behavior. In the long run, we're perhaps better served by striving for accuracy.

On a personal level, it is certainly unpleasant to discover that you are considered dull when you thought you were the second coming of Oscar Wilde, or mean-spirited when you thought you were sweet as pie, but being seen in too positive a light doesn't necessarily do us any favors. Research has found that people prefer to interact with those who rate them about the same as they rate themselves, even for negative attributes, and that people who consider themselves disagreeable will behave even more disagreeably to dispel the misconceptions of others who see them as agreeable. Numerous studies even find that married couples report being less satisfied and feeling less intimate when one spouse sees the other more favorably than that spouse sees himself or herself.

Everyone wants to be appreciated and admired, warts and all. In the end, the desire to have others know us the way we know ourselves can be more powerful than the desire to be put on a pedestal. When we see how others look at us, we want more than anything to recognize ourselves.

VI. MUCH OBLIGED

The challenges we face in finding our authentic self and choosing in accordance with it are considerable. One might say that we are trying to arrive at a state of homeostasis through a feedback loop between identity and choice: If I am this, then I should choose that; if I choose that, then I must be this. Ideally, as we get older, we should have to make fewer and fewer adjustments to bring into alignment how we see ourselves, how others see us, and how we choose. In practice, I'm not sure the "obligation" to choose—to return to Nikolas Rose— ever becomes easy and perhaps it puts an unreasonable amount of pressure on us. Unearthing the authentic self may require a degree of isolation and inward focus that simply doesn't appeal to most of us. And how many people are prepared to retreat to a cabin in the woods in order to live out Emerson's principles? Yet we are still consumed by the ideal of self-as-sculpture—our masterpiece, coherent and complete. Isn't there a more fruitful way to understand how choice shapes identity?

As we saw earlier in the chapter, American social networks

changed in the past with the rise of choice, and we can expect that they will continue to change as our choices keep growing. That does not mean, however, that we will become asocial creatures without any sense of community. The challenges we face when it comes to identity and choice exist precisely because choosing is not only a private activity but a social one, a negotiation between many moving parts. Choice requires us to think more deeply about who we are, both within ourselves and in the eyes of others.

If we set aside the statue of the perfect self, we might be able to see identity as a dynamic process rather than a static object. The chiseling, the carving out through our decisions, is what defines who we are. We are sculptors, finding ourselves in the evolution of choosing, not merely in the results of choice. When we change our thinking to embrace a more fluid process, choice will become no longer a force of destruction, an effort to break down what we don't want to be, but an ongoing, liberating act of creation. Our obligation, then, is to find the choice that makes sense today, that fulfills our needs given our immediate social context. Our choices are always interconnected with the choices of others, and we are known for our previous and current choices, not for the imaginary "perfect" self within. The writer Flannery O'Connor reportedly said, "I write to discover what I know." Perhaps we can take a page from her book and say, "I choose to discover who I am."

CHAPTER FOUR

Senses and Sensibility

I. OH, THE CHOICES YOU'LL MAKE!

Congratulations!
Today is your day.
You're off to Great Places!
You're off and away!

You have brains in your head.
You have feet in your shoes.
You can steer yourself any direction you choose.
You're on your own. And you know what you know.
And YOU are the guy who'll decide where to go.

Aim high. Follow your dreams. Go places! We first receive these messages when we're quite young, and they take on more significance as we grow older. When you're four and your parents read to you Dr. Seuss's *Oh, the Places You'll Go!*, it's entertainment and encouragement. When you get the same book as a present at your high school or college graduation, it's an incitement, a charge, a mission. If choice is about possibility, then it's also about responsibility. When "YOU are the guy who'll decide where to go," you had better read the map carefully and travel all the right roads.

But soon after setting off, you realize that the map is incomplete and inaccurate. Who made this thing? It doesn't give you a full picture of where your choices will take you, and sometimes you end up in very odd situations. So you start to make corrections and fill in the blank spots. Even so, it becomes evident that your journey won't be easy. You choose a job that you think will lead to professional fulfillment. It leads to financial success, but you're bored. You decide to move out of the city and get a bigger home. It has a beautiful garden and the neighborhood is quiet. This was supposed to be your path to a relaxed life, but the commute is raising your stress level. On the positive side, even though you knew your spouse for only a month before you got married, and you had always assumed you'd find married life very difficult, your relationship has turned out to be wonderful!

You're discovering that what you expect from your choices is quite often not what you get. Why is that, and are there ways to better align results with expectations? If we want to steer ourselves toward happiness, it's important to know why we make wrong turns, and how we end up disappointed by the very choices that were supposed to lead to Great Places. In this chapter, we'll try to come up with some answers to these difficult questions.

II. THE MARSHMALLOW MATTER

The little boy waits his turn, as he has been taught to do. One by one, the other kids are being led into another room by the serious but kind-looking man in the white coat. It feels a lot like going to the doctor, but his parents promised him there wouldn't be needles or other painful things. He's a little nervous anyway. When the man finally asks him to come along, the boy walks into the secret room and finds a whole bunch of delicious snacks—pretzel sticks, Oreo cookies, marshmallows—spread out on a table. Wow! The man asks him to point out the snack he would like to eat the most, and the boy chooses marshmallows.

"Good choice!" the man says. "Now, I actually have to go take care of something important in the other room." He hands the boy a tiny bell. "But here's what we can do," he continues. "You can have one marshmallow right now. If you wait until I come back, though, you can have two. While I'm gone, if you ring this bell then I'll come back right away, but if you do that you will only get one marshmallow. Do we have a deal?"

The boy thinks for a moment and then nods. He sits down, and the man takes one marshmallow from a tray and puts it right in front of him. Then the man leaves and shuts the door. The boy really likes marshmallows, and if one marshmallow is good, then two marshmallows are definitely better. He'll wait, just like he did before he came into this room. He swings his legs, looks around, shifts in the chair. Time passes. To him it seems like the man has been gone for *ages*. Did he say how long he would take? Maybe he's forgotten all about their deal and won't come back at all.

The marshmallow looks very good, even whiter and fluffier than it seemed at first. The boy rests his chin on the table and stares at that sugary piece of heaven. His stomach begins to grumble, and he wonders if he should just ring the bell. If the marshmallow is super-yummy, maybe one will be enough. He doesn't need two, does he? But if it *does* taste great, he might be sorry he didn't wait a little while longer. He goes back and forth like this until the marshmallow becomes irresistible. How could the man have left him alone for so long? It's not fair, and it's not his fault, and he deserves the marshmallow for being such a good boy. He's tired and on the brink of tears, so he reaches for the bell and gives it a good shake.

The "marshmallow studies," conducted in the late 1960s by renowned psychologist Walter Mischel, are widely known today for their exploration of how we resist—or give in to—temptation. The trials and tribulations of the four-year-old participants didn't last long: On average, the children waited only three minutes before ringing the bell. However, in those few minutes, the little boys and girls had to contend with the strong internal conflict between what they wanted immediately and what they knew would be better for them overall. Their particular struggle may strike adults as more funny than torturous, but we all know how frustrating it is to be in thrall to temptation.

Whether you're trying to hold out for the extra marshmallow or keep from spending money on that marvelous new piece of technology, the competing voices in your head tend to grow louder and more belligerent with time; to borrow from Oscar Wilde, yielding to temptations is often the fastest way to get rid of them, though you may very well regret your actions later. What's going on inside us when we're pulled in opposing directions? When we know that one option will lead to a better outcome, why do we yearn for the other? If you feel sometimes that you're thinking with two different brains, you aren't that far off. Humans do, indeed, have two interconnected and yet distinct systems for processing information and arriving at answers or judgments.

The first, which we'll call the automatic system, operates quickly, effortlessly, and subconsciously. It's a continuously running "stealth" program that analyzes sensory data and triggers feeling and behavior in rapid response. You may find yourself acting even before you know what's causing you to act. You might not even realize that you acted until a few seconds have passed. This is the system that urges your body to EAT MARSHMALLOW NOW, because the present moment is all it knows. Even a deliberate choice may be based on the output of the automatic system—perhaps a strong hunch or an attraction you can't quite explain.

In contrast, the reflective system, driven not by raw sensation but by logic and reason, is one that we have to turn on and tune into. Its scope extends beyond immediate experience, allowing us to factor in abstract ideas and contemplate the future in order to make choices. When using this system, we are much more aware of how we arrived at a particular conclusion. We say "X is true because of Y" or "To get to step 3, I must first complete steps 1 and 2." Reflective processing allows us to handle highly complex choices, but it is slower and more tiring than the automatic system. It requires motivation and significant effort.

When the two systems generate matching answers, there's no conflict. For example, the automatic reaction and the reflective reaction to a charging rhinoceros are one and the same: GET OUT OF THE WAY! All too frequently, though, the answers are different, and in such a situation, one must prevail over the other. If there's no time to be lost, we'll probably go with the automatic response; if there's no rush, we're much more likely to rely on our reflective powers. In the case of temptation, we may be aware that our desire is being fueled by the automatic system and that we'd be better off if we followed the reflective system, but just because we know the "right" answer doesn't mean we can bring ourselves to choose it.

In Mischel's studies, the children who were tempted to eat one marshmallow right away were experiencing the battle between the two systems. When most of them rang the bell within a few minutes of being left alone, the sound marked the victory of the automatic over the reflective. Since children don't have well-developed reflective systems, the results aren't surprising. But even adults, with their sophisticated reflective abilities, frequently don't resist the various "marshmallows" they encounter in life. Statistics show that infidelity is reported in nearly 30 to 40 percent of dating relationships and 40 to 60 percent of marriages; in one survey, 52 percent of college students indicated a moderate to high need for help in overcoming procrastination problems; and over 30 percent of workers have never saved money for retirement. Even when you know what you ought to be doing, what you would prefer in the long run, you can find yourself distracted and dazed by options that set off the automatic system. When the automatic reaction is particularly strong, you may feel controlled by some outside force: *I wasn't myself,* or *I don't know what came over me,* or *The devil made me do it.* To those who say you made a bad choice, you try to explain that it was more like an imperative. *Honey,* you say, *you've got to believe me. I had no choice. I could not do otherwise.*

Of course, that argument, even if it works, will get you only so far. After all, people do find ways to resist, and this ability may contribute to other successes. In the Mischel experiment, 30 percent of the children exercised enough self-control to hold out for a full 15 minutes, after which the man in the white coat returned and rewarded them with two pieces of their chosen snack. Follow-up studies found that the teenagers who had exercised self-control all those years ago went on to have stronger friendships, better coping skills, and fewer behavioral problems. They even scored an average of 200 points higher on the SAT than the children who had given in to temptation immediately. The pattern of superior performance continued well into adulthood: The self-controllers were less likely to smoke or use illicit drugs; they enjoyed higher socioeconomic status; and they completed more years of education. In other words, they seemed to be healthier, wealthier, and wiser. Though self-control may not be solely responsible for the positive outcomes, the correlation suggests that we shouldn't underestimate its impact on our lives.

On the other hand, it's disheartening when one imagines always forgoing instant gratification in favor of expected future gains. There's something to be said for spontaneity, indulgence, and throwing caution to the winds. A life focused too keenly on the avoidance of guilty pleasures may turn out to be severe and joyless. Most of us hope to save money without turning into Ebenezer Scrooge, work hard without becoming chained to the desk, and maintain our health without making the gym a second home. But finding the right balance can be quite challenging, especially because our desires and priorities "now" seem so different from—and usually more compelling than—whatever we may want "later." To see how you weigh present considerations against future ones, try the following thought experiment:

Someone offers you a choice between receiving $100 one month from now and $120 two months from now. What's your answer?

Then the same person offers you a choice between $100 today and $120 a month from today. Which amount do you choose this time?

Studies have found that in response to the first question, most people prefer to wait longer for the larger sum of money. However, in the second scenario, most of them settle for the lower amount instead of choosing to wait a month. Rationally, the two choices appear identical—in each case you receive $20 more for waiting one month longer—but in practice they don't feel the same because when the money becomes immediately available, the automatic system is engaged. Before, waiting an extra month for the extra money made *reflective* sense. But now, you can't help but think about what you could do or buy if you had the money this very minute! Wouldn't that be wonderful? Wouldn't that make you so much happier than the $120 you'd get a whole month later? This makes *automatic* sense.

If you choose $100 once in a blue moon to satisfy a particularly strong craving, you'll only lose $20 here and $20 there. But if you choose $100 most of the time, the costs will accrue over the many years of your life, and decades from now you may find yourself deeply regretful over just how much you threw away. The pleasures of surrendering to the automatic system can become addictive; you say, "Just this once," but it turns into nothing but an empty promise to yourself, a way to mark each loss. Most of us don't want to live this way, but what can we do about it?

Let's take a few pointers from the children who, even at age four, were able to resist the temptation to eat their snacks before the experimenter returned. The secret to their remarkable restraint was that they devised numerous strategies to combat their automatic response. Some put their hands over their faces so they couldn't see the tray of goodies in front of them. Others imagined playing with toys to avoid thinking about food. And a few managed to convince themselves that the marshmallows were clouds rather than melt-in-the-mouth treats. Using these tricks, the children physically or mentally hid the snack, thus removing the option of eating it. You can't be tempted by something that's not even there!

We know from further studies of Mischel's that intentionally deploying methods of distraction can work wonders. In variations on the original study, he gave the children toys to play with, asked them to think of fun activities while they waited, or he simply covered the snacks with an opaque lid. The average waiting times increased by up to 60 percent, and a majority of the children were able to resist ringing the bell. Through conscious application of these sorts of techniques, we too can conceal tempting choices. It seems like common sense not to work in the room that has the TV, even if it's turned off, or to put away the cookies in the cupboard instead of leaving them out on the counter, but we don't always do the very simple things that make self-control less of a struggle.

In addition to removing temptation, we need to think about how rigorously and in which cases we'd like to exercise self-control. Given your goals, what do you absolutely need to resist and what can you be more lax about? If you label too many things as threats to self-control, you'll find it almost impossible to get through the day, so the first step to success is to choose your battles. Like an athlete, you want to challenge yourself without damaging the very mind and body that allow you to compete. Ultimately, though, our goal should be to make the act of self-control less of a struggle in the first place, by bringing the automatic system in line with the reflective one. Because we aren't conscious of its activity, it's easy to treat the automatic system like an external force that interferes with our actions, but it is an essential part of us. Rather than trying to trick ourselves, we can teach ourselves, avoiding temptation until the act of avoidance itself becomes habitual and automatic.

III. PLAYING BY THE RULES

It's better to be overdressed than underdressed. When bargaining or negotiating, ask for more than you expect to get. Don't snack late at night. Go with what you know. Always try to see the other side of the argument. Spend no more than 35 percent of your income on housing. And for Pete's sake, don't call your ex after you've had a few drinks.

Rules of thumb like these usually serve us pretty well. They offer straightforward solutions to common problems, helping us save time and energy that would otherwise be spent mulling over options and possible consequences. Though not foolproof, they're generally reliable, and they make our complex and uncertain world a little easier to understand. When we're exhausted from fighting temptation and overwhelmed by the demands of choosing well, it can be a relief to turn to these rules—known formally as *heuristics*—for answers.

The fact is, though we make multiple decisions a day, every day, our choosing ability may not improve merely through repetition. Even with plenty of experience and knowledge, we often make choices that leave us disappointed. Heuristics seem to give us a way to choose that minimizes risk and increases the likelihood of satisfaction. Unfortunately, we're not as good as we think we are at recognizing when heuristics assist us and when they lead us astray. As a result, in spite of our best intentions and efforts, we may fail to choose the optimal course of action.

While we sometimes use heuristics consciously, they also operate at the subconscious level, generating snap judgments and hunches. We may not realize that we're employing a heuristic, and even if we do, we may believe that the heuristic is beneficial when it's actually detrimental. Missteps in the use of heuristics are known as decision-making biases, and an entire field of research has sprung up around these biases since their first appearance in the Nobel Prize–winning work of psychologists Daniel Kahneman and Amos Tversky. We'll now examine how four of the most common heuristics work—and how they can become biases—in order to take another step toward making better choices.

I.

The information in our memory bank affects what we pay attention to and consider important—a phenomenon known as "availability"—and this in turn affects our preferences. Say you're the Secret Santa for a colleague with whom you're only casually acquainted. You've decided to get him a tie, but you're not sure what colors he likes. So you try to remember which colors you've seen him wear most often in the past. This seems like a perfectly reasonable strategy, but the color that's most "available" in your head may not actually be the color your colleague wore the most.

We tend to have a better memory for things that excite our senses or appeal to our emotions than for straight facts and dry statistics. This means that you might overestimate the number of times your colleague wore a red tie, or underestimate how often he wore a gray one, simply because red is a brighter color. Similarly, you might ignore all the enthusiastic online recommendations for a new restaurant because one good friend told you that she recently ate the worst dinner of her life there. Majority consensus contradicts your friend, but her personal story and facial expressions are what you recall every time you walk by the restaurant.

Our decisions can also be affected by the vividness and tangibility of the consequences of each choice. Have you ever noticed that you spend with greater abandon when you use a credit card instead of cold hard cash? Research has shown that people are willing to spend significantly more when paying with a credit card than with cash—over twice as much in some studies. When we take bills out of the wallet and hand them over, our senses register that we now have less money. But when the cashier swipes a piece of plastic and gives it back to us, it feels as if we aren't paying anything at all.

Even the order in which we encounter options can affect their availability. We tend to better remember the first and last options in a group, so rather than focusing on the merits of each alternative, we may be influenced primarily by the position in which each appeared. This is why items displayed at either end of a store shelf sell more than those in the middle, and it's also the reason an interviewer might unwittingly pay more attention to the first and last candidates in a job interview.

II.

Every year, I tell my MBA students a near-legendary story about Roberto Goizueta, who was CEO of the Coca-Cola Corporation in the 1980s. When he was first appointed to the position, he discovered at a meeting with the senior vice presidents that the company management was celebrating: They owned 45 percent of the soft drink market! They seemed quite pleased with themselves and had set a goal of increasing shareholder value by about 5 to 10 percent in the next few years. Goizueta thought they were playing it too safe, so he decided to challenge their notion of growth. He asked them, "How much liquid does any given individual consume in a day?" Then he said, "How many people are there in the world?" Finally, the most important question: "What percentage of the entire liquid market—not soft drink market—do we have?" That number turned out to be a measly 2 percent.

By reframing the issue, Goizueta encouraged his colleagues to broaden their vision and think more creatively. They had been content with their modest view of the market and with the place Coca-Cola occupied within it; Goizueta showed them that the company's current position was less secure than they believed, but the good news was that there were many more shares to be won. This led to a dramatic shift in the company's mission, the results of which were awe-inspiring: In 1981, the total value of Coca-Cola stock was $4.3 billion; by the time of Goizueta's death in 1997, it had burgeoned to over $152 billion.

Clearly, the way we frame information for ourselves or for others can make a big difference in how we see and respond to choice. Every time we encounter new information or reexamine old information, we're influenced by its presentation. We can use framing to our advantage, but sometimes it has a negative impact on the quality of our decisions. For example, when framing highlights the costs of a given set of options instead of the benefits, we may become subject to bias. Research has consistently demonstrated that losses loom far larger in our minds than do gains. We do whatever we can to avoid losing the things that are most important to us, but we don't take similar risks to achieve gains because we worry that we might incur a loss instead. This seems natural enough, but it means that we're very susceptible to manipulation by presentation.

To see this in action, consider a famous study conducted by Amos Tversky and colleagues in which they presented patients, medical students, and doctors with statistics about the effectiveness of surgery and radiation therapy in treating cancer. The participants were asked which treatment they would prefer. Half of them were told that 90 percent of patients who underwent surgery survived the treatment, and 34 percent survived for at least five years afterward; all patients who underwent radiation therapy survived, but only 22 percent were still alive five years later. The other half were given the same information, but it was framed in terms of mortality rather than survival: 10 percent of patients died during surgery, and 66 percent died within five years; for radiation therapy, the figures were 0 percent and 78 percent, respectively.

Though all the participants were given identical statistics, the change in presentation had a remarkable effect on their decisions. With the survival frame, only 25 percent preferred radiation therapy to surgery, but with the mortality frame, 42 percent preferred radiation. When the possibility of dying during surgery was highlighted, people were more likely to select radiation therapy, even at the cost of decreased long-term survival. What's more, doctors were just as vulnerable to the framing bias as the other participants; despite extensive experience and training, they were unable to judge based purely on the numbers.

III.

A giraffe in the clouds, a scorpion in the night sky, the Virgin Mary on a grilled cheese sandwich—we find patterns everywhere. Our minds automatically seek order, and our tendency to establish relationships between different pieces of information plays an important role in decision-making. Drawing connections is vital to our reasoning abilities, but when we start to see patterns that don't actually exist or are more nuanced than we realize, we may end up choosing poorly.

Take, for example, the events leading up to the real estate price crash that precipitated a worldwide financial crisis and the worst recession in the past 75 years. Traditionally, owning a home was seen as a safe investment for the average American, unlikely to turn large profits but almost guaranteed not to lose value over time. The inflation-adjusted average home price stayed almost constant at $110,000 (in today's dollars) between the end of World War II and 1997. At that point, however, a new pattern emerged, with prices nearly doubling to about $200,000 between 1997 and 2006. When people saw this dramatic and consistent growth, they were convinced that prices would continue to rise in the future. A study by Robert Schiller and Karl Case found that in 2005, San Francisco home buyers expected prices to rise by 14 percent a year over the next decade. Some were considerably more optimistic, predicting yearly increases of up to 50 percent. Given this apparent pattern, many people decided that owning a home was well worth the risk of taking out mortgage loans with less than favorable terms.

There *was* a pattern underlying this jump in prices, but it wasn't the one that home buyers saw. The real pattern was that of boom and bust, or a "bubble," which occurs when popular enthusiasm for an asset begets more enthusiasm, pushing prices far higher than the true value. Eventually, the exaggerated value of the assets becomes clear, at which point everyone rushes to sell and the bubble pops. The pages of economic history are rife with bubbles: Single tulip bulbs sold for more than the average person's annual income during the Dutch tulip mania of the seventeenth century; the stock speculation of the Roaring Twenties contributed to the Great Depression; and the dot-com bubble threw the country into a recession less than a decade before the housing crash. Unable to see the forest for the trees—or the bubble surrounding the houses—people focused on trends that turned out to be unsustainable. Choices based on such short-sightedness, or "false-sightedness," often prove to be very damaging.

IV.

When heuristics don't yield the results we expect, you'd think we would eventually realize that something's wrong. Even if we don't locate the biases, we should be able to see the discrepancy between what we wanted and what we got, right? Well, not necessarily. As it turns out, we have biases that support our biases! If we're partial to one option—perhaps because it's more memorable, or framed to minimize loss, or seemingly consistent with a promising pattern—we tend to search for information that will justify choosing that option. On the one hand, it's sensible to make choices that we can defend with data and a list of reasons. On the other hand, if we're not careful, we're likely to conduct an imbalanced analysis, falling prey to a cluster of errors collectively known as "confirmation biases."

For example, nearly all companies include classic "tell me about yourself" job interviews as part of the hiring process, and many rely on these interviews alone to evaluate applicants. But it turns out that traditional interviews are actually one of the least useful tools for predicting an employee's future success. This is because interviewers often subconsciously make up their minds about interviewees based on their first few moments of interaction—say, reacting more positively to people who are similar in personality type or interests—and spend the rest of the interview cherry-picking evidence and phrasing their questions to confirm that initial impression: "I see here you left a good position at your previous job. You must be pretty ambitious, right?" versus "You must not have been very committed, huh?" This means that interviewers can be prone to overlooking significant information that would clearly indicate whether this candidate was actually the best person to hire. More structured approaches, like obtaining samples of a candidate's work or asking how he would respond to difficult hypothetical situations, are dramatically better at assessing future success, with a nearly threefold advantage over traditional interviews.

Not only do we try to confirm our existing beliefs, we're quick to dismiss information that threatens to prove them wrong. In a groundbreaking longitudinal study, psychologist Philip Tetlock, author of the book *Expert Political Judgment*, demonstrated that even experts exhibit this tendency. Throughout the 1980s and 1990s he asked hundreds of political authorities—political scientists, government advisers, pundits, and other policy wonks—from all parts of the ideological spectrum to predict the course of certain future events, such as whether relations between the United States and the Soviet Union would remain constant, improve, or deteriorate. As these events unfolded, Tetlock and his colleagues realized that even though the experts made predictions for a living, the vast majority of them performed slightly worse than they would have by choosing at random. And the ones who had greater confidence in their predictions were actually less accurate on average.

These experts, regardless of the specific nature of their worldviews and pet theories, were more willing to accept information that confirmed their beliefs than information that didn't. For example, those who subscribed to the "evil empire" view of the Soviet Union found all sorts of flaws in an analysis of newly released material from the Kremlin archives that suggested that Stalin had nearly been deposed by moderate factions of the Communist Party in the 1920s. The experts with a more pluralist viewpoint accepted these documents at face value. All told, the supposed experts were able to come up with numerous ways to turn being wrong into being "almost right." As a result, they stuck to their views instead of changing them to better fit the facts.

We do the same thing in our own lives, embracing information that supports what we already prefer or vindicates choices we previously made. After all, it *feels* better to justify our opinions rather than challenge them, to contemplate only the pros and relegate the cons to the back of our minds. However, if we want to make the most of choice, we have to be willing to make ourselves uncomfortable. The question is, if we *are* willing, how exactly do we go about fortifying ourselves against these biases?

IV. THE EXPERT'S EYE

Cal Lightman knows that the girl is afraid. He's certain the politician is hiding something. And that man on the phone should admit to his wife that he's cheating on her because the guilt is killing him. Within minutes, sometimes seconds, of observing complete strangers, and often without even engaging them in conversation, Lightman reaches pretty firm conclusions about them. Most of the time, he's right. As played by actor Tim Roth on the FOX network drama *Lie to Me*, Lightman is confident, abrasive, and maybe just a little crazy. By reading body language and "microexpressions," he solves crimes, saves lives, and generally does good, bringing the all-time total number of psychologists who are also television heroes to...one.

His remarkable talent may seem to be the stuff of TV fantasy, but the character is based on the very real Professor Paul Ekman, the "human lie detector" who boasts a 95 percent accuracy rate. Ekman's success is astonishing because lies are notoriously difficult to detect. To determine whether a person is lying, we tend to rely heavily on intuition. Unless we catch a lie on factual grounds, the only indicators of a person's dishonesty are tone of voice, body language, and facial expressions—signs that may be too subtle for us to consciously recognize but that can still evoke a strong gut feeling. The problem is that while we can practice our skills at evaluating others' truthfulness in social interactions, without clear feedback on whether our judgments are correct we don't know if we're erring on the side of gullibility or of distrustfulness. This means we're unable to improve over time. Though many people believe they're quite good at distinguishing truths from lies, almost no one in the general population performs with higher than chance accuracy. On average, even police officers, lawyers, judges, psychiatrists, and members of other groups that encounter more frequent and serious lies than ordinary people perform no better. What makes Ekman different?

The secret to his sixth sense is decades of practice and feedback. He has spent his career studying faces, and not just human ones. He began by tracking monkeys' facial expressions moment to moment, and he linked these expressions to the behaviors that followed, such as stealing from another monkey, attacking, or making a friendly overture. He later applied a similar concept to lie detection and discovered that liars give themselves away through "microexpressions," which last only milliseconds. Neither the liars nor the observers are usually aware of these microexpressions, but Ekman trained himself to detect them by diligently watching slow-motion tapes of known truth-tellers and liars—for example, students shown footage of gruesome medical procedures and asked to pretend they were watching a peaceful nature scene instead. By continually critiquing his performance, Ekman developed the ability to automatically detect and focus only on microexpressions, filtering out irrelevant body language and what the person was actually saying. His power may seem superheroic, but it was acquired by ordinary means.

Through creative self-teaching and hard work, Ekman found a way to combine the automatic system with the reflective one, allowing him to make snap judgments that are also highly accurate. His method, which we can think of as "informed intuition," captures the best of both worlds, combining the speed of reflex with the objective benefits that come from careful consideration and analysis. In fact, many people who excel in their fields, and have their remarkable feats regularly featured in popular books such as Malcolm Gladwell's *Blink*, rely on informed intuition. The best poker players use a combination of game strategies, knowledge of the cards in play, and a keen sensitivity to changes in body language to figure out if an opponent is bluffing. Trained and experienced airport security officers need very little time to home in on disembarking passengers who are smuggling drugs or other contraband. Even when it comes to discovering the physical laws that govern the universe, Albert Einstein wrote, "There is no logical way to the discovery of these elemental laws. There is only the way of intuition, which is helped by a feeling for the order lying behind the appearance."

You don't need to be an Einstein to reach this state of expertise-as-second-nature, but it doesn't come easy. In the words of Herbert Simon, a Nobel laureate and one of the most influential scholars of the century, "Intuition is nothing more and nothing less than recognition." The automatic system doesn't make predictions or apply theoretical knowledge; it reacts to whatever situation a person is currently facing. It will be accurate in novel situations only if they're similar to previously experienced ones, making an extensive body of hands-on expertise a prerequisite for developing informed intuition. Achieving a world-class expert-level understanding of a single domain, it takes an average of 10,000 hours of practice, or about three hours a day, every day, for ten years straight. And practice alone isn't enough. As we saw earlier, the considerable professional experience of doctors and political pundits doesn't necessarily protect them from framing and confirmation biases. You can't simply do X for three hours a day for ten years and expect to end up as the world champion of X. If you want to improve, you must continuously observe and critically analyze your performance: What did you do wrong? How can you do it better?

Whatever the domain, the end goal of this process of practice and self-critique is to acquire an informed intuition that reliably outperforms using the reflective system alone in both speed and accuracy. If you succeed, you'll be able to quickly collect and process the most relevant information in a given situation, all the while avoiding distractions that could lead to biased choices, and thereby determine the best course of action. Remember, though, that your informed intuition, no matter how sharp, will be limited to the specific domains into which you put the required time and effort. Also, it's difficult, if not impossible, to develop informed intuition in domains for which you don't have clear and measurable goals: i.e., explicit criteria for what constitutes success. When it comes to choosing, practice doesn't always make perfect, but it can help you cultivate genuine expertise if you go about it in the right way.

Of course, you can't become an expert at everything, so how should you improve your overall ability to choose? The key is to employ your reflective system to sort through your use—or misuse—of heuristics. Ask yourself how you arrived at a particular preference: Were you overly influenced by a vivid image or anecdote? Did you discard an option too quickly because it was framed as a loss? Is it possible you imagined a trend or pattern that doesn't really exist? Try to find reasons not to choose what you're immediately drawn to. Gather evidence against your own opinion. Though you won't always be able to engage in extensive reflection *before* you make a choice, it's worth your while to reconsider the choice later on. You may not be able to change it, but if you discover that you made an error, you can avoid repeating the mistake in the future. We're all prone to decision-making biases, but we're also capable of combating them through vigilance, persistence, and a healthy dose of skepticism.

V. THE TROUBLE WITH HAPPINESS

Let me tell you a story that has made the rounds among my colleagues at Columbia University. Once upon a time, former faculty member Howard Raiffa, a pioneer in the field of decision analysis, was offered a position at Harvard, which was considered a step up in prestige. In an attempt to hold on to him, Columbia countered with an offer to triple his salary. Torn between the two options, he decided to ask his friend, a dean at Columbia, for advice. The dean, rather amused by the question, suggested that Raiffa use the techniques that had earned him the Harvard offer in the first place: Break the decision down into its components, map the relationship between them, and do the math to determine which option was best for him. "You don't understand," Raiffa responded. "This is a *serious* decision."

The story may be apocryphal, but it gets at a basic truth: Personal happiness is always a very serious matter. It's all well and good to propose formulas and strategies to other people, but we're not sure we should trust them when our own long-term happiness is clearly at stake. We tend to feel that a mechanistic approach won't really account for the idiosyncrasies of individual happiness, but if we don't already know what will make us happy, how do we figure it out?

Benjamin Franklin laid an early foundation for Raiffa's work when he extolled the virtues of the pros and cons lists. When a friend wrote to him to ask for help with a tough decision, Franklin replied that he didn't have enough information to offer advice on *what* to choose, but he could still give advice on *how* to choose.

> When those difficult cases occur, they are difficult, chiefly because while we have them under consideration, all the reasons pro and con are not present to the mind at the same time....To get over this, my way is to divide half a sheet of paper by a line into two columns; writing over the one Pro, and over the other Con. Then, during three or four days' consideration, I put down under the different heads short hints of the different motives, that at different times occur to me, for or against the measure. When I have thus got them all together in one view, I endeavor to estimate their respective weights; and where I find two, one on each side, that seem equal, I strike them both out. If I find a reason pro equal to some two reasons con, I strike out the three. If I judge some two reasons con, equal to three reasons pro, I strike out the five; and thus proceeding I find at length where the balance lies....I think I can judge better, and am less likely to make a rash step; and in fact I have found great advantage from this kind of equation, in what may be called moral or prudential algebra.

Franklin's algebra seems simple enough, but does it work? Think back to the job search study I described in the previous chapter in which new graduates failed to realize that their priorities had shifted over time. As part of that study, Rachel Wells and I teamed up with Barry Schwartz to ask participants a little more about the jobs they ultimately chose. We were particularly interested in how the graduates who did everything objectively right in the job search process—speaking with their career counselors, parents, and friends more often; taking advantage of experts' rankings of the companies; applying for more jobs—compared to peers who took a more casual approach. After six months, the numbers were in favor of those people who analyzed their decisions more thoroughly. They had been invited to more interviews, received more job offers, and ultimately landed jobs with average salaries of $44,500; their less thorough counterparts were earning an average of only $37,100. However, despite earning 20 percent more, these graduates were actually less certain that they had made the right choice and less satisfied with their jobs overall. Though they had taken initiative and weighed the pros and cons of many options, their final choices didn't lead to greater happiness.

Perhaps the graduates who were more driven also had higher expectations. It's possible that their perfectionism was partly responsible for their lower levels of happiness, but that's not the whole story. The fatal flaw of the pros versus cons approach is that it focuses on concrete, measurable criteria, often to the exclusion of emotional considerations. Salaries and company rankings are easily compared, but how do we evaluate and compare two workplaces' atmospheres, or how comfortable we would be with our potential coworkers? Because our feelings can't be quantified, we might not account for them in the pros and cons lists, even if the larger part of our happiness is dependent on them. That may be what happened to the more thorough job seekers.

When deciding between job offers, most of us give a lot of weight to salary, even though money and happiness don't have a directly proportional relationship. Studies consistently show that money *can* buy happiness, but only up to a certain point. Once one's basic needs are met, the value of the additional material goods that come with greater wealth diminishes rapidly. The nationwide 2004 General Social Survey found that Americans earning under $20,000 per year reported being significantly less happy than those in a higher income bracket, but more than 80 percent still described themselves as "pretty happy" or "very happy." Above this tier, people are relatively happier overall, but further increases in income hardly make any impact. For the most part, people earning $100,000 are no more satisfied with life than those earning half that sum. Other studies have found that this trend—rising income without an attendant rise in reported happiness—holds true even for Americans who earn more than $5 million per year.

We may be too strongly drawn to higher salaries because our reflective system convinces us that more money buys greater comfort and security, which is an objectively better outcome. But the system may fail to include in the equation the psychic cost of the commute and of the loss of leisure time that often accompanies the bigger check. A study by Daniel Kahneman and colleagues found that commuting is by far the most unpleasant part of the average person's day, and spending even an extra 20 minutes in transit is one-fifth as harmful to your well-being as losing your job. You might consent to a lengthy commute because you want the larger house in the nicer neighborhood, perhaps with better schools, but these benefits rarely counteract the negative effects of longer travel time.

Because it leads us into temptation, the automatic system gets a bad rap, but maybe we should pay more attention to it when the question of happiness comes up. Tim Wilson and his colleagues at the University of Virginia conducted a study to test the following common claim: "I don't know a thing about art, but I do know what I like." Participants were asked to choose a poster to display in their homes. They had five options: a Monet, a Van Gogh, and three rather corny pictures of animals. Most people instinctively preferred the fine art, but when asked to describe their reactions, they found it easier to articulate reasons for liking the animal pictures. (Unless one has some formal education in art, it can be quite difficult to discuss Impressionist work in any detail. Talking about a smiling cow, on the other hand, is a breeze.) As a result, they began to favor the critters and chose them over the Impressionists. After a few months, however, their original preferences resurfaced: Three-quarters of those who put up an animal poster on the wall regretted seeing it every day; none of the participants who followed their original impulses and chose the Monet or the Van Gogh felt bad about the decision.

If justifying personal tastes is difficult, explaining romantic attraction is near impossible. As Blaise Pascal said, "The heart has its reasons of which reason knows nothing." Wilson and his colleagues observed this in practice when they asked partners in romantic relationships to fill out a questionnaire about how happy they were with each other. Some were asked to list as many reasons as possible for their relationship's current state and to think carefully about these reasons before completing the questionnaire. Other participants were asked to give whatever answers came immediately to mind. When the researchers followed up with the couples seven to nine months later to see if they were still together, they found that the intuitive ratings were highly predictive of the couples' success, but the ratings based on reasoned analysis were almost entirely unrelated. The people who analyzed their relationships thoroughly and concluded that they were doing very well were just as likely to have broken up as the people who reasoned that their relationships had serious imperfections.

The Wilson studies seem to nudge us toward relying on the automatic system for matters of the heart, but a study by Donald Dutton and Arthur Aron should give us pause. The study was conducted on two bridges in British Columbia. The first was wide and sturdy, with guardrails high enough to keep jumpers away, and anyone who did fall would land in the placid river only ten feet below. The second bridge, in contrast, was a spindly contraption straight out of an

Indiana Jones adventure. Suspended 230 feet above the rocks and rapids at a much rougher point in the river, it had low handrails and tended to sway with the wind, or whenever anyone crossed it.

As male sightseers crossed one or the other of these bridges, they were stopped in the middle by an attractive female experimenter who asked if they would be willing to take part in a study about the effect of the area's natural scenery on people's creativity. Their task, should they agree to participate, was to write a short story to accompany a photograph of a woman with one hand covering her face and the other outstretched. As each willing participant turned in his story, the experimenter gave her name and phone number to him on a piece of scrap paper and said that he should feel free to call "if he wanted to talk further about the purpose of the study."

Of course, the actual purpose of the study, which has since been dubbed "love on a suspension bridge," had nothing to do with creative writing. Instead, the goal was to explore how heightened emotions—in this case, fear—might be confused with other intense emotions—in this case, attraction toward the experimenter. It turns out that half of the participants who crossed the swaying suspension bridge called the experimenter later to "talk about the study"; of the men who walked the lower, more stable bridge, only one-eighth made the phone call. The stories written on the shakier bridge also contained more sexual overtones, as judged by reviewers who didn't know the context in which the two sets of stories were written. And in case you have any remaining doubts about the men's intentions, consider the fact that the callback rates were equally low for the two bridges when the study was repeated with a male experimenter.

How did people end up confusing the fear of falling to their death on the jagged rocks below with the feeling of being struck by Cupid's arrow? You see, the automatic system registers physiological responses, but it can't always figure out what's causing them. While fear and love seem to be completely different emotions, our bodily experience of them can be quite similar: The heart beats ever faster, the palms sweat, butterflies flutter in your stomach. Love at first sight might actually have a lot in common with the fear of falling.

The results of the bridge study can't be explained away as anomalous. In fact, we often look to the social context for clues about our emotional state. In a classic study conducted at Columbia in the 1960s, Stanley Schachter and Jerome Singer found that students who were injected with adrenaline (unbeknownst to them) could be incited by an experimenter to behave either playfully or angrily. Depending on how the experimenter manipulated the interactions, each student interpreted his physical, drug-induced excitement in one of two ways—"I must be having a great time!" or "I must be really angry!"—and then acted accordingly.

A former student of mine has firsthand experience of the strange relationship between context and emotion. While visiting India with a female friend of his, he was inspired by the suspension bridge study to conduct an experiment of his own. He had a romantic interest in this friend, but she didn't seem to be reciprocating. So he took matters into his own hands. A thrill ride through Delhi in a fast and dangerous auto rickshaw was just the thing, he thought, to get the blood pumping. She would surely connect her excitement to the person sitting right next to her, which would be him. The plan was practically foolproof! He waved down a speeding rickshaw being driven by a large, loud man in a turban. He gave directions that led them through narrow, noisy, and curved streets. His friend held on tightly, her eyes wide and her hair loosened by the wind. When they finally came to a stop, she stumbled out and smoothed down her clothes. "Well," he said, rather pleased with himself, "how was that?" She leaned close, looked him in the eye, and said, "Wasn't that rickshaw driver just gorgeous?"

It isn't easy to predict how others will react to a given situation. We even have trouble predicting our own emotions. When we try to determine how we'll feel in the future about the decisions we made today, we extrapolate based on our current feelings. In doing so, we often succumb to some of the same biases that we saw earlier in the chapter. For example, we tend to overestimate how intense our reaction will be because we focus on a vivid scenario, ignoring the larger context in which it will take place. Sports fans may predict that they'll be devastated if their team loses and overjoyed if it wins, but they don't factor in all the other elements of the day—weather, commute, deadlines at work, family dinner—that will contribute to their overall emotional state.

We also overestimate the duration of our feelings. If a promotion makes you incredibly happy today, you might believe it'll continue to make you incredibly happy two months later. But chances are you'll quickly become accustomed to your new job. Even winning the lottery doesn't raise people's long-term happiness. The encouraging flip side of this is that negative emotions associated with traumatic events—the death of a family member, being diagnosed with cancer, becoming disabled—also don't last as long as we think they will. The initial sadness or grief is profound, but we do recover over time.

To compensate for these biases, maybe we should follow the lead of experts like Paul Ekman. That is, we should analyze and improve our own performance by recalling our expectations, recognizing past inaccuracies, and making necessary adjustments in the future. But are we able to do this in the domain of emotion? Along come Tim Wilson and his colleagues, once again, to complicate things. Before the 2000 presidential election in the United States, Wilson and company rounded up some voters who cared very much about politics. They asked these voters how happy they would be if George W. Bush won or if Al Gore won. The day after Gore's concession speech, they contacted the voters again to ask them how they were feeling. Four months later, they asked the voters how they had felt (a) before the election, and (b) when Gore conceded. Neither the Bush supporters nor the Gore supporters accurately recalled their own feelings from the two earlier occasions. They overestimated the strength of their pre-election emotions. And for the post-concession reaction, Bush supporters remembered being much happier than they actually were and Gore supporters remembered being far sadder.

Apparently, we aren't much better at remembering how we felt in the past than we are at predicting how we will feel in the future. However, as we saw in the previous chapter, we need to believe that we are consistent, comprehensible individuals, so we construct stories about our emotions and opinions that make sense. For example, a participant in the above study might have thought to himself, "As a staunch Democrat, I must have been devastated when Gore lost." It's essentially the same way we predict our future feelings ("Of course I'll be devastated if Gore loses") or anticipate the feelings of others ("Bob's a committed liberal, so he'll be really upset if Gore loses"). The answers seem right, but in reality they're convenient fabrications. This is how we smooth out the rough edges of our true reactions and preferences, which are often quite inconsistent.

So we return to this question: If we don't even know our own minds, how do we figure out what will make us happy? We can temper the automatic system with the reflective system, and vice versa, but we still make mistakes. Perhaps, instead of looking for answers only within ourselves, we should examine what others have done in similar situations. Psychologist Daniel Gilbert, the leading expert on happiness research, writes in his book *Stumbling on Happiness*, "What's so ironic about this predicament is that the information we need to make accurate predictions of our emotional futures is right under our noses, but we don't seem to recognize its aroma." We tend to think that the experiences of others are mostly irrelevant because *our* circumstances and *our* personalities have no equivalents. "[W]e think of ourselves as unique entities—minds unlike any others," Gilbert writes, "and thus we often reject the lessons that the emotional experience of others has to teach us."

The saying goes that history repeats itself; personal histories do the same. We can gather the lessons of others' lives through observation, conversation, and by seeking advice. We can use the automatic system to find out who the happy people are, and the reflective system to evaluate how they got to be that way. Pursuing happiness need not be a lonely endeavor. In fact, throwing in our lot with others may be a very good way of coping with the disappointments of choice.

Near the end of *Oh, the Places You'll Go!,* Dr. Seuss warns that we are sometimes our own opponents in the game of life. When we're struggling against temptation, or when we feel let down by our own decisions, we may wonder how we can possibly win against ourselves. It's enough to make us want to wave the white flag of surrender, but we have to resist that impulse. We cannot completely opt out of choice because it is omnipresent in today's world. Our best bet, then, is to continue to study our complex relationship with it. As you read the upcoming chapters, which present more of the challenges of choice, remember that though the learning curve is steep at times, and though we're bound to stumble, we are capable of making progress with informed intuition and a little help from our friends.

CHAPTER FIVE

I, Robot?

I. NEUTRAL OBSERVER

We've been together in this book for several chapters now, and you've been a good sport, so I'm going to share a secret: Sometimes I like to turn my choice into someone else's problem. Given how many ways one can go "wrong" when choosing, it's tempting to pass off a choice I'm supposed to make as an opportunity for another person to express an opinion. This way, I don't have to take responsibility for the choice, and the person I ask often enjoys giving advice. I know you're raising an eyebrow, but it's not nearly as insidious as it sounds.

Take, for example, a trip to the manicurist, where I have to choose from over a hundred colors, roughly divided into four categories: reds, pinks, neutrals, and the more offbeat colors, like taxicab yellow or sky blue. Neutrals and reds are the most popular, and I personally prefer neutrals, even though I don't have strong opinions about color the way sighted people do. By definition, a neutral shouldn't carry much color, but there are still more than two dozen shades to choose from, including pinks, pearls, and champagnes.

"Which of these neutrals will look good on me?" I ask the manicurist.

"Definitely Ballet Slippers," she replies.

"Definitely Adore-A-Ball," the client sitting next to me counters.

"I see. How are the two different?"

"Well, Ballet Slippers is more elegant."

"Adore-A-Ball is more glamorous."

"And what colors are they?"

"Ballet Slippers is a very light pink."

"And Adore-A-Ball is a sheer pink."

"So how are they different?" I ask.

"Both would look great on you, but Ballet Slippers would look more elegant and Adore-A-Ball would be more glamorous."

If I were sighted, perhaps this is how my internal choosing monologue would go, but since I'm not, I eventually give up and tell them that I don't really understand. I can't help thinking, though I don't say anything out loud, that if they're grabbing for vague adjectives like "elegant" and "glamorous," there may not be much to separate the two shades. There is one thing the women agree on: "Trust us, if you could see them, you'd be able to tell the difference."

Would I? They could be right. After all, as the Indian proverb says, "What does a monkey know of the taste of ginger?" In other words, maybe I'm simply not capable of appreciating the subtle beauty of gradations of color. But before I could consent to becoming the monkey in this story, I had to test their claim. So I put on my researcher's cap and conducted a pilot study with 20 undergraduate women at Columbia University. These students were offered a free manicure, which included having their nails painted with either Adore-A-Ball or Ballet Slippers. Half the women were shown bottles labeled Adore-A-Ball and Ballet Slippers, and the other half saw the same colors in bottles labeled A and B.

In the group that could see the names of the colors, seven of the ten participants chose Ballet Slippers, while the rest preferred Adore-A-Ball. They described Ballet Slippers as the darker and richer of the two colors. In the other group, six chose A (actually Adore-A-Ball), describing *this* as the darker and richer of the two colors, while the others were evenly split between preferring B (Ballet Slippers) and being indifferent. Some couldn't tell the colors apart despite their best efforts; if not for the labels, they might have considered the two identical. In fact, in the group that saw the bottles labeled A and B, three participants thought we were playing a trick on them. They accused us of asking them to choose between two bottles of the exact same color.

Here's what fascinates me: The colors were practically indistinguishable, and yet, especially when they were given names, there *was* a difference. These women, more of whom chose the color Ballet Slippers when its name was visible, also unanimously preferred the name Ballet Slippers to the name Adore-A-Ball. This is unlikely to be mere coincidence. Rather, it seems that the name somehow made the color look better, or at least created a feeling of difference.

For me, the names couldn't make the colors look better or worse, so I simply wanted as objective a description of each color as possible. Ironically, I—the blind person—was concerned primarily with the visual properties of the color, while the sighted people were evaluating the color "package." I didn't care about the name—an adulterant, I thought—precisely *because* I couldn't see the color. But they were choosing not in a vacuum but in the context of a visual culture in which other people had packaged and positioned the product to make it as attractive as possible. Could it be that the color name, a seemingly superficial characteristic, had actually been designed to affect sensory perception itself? If yes, can we really trust our senses and the choices we make based on them? Since I had already taken a preliminary spin on the color wheel, I decided to pursue this line of questioning by following the rainbow.

II. YOU SAY CHICKEN, I SAY EGG

David Wolfe, I'm told, is a man of medium height and build in his late sixties. His smartly chic glasses, salt-and-pepper hair, and studiously maintained stubble all stand out against his Hamptons tan. When I first met him in June 2008, my assistant Snowden described him to me: He wore a tan three-button sport jacket over a black button-up shirt with tan-and-white linen pants. These were complemented by the snakeskin material of his loafers and the bright crimson pocket square tucked into the jacket. He was eye-catching but not flamboyant, which served him well as he stood at a podium, ready to address a roomful of some of the biggest names in fashion design, manufacture, wholesale, and retail.

Wolfe spoke about the increasing "wearability" of fashion trends and the current "style schizophrenia" within the industry. He praised the luxuries of resort wear, showcased necklaces the size of life preservers, and mourned the death of Yves Saint Laurent. But most important, and what his many listeners came to hear, were his predictions for the future, such as the assertion that a "little white dress" would soon become as essential to a woman's wardrobe as the classic "little black dress" has long been. He repeated his presentation every hour, on the hour, over the course of several days, each time to a different crowd of a hundred or more. These industry insiders, themselves dressed in everything from conservative taupes and beiges to zebra-print stilettos and bright blue stockings, listened avidly to his predictions about what people on the streets would be wearing not a month or a season but a year or two from now.

Exiting the Doneger Group headquarters, where Wolfe was giving his presentation, you would find yourself in the Garment District of Manhattan, an area in west Midtown that has functioned as a center of fashion design and manufacturing since the beginning of the twentieth century. To see the fruits of the lecture-room labors, however, you're better off strolling down Broadway in SoHo, a neighborhood farther downtown, where you're likely to find the sidewalks teeming with fashionistas. There, you spot a 20-something man wearing a light blazer the color of an apple Jolly Rancher. A few steps behind him, a woman in her 50s, jeans rolled up to midcalf, calls attention to herself with oversize red sunglasses and matching red socks. And teenagers, well, you know how they are. There's one lolling on a bench across the street, readjusting his multicolored eye patch.

Yet even in this riot of color and style, there are patterns. Bold primary colors seem quite popular, and you begin to notice many cool colors as well: green shirts, teal blouses, cerulean and azure dresses and skirts. The complements to these colors, such as mustard yellow and burnt sienna, also make several appearances. Floral prints are in, as are loose dresses. The influence of previous styles is apparent in the brightly colored leggings similar to those of the 1980s, but there are no bell-bottoms from the 1970s or baby tees from the 1990s. None of this, of course, would surprise Wolfe, who has made a prolific career of predicting the next hot thing.

After working in the trend-forecasting industry for almost 30 years, Wolfe joined the Doneger Group in 1990 as creative director. The Doneger Group is the biggest and foremost of the handful of forecasting companies that serve the fashion industry, which it studies at all stages of development, including design, merchandising, and retail, with an eye on providing its more than 1,000 clients with information that will most successfully drive their businesses. The advice offered takes a variety of forms: color palettes that may be popular in the coming years, "beauty books" filled with predictions for trends in cosmetics, and lectures like the one Wolfe gave.

Similar services are provided in the overlapping realm of color by the Color Association of America. Founded in 1915, the association meets twice a year to forecast the 24 colors that will be popular two years later in the categories of fashion for men, women, and children, as well as interior design, which includes furniture, appliances, dishware, and electronics. These color forecasts are then purchased by a wide range of clients: members of the fashion industry, who use them to design collections or to determine what to sell; Wall Street firms looking to spruce up their offices; tech agencies that want to use popular colors for website design; and other businesses simply trying to give some pop to their PowerPoint presentations.

The summer Snowden and I met Wolfe, we also attended the Color Association's committee meetings for women's and men's fashion. The Midtown Manhattan office is white from floor to ceiling, with swaths of fabric draped down one wall and bookcases full of art books lining another. The focal point of the room hangs on the wall in front of the central table. It is a giant square containing smaller squares of every color, appearing at first to be a close-up of a digital image or perhaps of a Chuck Close painting. In fact, it is a representation of the color spectrum. Natural sunlight from the many large windows mingles with the bright fluorescence of the fixtures overhead, fully illuminating the airy, impressive space. The committee members, including representatives from well-known and influential firms like Cotton Incorporated, Saks Fifth Avenue, and even the Doneger Group, convened here to share their color predictions for the fall and winter of 2009–2010.

Each made a presentation of a "color swatch," a poster board featuring sources of inspiration, usually with pictures of artwork, statues, models, pottery, still-life paintings, bicycle riders, flowers, leaves, and quirky, eye-catching objects. One swatch had a photo of a man with a goatee kissing a Dalmatian full on the lips. Another was full of round circles of unusual colors, like snowballs from a fairy-tale world. In addition to these images, the members shared stories or cited examples of what they believed were sign-of-the-times events and trends, cultural indicators that would soon color the world, literally. Sal Cesarani, head of S.J.C. Concepts, mentioned an exhibit of superhero costumes at the Metropolitan Museum of Art that would herald a new vogue for bright, saturated colors and comic book–inspired prints and patterns. Sherri Donghia, the head of the Donghia Furniture Group, spoke excitedly about the new Frank Gehry Building in Chelsea that serves as the headquarters for Barry Diller's new Internet technology firm. According to Nicolai Ouroussoff of the *New York Times*, the structure "looks best when approached from a distance. Glimpsed between Chelsea's weathered brick buildings, its strangely chiseled forms reflect the surrounding sky, so that its surfaces can seem to be dissolving. As you circle to the north, however, its forms become more symmetrical and sharp-edged, evoking rows of overlapping sails or knifelike pleats. Viewed from the south, the forms appear more blocky. This constantly changing character imbues the building's exterior with an enigmatic beauty." Donghia proposed that this protean building, the appearance of which seems to alter with the viewer's position and mood, would stimulate a desire for bright colors and a focus on individual perceptional experiences.

I couldn't quite grasp how such localized events and structures would influence the average person's color preferences. "Color me confused," I whispered to myself. Then Michael Macko, the VP Men's Fashion Designer at Saks, made a presentation to the committee on the theme of "Eco-lution," the idea that the environmental conservation movement would spur interest in the use of natural dyes, sustainable materials, and earth tones. This made more sense to me, though the evidence for all these claims was not overwhelming. Once each member had made his or her presentation, the committee synthesized the various predictions to create a single, definitive "color card."

In addition to consulting with one another, forecasters ask prominent fashion designers such as Calvin Klein, Ralph Lauren, and Michael Kors about their inspirations, and the designers are just as interested in what the forecasters have to say. Since it can take up to two years for a design to go from concept to finished product in stores, a peek into the future of fashion could increase a new clothing line's chances for success. Also, by speaking to forecasters, designers are able to glean information about their competitors, who are likely incorporating trend and color predictions into their work. Calvin Klein, for example, reportedly buys forecasts so he'll know what *not* to do. "I would say that there is not a successful designer in the world who does not buy trend information," David Wolfe said. "It's part of research and development if you're a fashion designer."

Retailers also have a clear interest in figuring out which styles will be popular. In the past, they did this by keeping track of what the major fashion designers debuted on the runways in Paris, Milan, London, and New York. Today, however, fashion weeks are held in every major city around the world, and thousands of micro-labels distribute through the Internet and word of mouth. So retailers rely instead on forecasters to consolidate and report the hottest trends, which have been shaped in part by the same forecasters' interactions with designers. The end result of this coordination is that the clothes on the store racks may share quite a few features, because even though they were created independently, they were all designed based on the same information. If scarlet is in and your favorite signal red is out, you're not going to find the latter no matter how hard you look, unless you rummage through bins of clothing from earlier seasons.

The "predictions" are edging ever closer to becoming their own causes. If designers believe that white will be the new black and so only make white dresses, or if the stores only order the white ones, then that's what consumers will buy. Even if you're trying to go against the grain or simply don't care about clothes, your choices will still be shaped by the trends of the moment. This is perfectly expressed by the fire-breathing fashion magazine editor played by Meryl Streep in *The Devil Wears Prada*. When a young assistant dismisses fashion as mere "stuff," the editor is more than ready to take her down a notch:

This…"stuff"? Oh, okay. I see. You think this has nothing to do with you. You go to your closet and you select out, oh,

I don't know, that lumpy, blue sweater, for instance, because you're trying to tell the world that you take yourself too seriously to care about what you put on your back. But what you don't know is that that sweater is not just blue, it's not turquoise, it's not lapis, it's actually cerulean. You're also blithely unaware of the fact that, in 2002, Oscar de la Renta did a collection of cerulean gowns. And then I think it was Yves Saint Laurent, wasn't it, who showed cerulean military jackets?... And then cerulean quickly showed up in the collections of eight different designers. Then it filtered down through the department stores and then trickled on down into some tragic Casual Corner where you, no doubt, fished it out of some clearance bin. However, that blue represents millions of dollars and countless jobs and so it's sort of comical how you think that you've made a choice that exempts you from the fashion industry when, in fact, you're wearing the sweater that was selected for you by the people in this room. From a pile of stuff.

We could even go one step further back and say that Oscar de la Renta made his gowns cerulean because the color forecasters predicted that the Season of Cerulean was upon us. The elaborate process of producing style, then, is perhaps not quite a conspiracy so much as a very chic version of the chicken-and-egg game: Which comes first, the customer or the designer? Do we make fashion, or does fashion make us? The more we think about the question, the more the answer slips through our fingers.

The various elements of the fashion industry and its auxiliaries largely operate by a "you scratch my back, I'll scratch yours" philosophy to promote their goods. Retailers like Saks Fifth Avenue give writers from *Cosmopolitan*, *GQ*, and similar magazines advance notice of the styles that will be appearing in their stores so that they can be featured in articles the instant they hit the shelves. Designers hold fashion shows and extend exclusive invitations to photographers and writers from magazines like *Vogue*. The magazine gets a scoop on the latest trends and the designers get some free advertising. Designers also arrange for their products to be featured on television shows and movies (you, too, can be the proud owner of a Carrie Bradshaw dress or a James Bond wristwatch!), and they often donate their latest creations to actors, musicians, and socialites like Paris Hilton. These celebrities are photographed by paparazzi at red-carpet premieres and nightclubs, and when they are splashed across magazine and tabloid covers, so are the clothes. Personal shoppers and interior designers meet with industry insiders over cocktails to determine what to recommend to their clients, and the list goes on. If there's one thing I learned from my meetings with people in the fashion industry, it's that everybody knows everybody else, and more often than not, they're all playing for the same team.

The goal is to expose consumers to the products through as many different media as possible, influencing them on multiple levels and taking advantage of the "mere exposure effect." As demonstrated in the 1960s by the research of Robert Zajonc, the more we are exposed to a particular object or idea, the more we like it, provided we had positive or neutral feelings toward it at the outset. In one study conducted in 1968, Zajonc showed Chinese characters to non-Chinese-reading people from 1 to 25 times, asking them to guess what they meant. He discovered that more frequent exposure to a character led to more positive guesses, for example, "happiness" rather than "horse" or "disease." Since seeing an unknown character multiple times provided no more information about its meaning than seeing it only once, this indicated that people's attitudes toward the characters themselves improved as a function of exposure. The mere exposure effect explains many facets of our lives, such as why it's so hard to find someone who can prepare our childhood favorites like Mom did, and it also holds when we see the latest fashion trends prominently featured in stores, catalogs, and finally on people we know.

In addition, when a trend emerges, it sends the message that it's becoming increasingly accepted. When we see the supplies of multiple independent retailers simultaneously shift in one way, we assume the demand has shifted as well. Of course, the change may actually be driven by the *prediction* of a future shift in demand, which may or may not materialize, but it still affects people's choices. The higher the exposure a product receives and the greater its perceived social acceptability, the more people will buy it, which in turn further increases its exposure and acceptability. Through this process, the predictions of the forecasters and fashion mavens are validated, making them seem like snazzily dressed seers. "The sneaky thing is, it's a self-fulfilling prophecy," David Wolfe admitted when I asked him about the fine line between predicting trends and influencing them. "It is the most convoluted avenue imaginable in terms of fashion, about manipulating choice, then presenting it. If I had to be honest: I am a manipulator."

What had started for me as an exploration of the complex relationship between language, color perception, and choice had turned into an odd and somewhat sinister whodunit. Had I uncovered a kind of scam, and if I had, who was to blame? Wolfe had made a confession, of sorts, but I wasn't ready to turn him in for crimes against the customer. On the one hand, he and other forecasters were claiming advance knowledge of customer choice and basing these claims on some rather dubious premises, such as the assumed influence of spandex-loving superheroes. On the other hand, they were making it easier for people like me to "choose" fashion trends and colors by reducing the number of options. They were taking the problem of cerulean versus turquoise versus lapis off my hands, and that was fine by me.

Remember the Color Association meeting I attended? The final predictions were distilled to a single "color card" with four categories. Color cards present a number of "stories" that create a narrative from a set of colors. In the Women's Color Forecast for the Fall/

Winter season of 2009–2010, the story "Muse" included colors called Erato (purple), Calliope (orange), and Clio (tile), while "Avant Garden" included Eden (turquoise), Crocodile (brown), and Verbena (green). The names served less as descriptors of the colors' properties than as shorthand for the connotations the forecasters want to convey to designers. For example, about naming a shade of green, forecaster Margaret Walch explained, "Now the color that we will name *Clover*, what are some alternative names that we could name it that would be equally accurate but perhaps don't appeal to people's psyches at the moment?...I could call it *Emerald* or *Irish Green*." The names and stories were part of packaging the color, and as I had noticed in the nail polish experiment, the package was quite important to those who could see the product. It would be easy for me to dismiss it as silliness, even to declare that in the land of the sighted, the blind woman is queen. But I have reason to believe that there are other cases in which I would be just as prone to manipulation as the next person.

III. THERE IS A DIFFERENCE

In an episode of the cable television show *Penn & Teller: Bullshit!*, the two magicians/entertainers took on the bottled water industry. After reviewing the evidence on the (lack of) differences in quality between bottled and tap water, they considered the question of taste. Bottled water manufacturers advertise their products as being not only better for you but better tasting than tap water, but when Penn and Teller ran a blind taste test on the streets of New York City, they found that 75 percent of the people preferred the taste of tap water to Evian.

For the second phase of their investigation, they moved indoors to a fancy restaurant. They hired an actor to play a "water steward," whose job was to present unsuspecting diners with a leather-bound menu of bottled waters with names like *Mount Fuji* and *L'eau du Robinet*, which cost up to $7 a bottle. He described the benefits of the various brands—for example, that one was "a natural diuretic and antitoxin"—and made recommendations. If diners decided to buy any of the water, he poured it into their glasses, then set the remainder of the bottle in an ice-filled wine bucket next to their table. He also solicited their opinions about the taste, and the diners agreed that their waters had been clearly superior to tap water, describing them as "crisper" and "smoother."

You may have already seen through this ruse: All water is "a natural diuretic and antitoxin," and *L'eau du Robinet* is just French for "tap water." Indeed, rather than having been bottled in exotic locations around the globe, all the ostensibly high-end waters shared a common and far humbler source: an outdoor faucet behind the restaurant. The water steward did the dirty deed himself with the help of a hose and some funnels, cackling for dramatic effect before he headed indoors to describe the many unique properties of the bottled waters to the customers.

Penn and Teller may have been more concerned with entertainment value than scientific rigor, but controlled studies have found the same basic results. In one study, researchers from Caltech and Stanford asked novice wine drinkers to sample and rate five different wines that ranged in price from $5 to $90 per bottle. In blind taste tests they enjoyed all of the wines about equally, but when shown the prices they preferred the more expensive ones. What the volunteers didn't realize was that they were actually drinking the same wine with a different price tag—and rating it as better-tasting when it was marked with the higher price.

Everything from the color of a product's logo—or of the product itself—to the shape of its packaging can change people's preferences in ways not captured by blind taste tests. Why should this be the case? Don't we know what we like? Well, as we saw in chapter 3, our choices are based as much on the identities they express as on their possible outcomes. When we say we prefer *L'eau du Robinet* or the more expensive wine, it could be a case of the emperor's new clothes—we don't want to appear to ourselves or others as having unsophisticated palates, or preferring a bottle of plonk to the good stuff. But could they affect our choices at a deeper level? Those of us who aren't tasting experts, i.e., most of us, need to rely on external information in order to choose well. And as we'll see next, some types of information are more informative than others.

Say you prefer bottled water because you believe it is more sanitary than tap water. You wouldn't be alone: Nearly half of bottled water drinkers buy the product partly or only because of concerns about tap-water safety. They are motivated not by white-coated spokespeople quoting statistics about how superior bottled water is but by images like the one on the bottle of Crystal Geyser Natural Alpine Spring Water sitting on my desk. One side shows the unspoiled Ossipee Mountains—the water's source—while the other side proclaims, "Always bottled at the spring to ensure quality, taste, and freshness. THERE IS A DIFFERENCE." Nearly every bottled water label boasts of a product that is "pure," "fresh," and/or "natural," which is visually illustrated, of course, with images of mountains, springs, glaciers, and other pristine water sources tucked away in the wilds. The implication is that any water not packaged in such a bottle is probably impure and unnatural, perhaps dangerously so. This advertising strategy seems simplistic, but it has been enormously successful. In 1987, Americans drank 5.7 gallons of bottled water per year on average; 20 years later, that number has nearly quintupled to 27.6 gallons, which is higher than the consumption of milk or beer.

Closer inspection reveals that the magic of bottled water is due mostly to smoke and mirrors. Nothing on the Crystal Geyser bottle actually claims that its water is of higher quality, or tastier, or fresher than what comes out of your kitchen tap, or out of the bottles of competitors. There may be "a difference," but what is it and compared to what? The legal term for this tactic is "puffery," which the

Federal Trade Commission (FTC) defines as those subjective claims that "ordinary customers do not take seriously." Puffery includes the hyperbole of the Energizer Bunny, as well as terms and phrases like "best," "revolutionary," "sophisticated," "gourmet," "you'll love it," "years younger," and a legion of other buzzwords that sound appealing but mean very little. Yet it's clear that people *do* take puffery seriously, at least enough to encourage marketers to continue using it when they see how it boosts sales.

Bottled water customers certainly must have bought into the puffery; they pay 1,000 times more on a per-gallon basis for the bottled "elixir" than they do for tap water. It turns out, however, that a quarter of bottled water brands *are* tap water, drawn from the same municipal water sources that supply homes and public water fountains. As for the rest, their labels are technically correct, but the products often fail to live up to implied promises. Poland Spring, for example, draws its water from man-made wells, including one beneath a parking lot and another squeezed between a dump and a former illegal sewage disposal site. Though these are both "springs" by definition—underground water sources that would have eventually come to the surface on their own—they sure aren't found in the idyllic locations called to mind by the labels on the bottles. In fact, federal quality standards for tap water are more stringent and more strongly enforced than the standards for bottled water, so it's possible any given bottle of water will be "different" in the wrong way (though both tap and bottled waters are perfectly safe in the vast majority of cases).

We like to think that the free market functions in a way that protects us from inferior or unnecessary products. After all, if the individual brands are all competing with one another, then it seems logical that in order to succeed they must develop superior products that people need. And wouldn't false or exaggerated advertising by one brand be pointed out and refuted by a competitor? Not when colluding with the "enemy" is more profitable than debunking the whole idea behind the product that you also sell. (Haven't we seen this kind of mutual back-scratching before?) Different brands may even actively cooperate with one another when they are owned by the same megacorporation, as is often the case.

For all the fuss over differentiating between them, it turns out that San Pellegrino and Perrier are both owned by Nestlé, along with 28 other brands of bottled water. As a result, you won't see the same level of advertising competition between them as you do between Coke and Pepsi. And since the two best-selling brands of bottled water in the U.S. are owned by Pepsi (Aquafina) and Coke (Dasani), you'd be just as unlikely to see them aggressively advertising their health benefits relative to soft drinks, one of the few claims they could legitimately make. This phenomenon is by no means limited to bottled water; Philip Morris and R.J. Reynolds, themselves subsidiaries of the Altria group and Reynolds American, respectively, control about 80 percent of the cigarette market in the United States. They carry 47 different brands between them, including Camel, Basic, Kool, Chesterfield, Parliament, Winston, Salem, Virginia Slims, and, of course, Marlboro. The majority of the cereals in the supermarket are produced by either Kellogg or General Mills, and the majority of beauty products can be traced back to either L'Oréal or Estée Lauder.

In almost every commercial arena, producers are merging, being taken over, or selling their brand names. The result is that these few megacorporations decide exactly how much variety their brands will offer long before they ever reach the shelves, and it's not in their interest to create true variety. Rather, they aim to maximize differences in image, thereby generating the *illusion* of variety and attracting the greatest diversity of consumers at the least cost to themselves.

A $1.30 bottle of Crystal Geyser contains water that comes from the same source as the water in a $1 bottle of Whole Foods' 365 Organic brand, and in fact many store brands at the supermarket can be differentiated only by label. Generic drugs, required by the FDA to have effects identical to those of the name brands, are cheaper, even though they are sometimes made by the same company, in which case they are known as "authorized generics." For example, the anticholesterol drug Simvastatin is branded as Zocor by Merck, but the generic pills are also made in Merck laboratories, may feature the Merck logo, and are sold in generic form through Dr. Reddy's Laboratories.

Even when the products aren't identical, they may still be more similar than we would expect. The Lancôme and Maybelline brands of cosmetics both belong to L'Oréal, despite having very different images and targeting different consumers. Their matte foundations are made in the same factories, are nearly identical in their composition, and according to "cosmetics cop" Paula Begoun, there's no detectable difference in performance. When you buy Lancôme Magique Matte Soft-Matte Perfecting Mousse Makeup at $37 instead of Maybelline New York's Dream Matte Mousse Foundation at $8.99, you're paying for something other than quality.

Companies get away with this because they control not just a particular product but also its ostensible competitors, making it very difficult for us to determine which differences are real and which are manufactured. We tend to assume that more expensive products are of higher quality; if a cheap product were just as effective, its makers wouldn't miss the chance to advertise this fact, would they? But when both brands are made by one company, it's more profitable to sell the same product under two different brands at different prices, fooling those with thicker wallets into paying more.

The cumulative result of these tactics is that though we may feel steeped in variety, we actually have far fewer qualitatively different options than we realize. This makes choosing a fraught process because we spend a lot of energy trying to sort through a plethora of options for no good reason, and we can't help but wonder if the wool is being pulled over our eyes. We turn to the Internet, the news, anything that might help us cut through the puffery so that we can make meaningful decisions. But even the most unbiased source can't promise that a new finding tomorrow won't reverse recommendations, so the more information we seek out, the more confused we become. Head spinning, you may relent and say, "I don't care if these forces are manipulating my choices. I'm thirsty, and I just want some water, and Crystal Geyser will do me just fine. It looks so pure and refreshing." Nobody wants to agonize over every little decision, and nobody should have to, but if choice is about freedom and exercising control, are we betraying ourselves by pretending that we make meaningful choices as consumers?

IV. THE RED PILL

The alarm clock goes off and you wake up, still tired from a late night. You fumble for the bottle of water on the nightstand, and after you take a swig, you focus your bleary eyes by reading its label: "…natural…fresh…environmentally responsible." Ah, you feel better already, though you could use some caffeine. Since you're out of coffee and don't want to wait until you head out the door to work, you shuffle into the kitchen and get a can of Coke from the fridge. What your mother would say if she could see you now! You gulp it down, smack your lips, and go to the bathroom to brush your teeth. The tube of toothpaste is thin, almost squeezed dry. Remember to pick up some Colgate when you go to the supermarket in the evening. In fact, maybe you should jot down a shopping list right now. You can spare a couple of minutes. So you pick up the pad by the phone, grab a pen, and plop down on the green sofa.

Just then the doorbell rings. Huh? You glance at the clock, and it's definitely too early for anyone to be at your door. Maybe you'll ignore it. You return to your list, but there's the ring again. You run your hand through your hair, adjust your pajamas, and walk to the door. Through the peephole, you see a man dressed in black from head to toe. He leans forward and pulls down his shades a little. You don't know why, but you feel he has something important to tell you.

If you open the door, your life will change, and not in a Publishers Clearing House kind of way. You take a deep breath and let him in.

"I don't know if you're ready to see what I have to show you, but unfortunately, we've run out of time," he says.

"Would you like something to drink?" you say. "A Coke, maybe?"

He frowns. "I'm trying to free your mind."

"Uh, thanks?" Maybe you shouldn't have opened the door after all. And yet you pay close attention as he goes on.

"All this," he says, "is a prison for your mind, a dream world built to keep us under control. You want to see what's real?" He reaches into his pockets, pulls out his hands, and places them palm up in front of you, a pill resting in the hollow of each. "You take the blue pill, the story ends, you wake up and believe whatever you want to believe. You take the red pill, you stay in Wonderland, and I show you how deep the rabbit hole goes. Remember, all I'm offering is the truth, nothing more."

The water and Coke aren't sitting well in you stomach. How do you manage to get yourself into these situations? You should know better. You should know better by now, so why are you reaching out for the red pill? You pop it into your mouth, and the lights dim and then go dark. For a moment, you've gone under and don't know where you are. And then you wake up.

———

The above scenario is freely adapted from the 1999 film *The Matrix*, which shows us a world in which the human race has been enslaved by artificially intelligent machines. As we make technological advances at breakneck speed, sometimes we can't help but wonder if *The Matrix* is predictive rather than speculative.

"This will really happen one day if we're not careful," say some voices.

"Oh, don't be ridiculous. That's the stuff of science *fiction*," say others.

"Fools!" says a vocal minority. "It has already happened. You think we're in control of our lives? We're not. There are forces all around us affecting our every move and changing the very fabric of reality."

Chances are, you find yourself in the first or the second group, or perhaps you move back and forth between the two. But consider for a moment the perspective of the mystery man who offered you the pills, who clearly belongs to the small third group. He may be paranoid, but that doesn't mean those forces aren't out to get him— and us. The grand mechanisms that direct our choices, often without our knowledge, can leave us feeling less than human. In *The Matrix*, humans retain their fleshy bodies, but those bodies are mere energy generators for the empire of the AI machines. Plugged into the Matrix, they are part of a program that constructs a seemingly normal life for them, while all the while they are being sucked dry for the benefit of their evil mechanical overlords. Thus, they are no more than machines themselves. The term "robot," which comes from the Czech *robota*, meaning "compulsory labor," could well apply.

We, too, might feel robotic if we think of ourselves as being subject to programming and control by the nefarious forces of capitalist industry. Choice? Hah! The only real choice we have is in deciding which pill to take. Should we take the red one? Should we call bullshit? Should we blame the marketers who try to take advantage of our biases, to create differences where few or none exist? Or should we take the blue pill, because if it *feels* real to the senses, how is it not real? If our brains process a rose by any other name as less sweet, the color rose by any other name as less vibrant, Coke in a different can as "less Coke," don't the differences become real to us? Should we travel to Wonderland or stay right where we are?

V. YOUR BRAIN ON COKE

A woman lies inside a giant machine as dark and cramped as a coffin. Her ears are assaulted by loud clicking noises that reverberate within the chamber. Her head is held immobile by a tightly fitted cage, a literal prison for her mind. She is fed through a tube that delivers precise doses of a simple carbohydrate solution. Only her eyes move, watching images flicker on a screen in front of her face. Strange devices in the walls beam waves through the air that penetrate her brain, allowing computers to eavesdrop on her thoughts. Has the world finally come to this? Should we have listened to the conspiracy nuts and end-of-the-world pamphleteers?

Actually, this is part of a harmless series of studies conducted in Houston during 2004, a different kind of blind taste test. The first step was straightforward enough: Participants had sips of either Coke or Pepsi squirted into their mouths without being told which was which, and then they were asked which they preferred. About half of them preferred Coke and the other half preferred Pepsi. About half of them also reported buying Coke in their everyday lives, and the other half said they bought Pepsi. The interesting thing was that people were just as likely to buy Coke but prefer the unlabeled Pepsi (or vice versa) as they were to match their purchasing decisions to their stated preferences. This finding came as such a surprise to the researchers that they reran the test several more times with new people to make sure the first time hadn't been a fluke.

If people were indeed choosing which soda to buy based on their taste preferences, they weren't doing a very good job. Flipping a coin and becoming a Coke customer if it came up heads, a Pepsi customer if it came up tails, would have had the same result. What was going on here? In the next step, the one that eerily resembles a brainwashing procedure in my description above, the original self-described Coke and Pepsi lovers were strapped into a functional magnetic resonance imaging machine (fMRI), which measures mental activity by using high-powered magnetic fields to track blood flow in the brain. It turned out that a part of the brain called the ventromedial prefrontal cortex, which is associated with evaluating basic rewards such as pleasant tastes, was more active when participants sipped the soda that they later reported preferring the taste of. In this case, they were evaluating each cocktail of caffeine, sugar, and flavoring in a purely sensory manner.

Of course, when we drink Coke and Pepsi in our lives, only very rarely are we performing blind taste tests. In a follow-up experiment, people again sampled sodas while being monitored by an fMRI machine. They were told that each sip might or might not be Coke, although it always was. Half the sips of soda were preceded by a picture of a Coke can, while the rest were preceded by a colored light, but this was not supposed to indicate anything about what the participants were drinking. The results showed that 75 percent of the people preferred the taste that was preceded by the Coke image rather than by the light, even though they were never drinking anything other than Coke. The presence of the Coke image also led to increased brain activity in other regions, the hippocampus and dorsolateral prefrontal cortex, both of which are used when people draw on previous emotional experiences. In other words, people were now "tasting the brand." As far as their brains were concerned, the Coke-associated sips really did taste better than the light-associated ones. Signals from the taste buds were overpowered by other brain activity when people saw that red can they knew so well. When this experiment was repeated with sips of Pepsi and the Pepsi logo, it did not produce a similar effect, suggesting that we don't have the sense of connection with Pepsi that we do with Coke. Why should this be the case?

Years ago, on a plane trip, I stumbled on a possible answer to this question. During the flight's beverage service, the passenger sitting next to me became agitated when the flight attendant told him they served only Pepsi products. "We don't serve Coke, sir," she said. "Would you like a Pepsi instead?" He most certainly would not! I asked the man whether he really could tell the drinks apart and if so, why did he prefer Coke to Pepsi? "I'm not really sure if I could," he said. "Coke's just always seemed right. I mean, Coke is like Christmas. What would life be like without Christmas?"

But why is it Coke, not Pepsi, that's like Christmas? Coke lists its ingredients as carbonated water, high fructose corn syrup, caramel color, phosphoric acid, caffeine, and natural flavors. So does Pepsi, and its "natural flavors" are almost identical in taste. The two brands do have some differences between them, notably that Pepsi is slightly sweeter and Coca-Cola still flavors its drinks with its namesake coca leaves (once the cocaine in them has been eliminated, of course), but these differences have been shown by standard blind taste tests to be negligible. So do we prefer Coke simply because our brains are addicted to its logo?

Since its invention in 1885, Coke has embedded itself, through aggressive and often ingenious use of advertising, in the minds of consumers and in the culture of America. Coca-Cola was one of the first companies to realize that image was even more important than product. Over the past century, the company has spent billions of dollars placing its ubiquitous trademark, that famous can colored a specific shade of red, in television commercials, magazine ads, and especially Hollywood films. A Coke sign has occupied the lower tier of 2 Times Square in Manhattan since 1932. The company sent 248 "technical observers" overseas during World War II to help bottle Coke behind the front lines. Norman Rockwell was commissioned to draw illustrations of all-American farm boys sipping Coke down at the ol' swimming hole. Remember the Coke commercial where young people from all over the world stood on a hilltop and sang a song that included the line "I'd like to buy the world a Coke"? That song became a top-ten hit. People were paying money to listen to an ad! Clearly, Coke is a lot more than just a drink.

In fact, along with whatever else it may stand for, Coke *is* Christmas. When you think of Santa Claus, what do you imagine? Chances are, you see a jolly fat man wearing a bright red suit and cap, black boots and belt, and a generous smile on his rosy face. This image of Santa Claus was created by Swedish illustrator Haddon Sundblom, who was commissioned by the Coca-Cola Company to draw advertisements of St. Nick delivering Cokes to the thirsty children of the world. "Prior to the Sundblom illustrations, the Christmas saint had been variously illustrated wearing blue, yellow, green, or red," Mark Pendergrast writes in *For God, Country and Coca-Cola*. "In European art, he was usually tall and gaunt, whereas Clement Moore had depicted him as an elf in 'A Visit from St. Nicholas.' After the soft drink ads, Santa would forever more be a huge, fat, relentlessly happy man with broad belt and black hip boots." Ever notice that Santa's suit is the exact same red as the label for Coke? That's not a coincidence: The Coca-Cola Company holds a patent on the color. Santa is clearly a Coke man.

And there's more. My own experience tells me that Coke is also freedom. Remember my trip to Berlin? In the midst of the celebrations that followed the fall of the Berlin Wall in November 1989, free cans of Coke were handed out. It was only when I was studying Coke's marketing campaigns over the years that I was reminded of the free Cokes. Yes, I did have a Coke on the day that was hailed as a triumph of freedom. I recall now that when I proudly held a colorful piece of the Wall, which I had chiseled myself, in my left hand, I also held a Coke in my right. Perhaps my own preference for Coke solidified right then, associated as it was with freedom and other American ideals.

At the unveiling of Times Square's new Coke sign in 2004, Michael Bloomberg, mayor of New York, said in a nationally televised broadcast, "This billboard really does stand for America as much as anything.... Coca-Cola has been a great partner with New York City and a great partner with America. It really has stood up for everything that's good." The consequence of being constantly exposed to these messages is that when we see the logo on a Coca-Cola can, we feel good, and these positive emotions augment the taste of the soda. Coke doesn't just taste like sugar and natural flavors; it tastes like freedom.

VI. THE 500-POUND GORILLA IN THE ROOM

The freedom lover (and Coke drinker) in you may be thinking that there must be something you can do to counteract all the money and energy devoted behind the scenes to anticipating or directing your every move. For one thing, you're going to start paying more attention. Yes, perhaps you'll sometimes have a crazed, wild-eyed look, but that's a price you're willing to pay to "free your mind." I'd like to be supportive, so let me alert you to the possible pitfalls of this strategy.

In the psychological study of attention, one comes across a famous short video clip of three students dressed in white and three dressed in black, with each team passing a basketball back and forth as the members constantly change positions. The goal for viewers is to count how many times the white team passes the ball from one member to another. If you'd like to participate yourself, which I recommend, you can view the video online at http://viscog.beckman. uiuc.edu/flashmovie/15.php.

———

There's a lot of activity in the video, so if you want your count to be accurate, you'll need to pay close attention to the white team for the entire duration. When you're done, read on.

———

The white team made 14 passes. Congratulations if you got it right or came close! By the way, did you notice anything slightly odd in the video? Perhaps you should go back and watch it again, this time without focusing on the white team. Read on when you're ready.

———

At about the halfway point in the video, a man in a gorilla suit calmly strolls in from the right into the center of the frame, turns directly toward the camera, and briefly beats on his chest before sauntering out to the left. If you're not watching with any particular goal in mind, this simian surprise is hard to miss. However, if you're paying attention to the white team and deliberately blocking out the black team's movements, the black gorilla seems to disappear.

The point of this exercise is that the scope of our conscious attention is often far narrower than we realize, so we prioritize by focusing on whatever's relevant to the task at hand. If you're reading this book in a room with a ticking clock, you probably weren't thinking about the noise until I mentioned it. (Sorry.) On the other hand, have you ever been sitting in the same room and suddenly realized it was quiet...too quiet? Then it hits you: That clock stopped ticking a while ago. How come we notice the absence of the sound but not its presence?

We saw in the previous chapter that our minds operate on two levels simultaneously: one conscious and reflective, the other unconscious and automatic. It's easy for our reflective systems to become overwhelmed with information, but the automatic system, being simpler, has a far greater bandwidth. As a result, we can subconsciously register information without becoming consciously aware of it. When you watch the video for the passes and miss the cameo by King Kong Jr., it isn't that you don't see him but rather that you don't *realize* you've seen him. In such situations, the automatic system takes note of the missed information; it also spontaneously interprets it and acts on its conclusion in the only way it can: by sending feelings or hunches up to the reflective system. We can have gorilla-size gaps in our conscious awareness of the world, yet still have our choices be strongly influenced by what resides in these gaps.

John Bargh, a social psychologist at Yale University, has spent his career studying the ways in which many of our judgments, opinions, attitudes, behaviors, impressions, and emotions form without our being consciously aware of them. In one of his most insightful studies, 30 students at New York University were each given scrambled sets of five words in random order—for example, "he, it, hides, finds, instantly"—and asked to construct a grammatically correct sentence using four of them. In one version of the task, each of the scrambled sets contained words related to descriptions or stereotypes of the elderly, such as worried, old, gray, sentimental, wise, retired, wrinkle, and even bingo and Florida. Care was taken to exclude any references to slowness, for reasons that will soon become clear. The other version used sets of words free of any particular association with old age, such as thirsty, clean, and private.

After participants finished the sentence-creation task, which they were told was meant to test their language proficiency, the experimenter thanked them for their involvement and directed them down the hallway to the elevator. As they walked from the doorway of the laboratory to the elevator, all the participants were secretly observed by a second experimenter who measured the length of time it took them to reach a piece of tape about ten meters down the hallway. Researchers discovered that on average, those who had constructed sentences using words related to the elderly took roughly 15 percent longer to reach the elevator than those who had seen the other set of words, even though none of the words either group saw were related to speed.

These results are interesting for two reasons. First, they show that the automatic system is tuned in and capable of complex mental activity. The participants' minds registered the pattern in the words related to the elderly, connected it with their preexisting knowledge that the elderly walk slowly, and applied the concept of walking slowly to their own behavior, all without their conscious knowledge. Even when explicitly asked, after completing the experiment, none of the students said that they had noticed words related to the elderly, and they didn't think that the sentence-creation task had affected their behavior in any way.

Second, the results demonstrate how subconscious influences can pervade all aspects of our behavior, even the ones we don't commonly see as choices. Ultimately, our walking speed can be under our conscious control, just as our body language, facial expressions, and style of speech can, but unless we make an effort to continually exercise this control, we'll defer to the dictates of the automatic system. In John Bargh's words, "Much of everyday life—thinking, feeling, and doing—is automatic in that it is driven by current features of the environment...without any mediation by conscious choice or reflection." Just like an iceberg, only a tenth of which is visible above water, our consciousness makes up only a small portion of our minds. In fact, the mind is more deeply submerged than an iceberg is; it's estimated that 95 percent of mental behavior is subconscious and automatic. Without conscious intervention, external forces can influence our choices with impunity.

Our minds don't organize stored information alphabetically or chronologically or by the Dewey decimal system but rather by its web of association to other information. As a result, being exposed to a particular piece of information also makes it easier to (or impossible *not* to) recall related information, and "information" in this case doesn't just mean facts but also includes things like how to move your hand, the taste of a lemon, and how you felt when you had your first kiss. We can deliberately take advantage of this system, for example by creating mnemonic devices to help study for a test, mentally retracing our steps to figure out where we could have left an elusive set of keys, or reminiscing about the past. Just as often, though, the associations come unbidden (and often consciously unnoticed) in response to some experience in our lives. Something that activates these automatic associations is known as a "prime," and its effect on our mental states and subsequent choices is known as "priming." Do you feel a twinge in your jaw as you imagine biting into a lemon wedge, or have you ever thought of an old flame after hearing "your song" on the radio years later? That's priming in action. When people enjoy the taste of Coke more after seeing the can, or when they thirst for a Coke after seeing an image of Santa, that's also priming.

None of the examples of advertising and other influences on our choices that we've looked at so far would be half as effective if it weren't for priming. Buying a product that a celebrity also wears allows us to feel a little more glamorous by association. We favor this brand of cough syrup in part because the handsome actor who isn't a doctor but plays one on TV is comforting to us when we're ill, even if we know that he doesn't know the first thing about what ails you. In fact, priming is one good reason nearly all ads ever produced feature the unusually good-looking: If beautiful people use Denham's dentifrice on TV, when we use it in real life, some of their attractiveness may rub off on us. As silly as that sounds, it makes perfect sense to the automatic system. Like a mental Google search, it pulls up a list of whatever is most related to an idea, whether the relation between the two is relevant to our needs or not. And as with Google, advertisers have become adept at taking advantage of the system to further their own ends.

Priming can have pervasive effects on our moods, perceptions, and choices. The associations primes create aren't particularly strong, but they don't need to be. Because we're unaware of their effects, we're unable to compensate for them in our conscious decision making. Moreover, the prime itself may be perceived only subconsciously, preventing us from realizing that we've been influenced. Subliminal messages are a classic example of this, though popular culture has greatly exaggerated their scope and power. (No, you didn't flunk out of school because the heavy-metal song you played backward told you to rebel against the system and worship Satan.) The truth is far more modest. Our emotions and choices *can* be subconsciously affected by simple words and images that appear on a screen for just 5 to 30 milliseconds, an incredibly short amount of time given that a typical blink takes 100 milliseconds. In one study, people who watched a short film in which the word "Beef" was flashed repeatedly were made hungrier by it than people who watched the same film without the prime, but they weren't hungry for beef in particular. While these true subliminal messages, which appear too briefly for us to consciously perceive even if we try, exist only in the laboratory, any stimulus in our lives can be functionally subliminal if we aren't paying conscious attention to it.

Does this mean that we *are* at the mercy of influences that we can't even detect unless we're hypervigilant, and perhaps not even then? Are we fighting some sort of losing battle against these insidious, brain-altering forces? Answering yes may make for a thrill ride of a movie, but it's a bit more complex offscreen. For one thing, the choices that have the largest impact on our lives are unlikely to be made in automaton mode. Few people (outside Las Vegas) wake up in the morning to find that they got married the night before without their conscious approval. The effectiveness of priming lies in its subtlety, not its strength, so it affects our choices on the margins rather than causing us to act against our strongly held values. A prime may influence whether you drink Coke or Pepsi, but priming alone will never lead you to sell all your belongings and spend the rest of your life in a monastery in the Himalayas.

On the other hand, even though our core values and attitudes are relatively safe from subconscious influences, the same can't always be said for the way we act out that core. The automatic system doesn't distinguish between incidental choices and highly consequential ones when forming and acting on associations, meaning that even the most important choices in our lives can be influenced in ways that run counter to our expressed preferences. For example, when we vote directly on a ballot initiative, it goes without saying that the choice should be based on our views of the issue and little else. But we might unwittingly allow the physical voting environment to affect the choice, as demonstrated by a study conducted by Jonah Berger, Marc Meredith, and S. Christian Wheeler. The study analyzed the results from the 2000 general election for the entire state of Arizona, including how people voted on the ballot initiative Proposition 301, which proposed raising the state sales tax from 5.0 to 5.6 percent in order to increase education spending. The researchers were interested in seeing if *where* people voted affected *how* they voted.

Elections in the United States are conducted at various polling locations such as churches, schools, and firehouses, and people are assigned to vote at whichever location is closest to where they live. The researchers found that the 26 percent of people who were assigned to vote at schools were more likely to support schools by voting yes on Proposition 301 than were those people who voted at other polling locations. To confirm that this effect was actually due to polling location rather than some other factor, such as pro-education people having deliberately chosen to live near schools, they conducted an online experiment that simulated the effects of voting in a school. People saw images of either schools or generic buildings as part of a supposedly unrelated personality test before being asked to indicate how they would vote on Proposition 301. Results showed that the people who were exposed to the school images were more willing to support raising taxes to fund education.

If we were absolutely sure of our opinions and resolute, perhaps we wouldn't be affected in this way, but most of the issues that ask us to consider our values are not easy to address in a black or white manner. We often find it necessary to find a balance between equally desirable or undesirable alternatives, and sometimes we don't even know what we really think about something until we're forced to confront it. The various locations in which we cast our ballots contain sensory cues—the smell of chalk dust at a school, the flame of a votive candle on a church altar—that can prime support for one side or another. For people who haven't yet decided how much they value additional school funding relative to a 0.6 percent increase in the price of the goods, or those who weren't even aware of the proposition until they stepped into the voting booth, primes may make an impact.

Choosing a candidate is an even more difficult voting decision. Rather than dealing with a single issue, we need to determine who will do a better job of running his or her jurisdiction overall. Aside from the difficulties in determining what the optimal set of policies for a candidate would be, and which candidate's platform matches it most closely, we need to consider the candidates' competence, trustworthiness, and a host of other personal factors. Even as we engage in reflective analysis of the pluses and minuses of the candidates, the automatic system injects information that may or may not be relevant to our analysis. The problem is that we have no filters to ensure that the final decision is based only on relevant information.

For example, we know that a candidate's appearance has little, if anything, to do with his or her ability, yet it affects our choices. A classic study of the 1974 Canadian national elections found that the most attractive candidates received over twice as many votes as the least attractive ones. And a 2007 study showed that about 70 percent of elections were won by the candidate whom people rated as more competent based solely on their appearance—even when they saw the candidate's photograph for only a tenth of a second. Additional studies have supported these results, also finding that elected officials are several inches taller and less likely to be bald than the population as a whole. This is by no means limited to politics; numerous studies have also found that height and salary positively correlated, especially for men, who earn about 2.5 percent more per inch of additional height, and that highly attractive people of both sexes earn at least 12 percent more than their less attractive coworkers. In fact, physical appearance has a greater impact even than job qualifications on whether a person will be hired following a job interview. And attractive defendants in criminal cases receive lighter sentences and are twice as likely to avoid jail entirely.

In none of these cases have people said that appearance is a factor in their choices. Of course, few people would admit or even acknowledge to themselves something that shallow and unjust. Most of the time, they probably aren't even aware of these biases when they occur. Attractiveness and skill in one's field of expertise are naturally linked in our minds since both are desirable traits, which means that exposure to one will prime the other. These associations are further reinforced by culture—everything from Cinderella to, well, practically every television and movie hero to date. When telling a story they're effective as wish-fulfillment, or as a quick and convenient way to sketch a character without giving a lengthy back-story, but as a side effect, these associations can automatically be applied to our real-world judgments as well. Suntans and bald spots probably aren't valid factors to consider in any domain aside from fashion photography, but they still manage to sneak in around the edges of even serious decisions.

The effects of priming itself are seldom dramatic, but a subtle shift in people's behavior can have a tremendous impact on the world. Remember the infamous presidential election of 2000? With every state but Florida reporting, Al Gore led the popular vote and had 267 confirmed electoral votes to George W. Bush's 245. Either candidate needed 270 electoral votes to win, which meant that Florida's 25 electoral votes were the key to the presidency. The final result wouldn't be known until more than a month past Election Day, though, both because the race in Florida was incredibly tight and because poor ballot design had resulted in a large number of voting errors. Confusing "butterfly ballots" in Palm Beach County apparently caused thousands of people to vote for Pat Buchanan instead of Al Gore, and thousands more punch-card ballots were disqualified because the paper "chad" that voters were supposed to punch out didn't detach enough for automatic vote-tallying machines to read it. These controversies led to a series of recounts that eventually led to a Supreme Court judgment. When the dust settled, Bush was declared the winner in Florida by exactly 537 votes, although under other proposed tallying methods the vote could have been 171 in Gore's favor instead.

What's amazing is that this confusion of butterfly ballots and hanging chads may not have been the deciding factor. These are legitimate examples of user-unfriendliness, the kind that a good ballot designer should have seen coming a mile away, but the shift in behavior that may have clinched the election could have been due to Bush's name being at the top of the ballot. There was no diabolical reason behind this, or even partisan scheming. Ballot ordering varies wildly from state to state, probably because nobody considers it very important. Some list candidates alphabetically by name, others alphabetically by party, and still others list incumbents first. Only a handful of states rotate ballot order between precincts, ensuring that all candidates will be represented equally. In Florida, it was a regulation that the candidate who belongs to the current governor's party will appear first on the ballot, and because the governor of Florida in 2000 was George W. Bush's fellow Republican (and brother) Jeb Bush, George got top billing.

Why would this matter? Stanford professor Jon A. Krosnick conducted a recent series of studies on the 2000 presidential elections in Ohio, North Dakota, and California. These three states all rotate ballot order, allowing researchers to measure how many people vote for a candidate when his name is first on the ballot versus lower down. They found significant benefits for whoever came first, whether Bush, Gore, Buchanan, or Nader. The largest effect was an incredible nine-and-a-half-point advantage for Bush in California, and the average benefit across all candidates and states was 2 percent. In politics, 2 percent is a huge difference, the kind for which candidates fight tooth and nail. The margin of Kennedy's victory over Nixon in 1960 was 0.2 percent, for example. Although it wasn't possible to measure how much Bush benefited from this effect in Florida because his name always came first, if we conservatively assume a 1 percent advantage—half of the overall average—he received about 50,000 additional votes by the sheer luck of being listed first on the ballot. If the ballots had been rotated and these votes split with Gore, all the hanging chads in the world wouldn't have helped Bush, and the world might be a different place today.

VII. NETWORK

We want to make meaningful choices in our lives, but how do we do that when others manipulate the social value assigned to the options, our beliefs about which options are best, and our senses and emotions? In some ways, the comparison of our world to that of *The Matrix* may be more apt than we'd like to believe. According to Morpheus, the leader of the resistance, the Matrix is a "neural interactive simulation." In the context of the movie, such a simulation is very bad indeed. The human character who doesn't acknowledge this, who knows the truth but thinks that perhaps the comforting illusion created by the Matrix has its charms, is not only a disagreeable person but a traitor. His name is Cypher, and after many years in the resistance, he decides to betray his friends so that the machines will put him back in the Matrix: "Ignorance is bliss," he says. In name, in attitude, in deed, Cypher is opposed to meaning and, by extension, truth. But it is much easier to set up a villain when a clear line can be drawn between "us" and "them." When everyone is in on it, when we collectively create our systems of choice, is it even possible to separate what's "real" from what's not?

One could argue that in our world, each brain acts as a node, an individual neural interactive simulator, in a giant network of simulators. The sum of the activity of all these simulators creates our world, and each person perceives that world through his or her own simulator. The only way to avoid the influence of the other simulators would be to opt out of the network, to sever all connections, to live only in one's own head.

I'm not suggesting that we ignore all the effects of advertising, priming, and so on by dismissing them as the natural and unavoidable result of social interaction. It is absolutely worth our while to critically examine the various actors and directors that influence our decisions. But we don't need to choose between a red pill and a blue pill—between hyperawareness and blissful ignorance. Becoming aware of a potential influence on our behavior doesn't necessarily mean we should make decisions that oppose it. For example, a pro-conservation poster that uses a close-up picture of a baby seal is certainly emotionally manipulative (unless you have an irrational fear of baby seals), but if it gets you to reduce your carbon footprint, should you worry about the manipulation? If you prefer Coke to Pepsi, learning that this preference is due to their ad campaigns rather than to their formulas won't change the fact—at least not in the short term—that Coke simply tastes better to you. You might decide to switch to a generic cola and save yourself a few bucks, and slowly retrain your brain to like the generic just as much as the Coke, but you might also decide that not only do you enjoy Coke, you enjoy enjoying Coke, and since as far as you know, the company isn't bottling its soda using child labor, this is one battle you'd rather not fight.

We tend to have a knee-jerk negative response to anything that seems to want or have control over us. We worry that if we give up *any* control, we may eventually become nothing more than robots. Our anxiety is not always unwarranted, but too much of it is counterproductive. The problem may lie in the fact that we tend to put choice on a pedestal, so much so that we expect to be able to bend everything to our will. We would serve ourselves better by separating the influences that conflict with our values from the influences that are basically harmless. We can then consciously examine our reasoning process to combat some of the covert effects of the negative influences.

Yes, we can accept a little manipulation of the taste buds. And maybe we don't mind buying that teal sweater, even if it's not exactly what we had in mind. But when our voting is affected by factors we're not even aware of, the prospect of mind control doesn't seem like science fiction anymore. If the democratic process can be so easily undermined, who's really in charge? That's worth making a fuss over. By focusing on things that really matter, we avoid running ourselves ragged over decisions that are simply not important in the long run. The energy we save can be channeled into our reflective system, which needs to operate at its highest level to deal with the many choices that we're about to encounter in the next chapter.

CHAPTER SIX

Lord of the Things

I. STUCK IN A JAM

Have you heard of the famous jam study? Perhaps you vaguely recall reading about it in a newspaper article awhile back, or maybe someone brought it up at a cocktail party. If you don't know about it, you will very soon. Quite a few people have told me about the study, and some of them have even given serious thought to it. When I met with the head of Fidelity Research, he explained it as follows: "Consumers think having more choices is great, but they're less likely to buy a jar of jam when they have to choose from a larger array. We offer our clients up to 4,500 mutual funds, so this study provides a mantra for us: NARROW IT DOWN. We're constantly advising our employees to NARROW IT DOWN for the clients." He added, "We have slides. I'll send them to you."

Then there was the McKinsey exec who said that because of an internal memo regarding this same study, consultants now practice the 3 x 3 Rule, in which the client first chooses from among three choices, which can lead to another set of three choices, culminating in no more than a third set of three options. This rule of thumb for presenting people with choices is also used by bank brokers, personal shoppers, and Wall Streeters, proving the broad appeal and utility of putting a cap on how much choice customers have.

And such encounters with enthusiastic jam study disciples weren't limited to boardrooms and business meetings. Once, during the course of a long flight, I was having a conversation with the woman seated next to me about how exasperating a basic task like grocery shopping had become. "There's just too much choice out there these days," she sighed, then proceeded to share with me the details of some research she'd recently read about in a *New York Times* editorial. Apparently, she told me, a few years back someone had done a study in a supermarket, using different flavors of jam. It turned out that when people were given a smaller number of flavors to choose among, they were actually more likely to buy a jar of jam than if they had been given a wider variety of options. She couldn't remember all the details, she said, but it had stuck in her head because it seemed to give credence to what she'd been feeling all along.

More often than not, people I've talked to over the years seem to agree with my seatmate on the flight that there might just be something to this curious notion of excess choice. But reactions to the study are not always so positive. Various people have attacked the results in books or on talk shows, and I'm told that Rush Limbaugh once made it the focal point of a rather heated tirade. Such ideas, they argue, are blatantly anti-freedom! Anyone who perpetuates them must be in favor of authoritarianism, Nazism, communism—the list goes on. How dare anyone suggest that choice isn't a universal good?

Since I'm the one who conducted the jam study, I'm the one making that suggestion. But the study hardly seems mine anymore, now that it has received so much attention and been described in so many different ways. I hadn't anticipated the response, and I'm still trying to understand it. From the various versions people have heard and passed on, a refrain has emerged: More is less. That is, more choice leads to less satisfaction or fulfillment or happiness. The revelation that an abundance of choice doesn't always benefit us has gradually seeped into the broader culture, spreading like a juicy bit of gossip or a scandal. "Have you heard the news about choice?" "I know! Can you believe it?" The idea grabs people, with its seeming contradiction, its counterintuitive premise. It *sounds* wrong, but doesn't it—at least some of the time—*feel* right?

We all know that we want choice and like having options. The word "choice" almost always carries a positive connotation; conversely, to say "I had little or no choice" is usually to apologize or to explain one's unfortunately limited predicament. We assume that if having choice is good, having more must be better. For all of its positive qualities, however, a wide variety of choice can also be confusing and overwhelming, leading us to throw our hands in the air and exclaim, "I don't know! There are just so many options! Can I get some help here?" Rather than give in to frustration, how can we navigate the downsides of the proliferation of choice? What actually happens to us when we're faced with an overwhelming array of options, and what sorts of problems can arise as a result?

II. BACK TO THE DRAWING BOARD

Let me take you back to chapter 2, to the studies I did with Asian American and Anglo American children. You'll recall that the Asian American children performed best when solving puzzles that they thought their mothers had chosen, whereas Anglo American children performed best on puzzles of their own choosing. I left out the preliminary steps I took to prepare for these studies, but I'd like to return to them now, because that's where the story really begins.

In keeping with the rigors of scientific inquiry, before comparing the effects of choice on the two groups of children, I needed first to show that choice was, in fact, beneficial for Anglo American children. Decades of theory and research argued for the positive effects of choice on motivation, so I assumed I'd have no trouble demonstrating this in my own study. I was, of course, wrong.

My investigation began with three-year-olds at preschools in Palo Alto. I set up a room filled with toys. Legos? Check. Etch A Sketch? Check. Slinky, Tinkertoys, jigsaw puzzles, crayons? Yup, you name it. A child was brought in and told he could play with anything he wanted. Once he was done, it was someone else's turn. This child, however, was told exactly what to play with and was not permitted to switch. Then another child had a go, and so on down the line. By the end, half of the children had been given a choice and the other half had not. One of these groups played enthusiastically and expressed disappointment when time was up; the other was dis-engaged, listless. Which children were in which group? The answer seems obvious: Since choice is motivating, the children who chose their toys must have enjoyed themselves more. Why, then, did I observe the opposite?

As a young doctoral student hoping to impress my adviser, Mark Lepper, I was determined to overcome my apparent incompetence and achieve the "right" results. I repeated the experiment, to no avail, so I decided to make some changes. Perhaps I simply needed better toys, and more of them. I raided the counters and shelves of specialty stores, gathering up the latest, most unusual and innovative toys. Soon the room was stocked with more than a hundred different options, and I was sure that any kid—no matter how picky—would find something new and exciting to play with. But matters only got worse, as the children who were allowed to choose grew even more bored and restless and anxious to escape. It was back to the drawing board for me.

I pored over the seminal papers on the power of choice (at least for Westerners, since these studies were conducted mostly in the United States with white male participants), searching for any detail I might have missed. I read again that people of all ages were happier, healthier, and more motivated when given choices, even limited ones, such as which night to watch a movie or which puzzle to solve. If you believed you had choice, you benefited from it, regardless of whether you actually exercised it. And if a small amount of choice—or just the belief you had choice—was a good thing, as the experimental evidence showed, then *more* choice was probably wonderful. This extrapolation made enough logical sense that it was never tested; none of the key studies offered more than six options to the participants. The first of these studies had used six as a convenient, manageable number, and later studies followed suit, because if it ain't broke...

Taking my cues from the earlier research, I designed a new series of experiments. This time, first- and second-grade students were brought into a room, one at a time, and asked to draw with markers. Some of them were given two choices: Pick one of six different subjects (e.g., animals, plants, houses) and one of six different colors. The others were told what to draw and which color to use. Now I saw the result that had eluded me in my first study. The choosers wanted to spend more time on the activity, and they produced better drawings—as judged by independent observers—than the nonchoosers. By showing that choice conferred an advantage upon Anglo American children, I had laid the groundwork for the comparative study with Asian American children. I was relieved but also curious about the unexpected results of the toy study. Why didn't those children benefit from choice in the same way that the children in the drawing study did? Were they too young to have developed much skill at making decisions on their own? Or was I on to something much bigger—a side of choice that hadn't yet been explored? To find out, I needed to take a closer look at the number six and uncover its secret compact with choice.

Luckily for me, George Miller, currently professor of psychology at Princeton, had already done much of the legwork. In his 1956 paper "The Magical Number Seven, Plus or Minus Two: Some Limits on Our Capacity for Processing Information," Miller writes that he has been "persecuted by an integer." It seems to follow him everywhere, and he's convinced that "[t]he persistence with which [it] plagues [him] is far more than a random accident." Yes, there are "the seven wonders of the world, the seven seas, the seven deadly sins, the seven daughters of Atlas in the Pleiades, the seven ages of man, the seven levels of hell, the seven primary colors, the seven notes of the musical scale, and the seven days of the week," but what really concerns Miller is the relationship between this number and the amount of information each one of us can cope with at any given time.

For example, when people are shown shapes of various sizes for a short time and then asked to number them in order (1 for the smallest, 2 for the second smallest, and so on), their ratings are highly accurate up to seven unique sizes. But if they're shown a greater number, they become increasingly likely to make errors, rating two different objects the same or rating the same object differently on separate occasions. Studies have found a similar limit on our capacities for a wide range of perceptual judgments, such as determining—or distinguishing between—the positions of points, the direction and curvature of lines, the hue and brightness of objects, the frequency and volume of tones, the location and strength of vibrations, and the intensity of smells and tastes. For each of the senses, most people can handle only five to nine items before they begin to consistently make errors in perception. As the number of items grows, there might—on average—be less of a difference between any two of those items, but this alone does not account for our difficulties: People can easily distinguish between any of five high-frequency tones or any of five low-frequency tones, but they become confused when asked to distinguish between all ten. Since it should be a snap to tell the high-frequency tones from the low-frequency ones, the problem lies not in the particular qualities of the tones but in their total number.

We also falter if we try to keep track of multiple objects or facts simultaneously. When 1 to 200 dots are flashed on a blank screen for a fraction of a second, and people are asked how many they've seen, they're able to give correct answers for up to six dots or so. After that, they start estimating. And if we try to store more than seven simple units of information, like numbers or words, in short-term memory, pretty soon bits and pieces begin to crumble away.

When we choose, we rely on many of the aforementioned processing skills. We have to notice all the options, compare them to figure out the differences, remember our assessments, and then use these assessments to assign rankings. Due to our limitations, each step becomes more and more overwhelming as the options increase. So although children were able to deal with six options in the drawing study, the hundred options in the toy study must have left them baffled. The "failure" of the first study led me to Miller, and Miller's strange persecution led me to the realization that an important and interesting facet of choice had been heretofore overlooked. It was high time someone explored the effects of large versus small amounts of choice on our everyday decisions. That's how the jam study came about.

III. THE GOLDEN MEAN

In 1925, Prussian immigrant Gustave Draeger opened a delicatessen in San Francisco. Thanks to hard work and enterprise, the business grew quickly. After Prohibition ended, he set up a small chain of liquor stores, and by the time he retired, Draeger had established San Francisco's first supermarket. His sons took over and expanded further, closing the original store but adding several new ones. As a graduate student, I often visited the Menlo Park Draeger's, well known for its awe-inducing shopping experience. The carved oak columns in the atrium, the black marble countertops and dark ceramic floor tiles, the wine section lined with 20,000 bottles—these were just some of the elements that transformed a grocery store into a grand theater for acts of consumership (frequently documented by camera-wielding Japanese tourists).

You could buy the best pots and pans to whip up recipes from any of the 3,000 cookbooks also on sale, and you could pick up some pointers at the cooking school on the second floor. Or if you were too hungry to wait until you got home, the in-store restaurant served $10 gourmet burgers. (Bear in mind that this was 1995, when a McDonald's burger cost 85 cents.) Walking down and across the many aisles, you'd see 15 types of bottled water, 150 sorts of vinegar, nearly 250 mustards, 250 different cheeses, over 300 flavors of jam, and 500 kinds of produce. The olive oils were more modest in number—only 75 options—but not in price; some of them, aged for a hundred years or more, were displayed in a locked glass case and cost more than $1,000 a bottle. All of this variety, emphasized in the advertising, was a source of pride and distinction for Draeger's. To introduce people to it, tasting booths were often set up with 20 to 50 different samples of some product. The store was undoubtedly attracting attention for its unparalleled selection, but was that attention translating into sales?

The manager, a firm believer in the benefits of choice, was just as interested as I was in the answer to this question. I convinced him to let me conduct a study with a tasting booth of my own. (We kept it a secret from the employees in order to avoid interference; for example, attempts to influence the customers.) My research assistants and I pretended to represent Wilkin & Sons, supplier of jams to the Queen of England. We chose this brand because we wanted variety and high quality, and we picked jam because it's easy on the tongue, unlike mustard or vinegar, and most people enjoy it, or at least don't seem to mind it.

The booth was set up near the entrance, where it was most likely to catch the eyes of shoppers, and it was run by Irene and Stephanie, two affable Stanford undergrads. Every few hours we switched between offering a large assortment of jams (photo below) and a small one (next page). The large assortment contained 24 of the 28 flavors made by Wilkin & Sons. (We removed strawberry, raspberry, grape, and orange marmalade so that people wouldn't just choose what was most familiar to them.) The small assortment consisted of six jams plucked from the large assortment: kiwi, peach, black cherry, lemon curd, red currant, and three fruit marmalades. Another research assistant, Eugene, positioned himself behind some impressive cookware near the booth. From there, he observed people entering the store and recorded how many stopped to sample the jams. He found that 60 percent were drawn to the large assortment but only 40 percent to the small one. (Such was his dedication, he risked arrest to acquire this data; store employees thought he was trying to shoplift the $300 Le Creuset pans behind which he was lurking.)

Meanwhile, at the booth, Irene and Stephanie encouraged customers to taste as many jams as they liked. On average, they tasted two jams regardless of the size of the assortment. Then each person

was given a coupon valid for one week that knocked $1 off any sin-
gle Wilkin & Sons jam. Most of the people who decided to buy a
jar did so on the same day they received the coupon. Because we
weren't selling the jams at the booth, customers had to go to the jam
aisle, make a selection, and pay for it at the register. In that aisle, they
might have noticed an employee with a clipboard taking inventory.
In fact, he was another member of our team, Mike, and yes, he was
spying on the customers. He noted that people who had sampled the
large assortment were quite puzzled. They kept examining different
jars, and if they were with other people, they discussed the relative
merits of the flavors. This went on for up to ten minutes, at which
point many of them left empty-handed. By contrast, those who had
seen only six jams seemed to know exactly which one was right for
them. They strode down the aisle, grabbed a jar in a quick minute—
lemon curd was the favorite—and continued with the rest of their
shopping. When we tallied the coupons (the bar codes let us know
which assortment each buyer had seen), we discovered the following:

30 percent of the people who had seen the small assortment decided to buy jam, but only 3 percent bought a jar after seeing the large assortment. Even though the latter attracted more attention, more than six times as many people made a purchase when we displayed the smaller set of jams.

When I shared these findings with the manager, he ruminated on the implications. Everyone could agree that the Draeger's experience was mind-boggling, but what did this mean for how the store should be run? For many people, having one's mind boggled was the whole *point* of going to Draeger's; it wasn't just shopping, it was entertainment. But in order to thrive, the store required more than just visitors and spectators. A significant portion of the people walking through the doors had to be turned into paying customers, but the fantastic variety seemed to favor browsers over buyers. How could the manager ensure that the very choice that brought the masses in didn't end up pushing them out without so much as a jar of jam for a souvenir? One way to do this, he decided, was to use tasting booths not to showcase variety, which was already evident everywhere in the store, but to highlight a few options for a given product or brand. Thus, the tasting booth became an optional aid in the choosing process rather than a mere sideshow.

As the years have passed, the challenges posed by choice, both to customers and to managers, have only grown. In 1994, the year I had my first inkling that there might be such a thing as too much choice, over 500,000 different consumer goods were already available in the United States. By 2003, the number had increased to nearly 700,000, an upward trend that shows no signs of letting up. Technological advances frequently introduce new categories of products into our lives. Some of them—cell phones, computers, digital cameras— become indispensable, and soon enough the options proliferate. Just as importantly, not only are there more goods on the market, there are more ways to get at them. The typical supermarket, which carried 3,750 different items in 1949, now boasts some 45,000 items. Walmart and other "big-box" retailers offer smorgasbords of over 100,000 products to Americans in just about every part of the country. And if you don't find what you're looking for within a few blocks, you'll certainly find it with a few clicks. The Internet extends your reach well beyond local venues, providing access to the 100,000 DVDs on Netflix.com, 24 million books (and millions of other products) on Amazon.com, and 15 million singles on Match.com.

The expansion of choice has become an explosion of choice, and while there is something beautiful and immensely satisfying about having all of this variety at our fingertips, we also find ourselves beset by it. We think the profusion of possibilities must make it that much easier to find that perfect gift for a friend's birthday, only to find ourselves paralyzed in the face of row upon row of potential presents. Which one is really her? Which one is truly the "perfect" gift? This one is good, but how do I know that there isn't something better someplace else, and have I, by now, looked hard enough for it? We exhaust ourselves in the search, and something that should have been a joy—celebrating a loved one—becomes a chore. But can we really complain? This abundance, which many of us take for granted, is not available to everyone. When we question it, we might be accused of looking a gift horse in the mouth, or somebody might offer to play us the world's saddest song on the world's smallest violin. Moreover, whatever our reservations about choice, we have continued to demand more of it. These demands have not gone unheeded, and one can't deny that all this choice does come with certain benefits.

For one thing, if you know exactly what you're looking for, it's much easier to get your hands on that original version or out-of-print edition or rare recording. Of all the sales made by online retailers like Netflix, Amazon, and the Rhapsody music service, 20 to 25 percent are items too obscure to be stocked by most brick-and-mortar stores. Whereas the final book in the Harry Potter series sold 11 million copies on its release date alone, each obscure item might sell no more than a hundred copies a year. But a million books that sell only 100 copies apiece assemble into as strong a force as 100 books that sell a million copies apiece. This phenomenon was named "the Long Tail" and discussed in a book of the same name by *Wired* magazine editor in chief Chris Anderson. The term describes the following: a bar graph of retail items, ranked from highest to lowest number of sales, with the worst-selling items forming a long, thinning tail that stretches far to the right.

This phenomenon is good news for retailers. Those rare items that make up the tail significantly boost the total number of sales, and they're often more profitable because the makers settle for lower royalties. As consumers, we're all excited to find the unusual and little-known products we want that don't seem to be available anywhere else. That being said, most of us still do the bulk of our buying among the most popular products, known as "head" items because of their position at the opposite end of the graph. Even when we do buy something obscure from the tail, these purchases are made in addition to popular, mainstream items we're already getting.

People often refer to the Long Tail as evidence that we're not overwhelmed even when faced with millions of options. But we see this effect only for items that are clearly different from one another, like books or songs, not to mention that consumers can amass thousands of such choices over the course of their lives. When one alternative is not easily distinguishable from another, and when the goal is to find the single best item—who needs a library of flossing options?—more choice isn't as useful or as attractive anymore. It simply creates noise, hampering our ability to focus. We can spend inordinate amounts of time deciding between things with exactly the same purpose: If there's such a vast assortment laid out before us, doesn't it feel as if we should give it some consideration? One wonders, though, just how many types of shampoo or cat litter a supermarket can support before the options become redundant.

Some companies have tested this idea, putting the "more is less" mantra into practice. When Procter & Gamble winnowed its 26 varieties of Head & Shoulders antidandruff shampoo down to 15, eliminating the least popular, sales jumped by 10 percent. In a similar move, the Golden Cat Corporation got rid of its ten worst-selling small-bag cat litters, which led to a 12 percent bump in sales and also cut distribution costs in half. The end result was an 87 percent profit increase in the small-bag litter category.

Chances are that quite a few other companies could benefit from reducing the amount of choice they offer customers. Though this may seem risky, it is favored by a growing body of evidence. Since the publication of the jam study, I and other researchers have conducted more experiments on the effects of assortment size. These studies, many of which were designed to replicate real-world choosing contexts, have found fairly consistently that when people are given a moderate number of options (4 to 6) rather than a large number (20 to 30), they are more likely to make a choice, are more confident in their decisions, and are happier with what they choose.

However, we cannot simply declare that we should henceforth restrict ourselves to no more than the 7+/−2 options suggested by George Miller's findings. You probably wouldn't have to think very hard to come up with a counterexample in your own life where you clearly benefited from more choice. In practice, people can cope with larger assortments than research on our basic cognitive limitations might suggest—after all, visiting the cereal aisle doesn't usually give shoppers a nervous breakdown. To the contrary, the superfluity of the American supermarket can feel filling and *ful*filling. In Don DeLillo's novel *White Noise*, the narrator reflects on his and his wife's supermarket experience.

> It seemed to me that Babette and I, in the mass and variety of our purchases, in the sheer plenitude those bags suggested, the weight and size and number, the familiar package designs and vivid lettering, the giant sizes, the family bargain packs with

Day-Glo sale stickers, in the sense of replenishment we felt, the sense of well-being, the security and contentment these products brought to some snug home in our souls—it seemed we had achieved a fullness of being that is not known to people who need less, expect less, who plan their lives around lonely walks in the evening.

He is comparing his own brimming shopping cart to the "single lightweight bag" of his bachelor friend, but he also seems to be speaking more broadly of the comfort of "plenitude," of how it feels like a blessing. The pleasures of consumerism may be fleeting, and perhaps based primarily on distraction and delusion, but in certain moments, they feel so right. As readers of the book, we may find the narrator's experience shallow and distasteful, but he clearly enjoys and values it. And yet, at the same time, even for him the supermarket is a place "awash in noise. The toneless systems, the jangle and skid of carts, the loudspeaker and coffee-making machines, the cries of children. And over it all, or under it all, a dull and unlocatable roar, as of some form of swarming life just outside the range of human apprehension." Some of that white noise, I think, is our own mental hum as we try to cope with everything that is available to us.

The amount of choice we can handle depends partly on the characteristics of the options on offer. When we choose frequently and can choose multiple items, as mentioned above for the Long Tail, no single choice is very important, so it's not necessary to fully evaluate them. As a result, 100 mp3s, for example, won't be nearly as overwhelming as 100 mp3 players. It seems, then, that we can get by fairly well for certain kinds of choices. But for the many other decisions that we're asked to make in the face of nearly endless options, how can we save ourselves from being driven to distraction, even madness, by the noise?

Developing expertise in a given domain is one remedy for coping with a multitude of choice. Expertise enables people to understand options on a more granular level, as the sum of their characteristics rather than as distinct and indivisible items. For example, the same object could be understood as "a car," "a sports car," or "a Ferrari Enzo with a V12 engine" depending on a person's level of expertise. This additional level of detail lets people sidestep their cognitive limitations on information processing in several ways, resulting in significant benefits for the amount of choice they can handle. First of all, comparing items on multiple dimensions exponentially increases the number of unique items that we can distinguish between. In one of the studies described by Miller, people were able to distinguish seven audio tones only when they varied only in frequency, but when the tones also varied in features like intensity, duration, and spatial location, people were able to distinguish 150 different tones without error.

Moreover, people can develop preferences for attributes rather than entire items, allowing them to quickly eliminate the vast majority of the options and focus their attention on the remaining few. To continue with the car example, a person might decide that he's in the market for a German station wagon that's under $30,000, has folding rear seats for extra cargo storage space, and ideally has a sunroof, too. The more specific one's preferences, the easier the choosing task becomes. An expert who knows exactly what he wants can effortlessly choose from even an immense assortment.

Together, these effects of expertise can produce remarkable results. When we learn, through study and practice, to simplify, prioritize, and categorize elements and to recognize patterns, we are able to create order in seeming chaos. For example, chess masters throughout history have performed stunts like playing and winning 20 games at once, sometimes even while blindfolded. How do they do it? First, of course, it's the tens of thousands of hours of practice, which allows them quickly to extract the relevant information from the board: lines of attack, avenues of escape for the king, and so on. Given their informed intuition, they know how to separate the wheat from the chaff, zeroing in on which moves are and aren't worth considering in a given situation. So by considering only the most viable tactics, they can plan multiple moves in advance with relatively little mental effort. Some of these configurations even have names, like "the Sicilian Opening" or "Boden's Mate," and an expert can draw on the collective wisdom of previous grandmasters' responses to these situations. Essentially, they win by playing smarter, not harder.

That the chess masters' impressive recollection is based on cognitive efficiency and not (entirely) on superhuman feats of memorization was demonstrated by studies that tested masters against novices on their ability to remember and reconstruct a board of chess pieces after observing it for only five seconds. The masters easily outperformed the novices, in some cases placing 23 or 24 pieces out of 25 correctly on the first try, but only when the configurations they were shown could have occurred naturally during the course of a game. When the pieces were placed randomly, the experts did no better than the novices, getting only two or three correct on the first try.

As we can see from the nature of expertise, when talking about choice it's important to make a distinction between the number of options available in the environment and the number actually faced by the chooser. Both experts and novices would be overwhelmed if they tried to directly compare and choose from a hundred options, so they need to simplify their choosing processes somehow. The difference is that experts can simplify their own choices, which in turn allows them to take full advantage of the opportunities provided by more choice. Novices, on the other hand, are reliant on choice providers to reduce the number of choices they provide, in which case they'll benefit—but not as much as the experts. If providers keep offering lots of choice, they'll eventually be overwhelmed.

What can the consequences be when novices are faced with more choice than they can handle? Or when it doesn't seem possible to develop expertise? After all, chess is a closed and coherent system, with clear rules and one very clear goal: Capture the king. Even so, it takes a great deal of effort to master. What happens when we're uncertain of our goals or of the process by which we should achieve them? In these cases, it's much more difficult to become an expert. What then? Up to this point, we've considered effects of too much choice that seem fairly benign, like wasting several minutes in the jam aisle or a rather embarrassing defeat of a blindfolded chess master, but they're benign only because the choice contexts themselves aren't especially consequential. As we'll see next, the experience of "choice overload" is present in more important and more complex decisions as well, such that too many options can harm people's financial security and health.

IV. THE ROAR OF PLENTY

In 1978, a new class of retirement plans, known as the 401(k), became available to American workers. Whereas traditional pension plans were funded by the employer, these "defined contribution" plans encouraged the employee to invest a portion of his own salary in a range of mutual funds, the earnings of which would become available after retirement. They solved many of the problems of pensions, which were often underfunded and couldn't be transferred if the employee switched jobs, and they offered the employee more control over his financial future. Today, the 401(k) is the dominant form of retirement investing in the United States: Almost 90 percent of the people who have some form of retirement plan are covered solely or in part by defined contribution plans.

Like other long-term investments, 401(k)s reap the benefits of compound interest. Prices may fluctuate wildly in the short term, especially in the stock market, but booms and recessions balance out in the long term and produce dramatic cumulative returns. Even after the stock market lost about 40 percent of its value in 2008—the worst loss since the Great Depression—the 25-year annual average return of the S&P 500 stock index was still about 10 percent. At those rates, if a 25-year-old employee contributed just $1,000 to the S&P each year, by the time he retired at age 65, his total contribution of $40,000 would have become $500,000. These numbers don't account for inflation, but since inflation affects savings just as much as it affects investments, 401(k) plans still have more than a tenfold advantage over stockpiling money in a bank account.

In addition, your contributions to the plan and the returns earned are both tax-exempt until you retire and begin to withdraw money. For the average American, this is equivalent to contributing an additional 20 percent to the fund as compared to investing in the market with the same amount in after-tax dollars. Moreover, most employers match employee contributions with money of their own. The match percentage and cutoff vary by company, but dollar-for-dollar matching up to several thousand dollars is not uncommon. This means that our young employee's $1,000 yearly contribution effectively becomes $2,000, turning him into a millionaire by retirement. Given these incentives, if you know nothing about investing, randomly picking funds for your 401(k) is still a better financial move than not participating at all. So why doesn't everyone sign up?

In 2001, I received a call from Steve Utkus, the director of the Center for Retirement Research at the Vanguard Group, one of the largest mutual fund companies in the country. He told me that an analysis of the retirement investment decisions of more than 900,000 employees covered by Vanguard had revealed something disturbing: The percentage of eligible employees participating in 401(k)s had been in steady decline and was currently down to 70 percent. Concurrently, the average number of funds in each plan had been gradually rising. He had recently read my paper on the jam study and was wondering if these two trends might be related. Were the employees suffering from too much choice?

With my colleagues Gur Huberman and Wei Jiang, both professors of finance, I examined the investment records in order to answer his question. We found that an increase in the number of options *did* have a significant negative effect on participation. As the graph shows, participation rates quickly fell from a high of 75 percent for the smallest plans, which had four funds, to 70 percent for the plans with 12 or more funds. This rate held until the number of options exceeded 30, at which point it started to slide again, reaching a low just above 60 percent for plans with 59 funds.

It's unlikely nonparticipants muttered that there were too many choices and then actively opted out of their 401(k)s. Rather, quite a few of them probably intended to enroll as soon as they'd done some research and figured out which funds were best for them. After all, it's easy to sign up on the spot when you have only five choices, but when you have 50 it seems reasonable to mull things over for a while. Unfortunately, as you keep delaying the decision, and days turn into weeks, and weeks into months, you might forget your 401(k) altogether.

Okay, so some employees were overwhelmed by the number of options and didn't participate. Clearly, having a lot of choice did not work in their favor. But what about the people who *did* participate? They were perhaps more knowledgeable and confident about investing, and maybe they were able to take advantage of all those options.

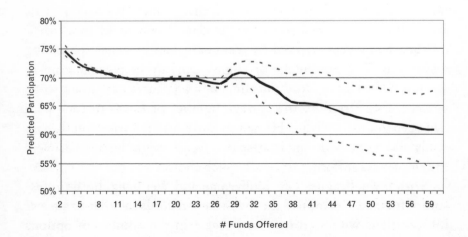

However, when Emir Kamenica, an economics professor at the University of Chicago, and I examined the funds that participants had chosen, we found that this was not actually the case: More choice had, in fact, led to worse decisions. Stocks composed the largest category of funds in these 401(k)s, and as the total number of funds in a plan went up, the plan became increasingly stock-heavy. Given these facts, we expected that even if people were picking funds out of a hat, they would be investing more in stocks as their options increased. But the exact opposite was true: For every set of ten additional funds in a plan, 2.87 percent more of the participants avoided stocks completely, and the rest allocated 3.28 percent less of their contributions to stocks, preferring bonds and money markets instead.

Why were we troubled by our findings? Well, 401(k)s are designed for long-term investing, and that's where stocks shine. Looking at 25-year averages, stocks reliably outperform bonds and especially money markets, which may not even keep up with inflation. Yet in our study, even the employees in their late teens and early twenties, who could afford more risk, gave short shrift to stocks as the number of funds in their plans increased. It seems that learning about all the funds was too complicated, so people tried to reduce the options by pushing the largest category—stocks—to one side. In doing so, they may have compromised their future financial well-being. They did make one exception: They bought more stock in the companies where they worked, perhaps due to familiarity or loyalty. But this is generally a risky move, because if your company goes bankrupt, you lose both your job and a good portion of your nest egg, as any former Enron or Lehman Brothers employee can tell you.

Let's consider the possibility that people don't take advantage of choice for retirement investing because even though it is an important decision, it's one that doesn't have any immediate impact on the chooser. Without a tangible payoff in the present, you may simply not be motivated enough to carefully and thoroughly assess your options. But perhaps you'd work hard to reap the benefits of more choice in a domain that's equally important and affects your current well-being? Unfortunately, even when it comes to health insurance, we don't seem to handle choice too well.

Remember President George W. Bush's push for Medicare reform? It resulted in the addition of a program called Part D to the federal health insurance program for senior citizens. Part D was created in December 2003 to compensate for the increasing role and cost of prescription drugs in modern health care by subsidizing them. Seniors choose from a variety of coverage plans offered by private companies, and the government reimburses the companies for the costs. In particular, Bush lauded the increase in choices provided by the program as a cure-all for Medicare's ills. "A modern Medicare system must offer more choices and better benefits to every senior— all seniors," he asserted. "The element of choice, of trusting people to make their own health care decisions, is essential." The logic behind offering a wide variety of plans held that "[t]he more options a senior has to choose from, the more likely it is that the benefit is going to be tailored to his or her needs."

For many participants, Medicare Part D has led to a 13 percent reduction in out-of-pocket costs, and according to one study, an increase in the purchase of prescribed medication. These benefits are considerable, but the program has fallen short in other ways. As with the 401(k)s, many of the people who stood to gain from enrolling failed to do so. The initial enrollment deadline for Medicare beneficiaries, March 15, 2006, came and went, and 5 million of the 43 million eligible seniors had not enrolled. All was not lost as they could join at a later date, but they would have to pay higher monthly premiums for the rest of their lives.

Still, you might say, nearly 90 percent of the seniors had enrolled. Isn't that success? In fact, almost two-thirds were enrolled automatically by their insurance providers, with many randomly assigned to plans that did not necessarily meet their prescription drug needs. Of the people who had to *choose*, 12.5 million enrolled and the remaining

5 million did not. Enrollment rates were dismal for those who most needed Part D—the low-income individuals eligible for full prescription drug coverage at no personal cost. If they enroll now, they'll incur late penalties they can ill afford; if they don't, many will have to forgo medication that they can't pay for on their own. Either way, they're in trouble.

Seniors were supposed to be able to benefit from choosing their own plans, and from the increased variety available to them, but the choice itself became a major obstacle to enrollment. There were dozens of plans, ranging from 47 in Alaska to 63 in Pennsylvania and West Virginia, and elderly people, many of them with poor eyesight and limited computer skills, had to go online to find the list of attributes for each plan. Then they had to figure out how the plans differed from one another, which seemed to require superhuman puzzle-solving abilities. Plans varied in multiple ways: drugs covered, generic drug policy, co-payments, monthly premiums, annual deductibles, and on and on. Different companies offered plans with the same characteristics but at different prices, and these characteristics could change from one week to the next.

Marie Grant, a retired nurse from Cleveland, recalls her frustration with Part D: "I never understood the whole mess.... I'm so mad. All these different plans." Martha Tonn, a retired teacher from Wisconsin, "felt it was too much, too overwhelming." They're in good company, because 86 percent of seniors and over 90 percent of doctors and pharmacists agree that Part D is much too complicated. A substantial number of seniors trying to enroll in Medicare couldn't even discern which option offered the same benefits they already had, let alone which plans would be an improvement or how they could tailor any of them to fit their own needs. To be sure, any attempt to compare 63 options will test our cognitive limits—but there's more to the story than just our ability to process the different choices. Bush and other architects of the program focused primarily on quantity, but unfortunately, in doing so, they paid far less attention to the quality of choices included, and whether these choices were meaningful in terms of improving people's lives.

When it comes to making challenging and consequential decisions like how to invest in a 401(k) plan or how best to take advantage of the Medicare Part D subsidy, we've seen that a focus on simply increasing the available choices can backfire and lead to decisions that harm rather than help. But wait, you might say. Certainly in such cases, we can take more care in both providing and evaluating choices. On the whole, though, aren't we still better off keeping our options open?

V. OPEN SESAME

"When one door closes, another opens." This phrase is often used to console people when something they desire slips through their fingers, and in the long run it tends to work. But it can be cold comfort in the moment of vanished possibility; as the second half of the saying goes, "We often look so long and so regretfully upon the closed door that we do not see the one which has opened for us." We focus so keenly on those alternatives that are lost to us because, more often than not, we prefer to keep all of our doors wide open. As we saw in chapter 1, even animals actively seek more options rather than fewer, despite the fact that there's no additional benefit to, say, having multiple buttons to press for food instead of just one. We can't help but feel cheated, knowing that there are opportunities that have been closed off to us, so why limit ourselves?

Consider the findings from a study conducted by Dan Ariely, author of the 2008 book *Predictably Irrational*. Participants played a computer game in which they saw three colored doors on the screen—red, blue, and green—and could open any one of them by clicking on it. Once a door was open, they could click inside to gain or lose a random amount of money. Alternatively, they could click on a new door to open it instead and close the previous one. The participants were given a total of 100 clicks, and their task was to use this limited number of clicks to earn as much money as possible. The amount at stake was higher for some doors than others, but in the end, all three doors averaged out to earning three cents per click. Mastering the game and earning the largest possible payout ultimately required realizing that no door was better than the others and simply clicking the open door as many times as possible.

But there was a twist. For some participants, the unopened doors would slowly shrink and then disappear completely after 12 clicks in the open door. If they initially chose the blue door, for example, and started clicking inside to earn money, the red and green doors would simultaneously begin to dwindle in size. Participants could spend a click to switch to one of the vanishing doors, say, the red one, and it would restore to its full size. But once they did so, the previously opened blue door and the unopened green one would proceed to shrink. This created a dilemma: If they kept the other doors from disappearing, they'd be losing clicks that could otherwise be used to earn money, while if they let the doors disappear they'd risk potentially losing out on a higher-paying door than their current one. It turned out that these participants used over twice as many clicks on switching doors compared to the people whose doors were in no danger of disappearing. Unfortunately for them, frantically clicking around just to keep all of the doors in sight significantly cut into their overall earnings.

The most surprising result occurred when the participants were told in advance that all three doors offered the exact same average payoff, making it obvious that there was no financial benefit to changing doors. Even then, the people in the disappearing door condition spent more clicks switching around, though doing so clearly cost them money in the end. Keeping doors open—literally in this study and metaphorically in our lives—seems to be very important to most of us. But as the study illustrates, we can't have our cake and eat it, too; if we want to maintain a wide range of alternatives, something has to give, whether it be our time, our sanity, or our bottom line. While the costs may have been relatively minor in the disappearing door game—a few cents here or there—the important thing to realize is that there are consequences to keeping our options open.

The ability to choose well seems to depend in no small part upon our knowing our own minds. And when we ask for more choice, we seem to be saying, "I know what I want, so however much choice you give me, I will be able to pick out the thing that I want." We firmly believe that no matter how many alternatives we're given, ultimately we'll know which door we prefer to walk through. Yet, paradoxically, asking for more choice is also an admission that we don't always know what we want, or that we are changeable enough that we cannot know what we want until we are in the moment of choosing. And it's clear that after a certain point, the amount of time and energy directed toward choosing counteracts the benefits of the choice. So why do we persist in our pursuit of greater choice?

In many cases we'd suffer from being limited to any single item, no matter how much we enjoy it. Imagine eating your favorite food, whatever it might be, for breakfast, lunch, and dinner 365 days a year. You would eventually become sick and tired of it, a process known as satiation. Satiation applies only to the specific option and ones similar to it, though, so other foods would remain just as tasty and would therefore eventually become preferred, at least for a while until you regained your appetite for your original favorite. Indeed, decades of research involving everything from pudding to pizza rolls have shown that people will eat more and enjoy it more when given a variety of foods and flavors to choose among than when given a single option.

Satiation and its associated need for variety affect many aspects of our lives, from our favorite movies to our friends and romantic partners. Depending on the onset speed and duration of the satiation, the choice set may need to be quite large. We all know people who never reread a book, watch a movie more than once, or order the same dish again at a restaurant, for example. For these reasons, even if a larger number of options makes each individual choice more difficult, it can still be beneficial overall by helping people find backup choices for when they're tired of their favorites. However, as Ariely's study shows, valuing the *condition* of having options over the *quality* of the options can sometimes lead to decisions that don't serve us well.

Our penchant for variety may be an evolutionary adaptation, perhaps to encourage us to eat balanced diets instead of filling up on the most convenient foods and developing scurvy or some other nutritional deficiency. One could say that we have a natural "buffet" mentality; we like having easy access to a little of this and a little of that, and a helping of that other one, please. Unfortunately, the larger the buffet, the more likely we are to overconsume in an attempt to take advantage of all that variety. A study by the USDA found that as the total amount and variety of food in the United States increased in recent decades, average food consumption rose at an even faster rate—not just for junk food, but across all categories, including fruits and vegetables. We see similar trends in other areas, such as the increasing amount of time we spend in front of TV and computer screens as channels and websites multiply. According to Mike Shaw, president of sales and marketing at ABC, the average American now watches four and a half hours of TV per day. A Stanford study found that the average Internet user spends two hours a day online while at home, and this time spent online cuts the most into time that would otherwise be spent with family.

The "muchness" that so attracts us is often not to our advantage. In some cases, we might give up the best option(s) for a wider range of inferior options, as we saw in the open doors study. Or we might give short shrift to our health and loved ones as we revel in the multitude of options. Not only that, but even when we have no trouble identifying the best choices from a very large set, and even when we are able to exert control over our buffet-loving minds and bodies, we still have to contend with another problem. The more choice you have, the greater the number of appealing options, no matter how discriminating your tastes. At some point, you simply won't have enough space or money or time to enjoy all those options. So you'll have to make some sacrifices, and each of these carries a psychological cost. Your enjoyment of the chosen options will be diminished by your regret over what you had to give up. In fact, the sum total of the regret over all the "lost" options may end up being greater than your joy over your chosen options, leaving you less satisfied than you would have been if you had had less choice to begin with.

Have you ever experienced the equivalent of TiVo guilt? Originally you believed that your DVR—a wonderful little invention that allows you to automatically record, store, and organize television programs—would free you to work late or make dinner plans without feeling that slight twinge of regret in missing your favorite shows. You were pleasantly surprised that it even suggested new programs you might like based on your current interests, and would record those for you, too. But then you realized that it was all too easy to ask TiVo to record many more things than you could watch, or at least, enjoyably watch. And that pang of guilt returned: Do you delete the recorded shows that are piling up unseen? Or do you suffer through a marathon TV-watching session that's motivated more by duty than interest?

Another way in which greater choice can lead to greater regret is the very fact that it *does* increase the potential benefits of choosing well, even as it makes the process of choosing more difficult. When the options are few, we can be happy with what we choose since we are confident that it is the best possible choice for us. When the options are practically infinite, though, we believe that the perfect choice for us must be out there somewhere and that it's our responsibility to find it. Choosing can then become a lose-lose situation: If we make a choice quickly without fully exploring the available options, we'll regret potentially missing out on something better; if we do exhaustively consider all the options, we'll expend more effort (which won't necessarily increase the quality of our final choice), and if we discover other good options, we may regret that we can't choose them all. This dilemma can occur for choices from the mundane, like picking a restaurant, to the highly significant, like whom to marry or what career to pursue.

We're aware of the positive effects of choice but not the negative ones, so we attribute any harm caused by too much choice to some other cause, perhaps even to too little choice. After all, at first glance it seems that the best solution to not being able to find the perfect option is to add more options—but an excess of possibilities can keep us from being happy with our choices. As a result, we may see choice as a solution to problems of which it is actually the cause.

If the difficulty of choosing isn't resolved by adding more options, then perhaps the solution is just the opposite: to come up with a more effective algorithm for eliminating choices. Not quite. Choosing is not simply a mathematical problem. Perhaps the main issue with increasing choice is that it betrays our expectations. These expectations—that it will allow us to "realize" ourselves, to be and have all that we ought to be and have—are turned back on to us. If I have so much available to me, I should be able to make the best of it; I can no longer use the excuse that I didn't have a choice. When we ask for more choice, we also become subject to more choice. In this way, as choice grows, it acquires a life and character of its own. It makes demands on us to be better, to do better. These demands extend beyond the computational and rational to the emotional and, one might argue, even the existential.

Alexis de Tocqueville, the French thinker who keenly chronicled early American society, described the consequences of ever-increasing choice more than 170 years ago:

In America I have seen the freest and best educated of men in circumstances the happiest to be found in the world; yet it seemed to me that a cloud habitually hung on their brow, and they seemed serious and almost sad even in their pleasures.... They clutch everything but hold nothing fast, and so lose grip as they hurry after some new delight.

We can draw a long and somewhat crooked line from de Tocqueville to *The Simpsons*, a trenchant satire of American life and a cultural touchstone. In the season 5 episode "Homer and Apu," Marge takes Apu shopping at a new supermarket: Monstromart ("Where Shopping Is a Baffling Ordeal"). From the towering shelves lined with gigantic containers, Marge selects a large brown box. "That's a good price for twelve pounds of nutmeg," she says with pleasure.

Apu's eyes widen. "Oh, great selection and rock-bottom prices," he says. "But where is the love?"

Just then a voice comes over the loudspeaker, as if in response to Apu: "Attention, Monstromart shoppers. Just a reminder that we love each and every one of you."

"Awww," exclaim most of the shoppers, their eyes turned up to the loudspeaker. Apu, however, is not impressed. Only he sees what we see: a strange landscape in which people are dwarfed by products, where a human-size bottle of pancake syrup ghoulishly blocks the way, and where—when massive jugs of cranberry juice topple over and crack—their contents rush down the aisle like a river of blood. It's so ridiculous, it's funny. But a real Monstromart—a mutated and steroid-pumped version of the supermarkets of *White Noise*—would most likely be a "serious and almost sad" place to seek our pleasures.

VI. THE WELL-ORGANIZED CHOICE

But take heart! The proliferation of "new delights" need not be dire news for us. I believe that we *can* take advantage of the promises of choice, that we can benefit from choice instead of succumbing to its demands, if we commit ourselves to some reeducation and training. In learning how to negotiate both the computational and the non-computational demands of choice, it seems to me that there are two important first steps. To begin with, we have to change our attitudes toward choice, recognizing that it is not an unconditional good. We must respect the constraints on our cognitive abilities and resources that prevent us from fully exploring complex choices, and stop blaming ourselves for not finding the very best option every time. In addition, when possible, we must increase our expertise in order to counteract the limits on our cognitive abilities and resources, enabling us to obtain the most benefit from our choices with the least effort.

Developing expertise carries costs of its own, though. We can become experts in some areas, like speaking a language or knowing our favorite foods, simply by living our lives, but in many other domains expertise requires considerable training and effort. What's more, expertise is domain specific, as seen by the chessboard memorization studies. The expertise that we work hard to acquire in one domain will carry over only imperfectly to related ones, and not at all to unrelated ones. In the end, as much as we may want to become experts on everything in our lives, there simply isn't enough time to do so. Even in areas where we could, it won't necessarily be worth the effort. It's clear that we should concentrate our own expertise on those domains of choice that are most common and/or important to our lives, and those we actively enjoy learning about and choosing from.

But what can we do when we want to choose well in an area in which we have no expertise? The obvious answer is to take advantage of the expertise of others, although this is often easier said than done when it comes down to the details. If you're a choice provider, it's not always clear how to balance giving effective assistance to inexperienced choosers without chasing experienced ones away. If you're a chooser, the difficulty is in knowing what features of a set of options will be effective at improving your choices and which ones will only make you more confused.

People have a tendency to assume that since they know their own preferences best, they should be the ones to ultimately make their choices. This is true in cases where preferences may vary extensively from person to person, as at a restaurant or video store, but in many cases we all have generally the same preferences. When it comes to investing for retirement, for example, everyone has the same goal of getting the best return, but the difficulty is in knowing how to get there. In these cases it's often simplest to rely on an expert's recommendation, as long as choosers can be confident that the experts have their best interests in mind.

To return to the dilemma of investing for retirement, let's look at what happened when Sweden privatized its social security program in 2000, essentially switching the entire country from pensions to defined contribution plans. Swedish workers had a portion of their income automatically withheld by the government and were able to choose to invest it in one or more of over 450 different mutual funds, or else it would be placed in a default fund designed by the government to meet the average investor's needs. The government actively discouraged people from going with the default through a massive advertising campaign encouraging them to create their own portfolios instead, and it proved effective: Two-thirds of people actively chose their own funds.

However, an analysis of the program by economists Henrik Cronqvist and Richard Thaler found that this encouragement was misguided, as the people who chose for themselves exhibited a number of decision-making errors that ran counter to their interests. They had an unbalanced investment strategy, putting nearly all of their money in stocks and ignoring bonds and other assets. Further, their stock portfolios heavily favored Swedish stocks, stock in the companies where they worked, and whatever stocks were hot at the time. In general, they chose the options that were familiar to them from the news or their daily lives rather than taking the time to build diversified portfolios that were tailored to their individual needs. As a result, their choices consistently underperformed the default fund, by 10 percent after three years and 15 percent after seven.

In retrospect it's clear that the government should have steered inexperienced investors toward the default fund, not away from it. This is an area where choosers would have benefited most from closely following the recommendations of experts. On the other hand, compared to the plans I examined as part of the Vanguard study, none of which had a default option, the Swedish government did the right thing by having a default fund in the first place, and by designing it intelligently rather than setting it to something simple but less beneficial, like a money market fund. Congress recently passed legislation that allows employers in the United States to do something similar, automatically enrolling their employees in a 401(k) plan unless they opt out. Automatic enrollment is highly effective at increasing participation rates, to more than 90 percent according to one recent study, since it reaches those people who intend to participate but would otherwise procrastinate or who simply aren't aware of the plans.

When individual goals and preferences vary, turning choice into a collaborative activity, one in which you rely on and interact with many other people, is yet another way to cope with choice. Take the Best Cellars chain of wine stores, a great example of a retailer working with choosers to make the decision process as easy as possible. In contrast to the typical wine store, with racks and shelves filled with thousands of bottles organized by the region of origin or the type of grapes used, Best Cellars offers just 100 different wines in its stores, with each wine preselected for quality and reasonable price. What's more, the wines are divided into eight categories with self-explanatory names like "fizzy," "juicy," and "sweet." More detailed information about each wine is clearly displayed above the bottles, and the staff is willing to make recommendations in nontechnical terms. It's not a store designed to cater to connoisseurs or those shopping for a special occasion, but for the average, everyday consumer, it's hard to beat.

We can also take advantage of the wisdom of crowds, as well as the wisdom of experts, to make better choices. The Zagat restaurant guide is one example, scoring restaurants based on the opinions of multiple amateur restaurant-goers rather than of individual critics. The online retailers who've taken advantage of the Long Tail also owe much of their success to customer reviews and recommendations, and consumers can increase these benefits even further by focusing on the pockets in the crowd that are similar to them. Amazon.com tells you that "customers who bought this item also bought" dozens of other products that might be of interest to you, and Netflix.com offers intelligent movie recommendations by using your own previous ratings of movies to find other members with similar tastes, then suggesting movies that they rated highly but you haven't yet seen. (Netflix makes finding new movies so simple that it's easy to go wild, recklessly adding movies to your queue until you wind up with more than you could hope to watch in the next ten years. If you're not careful, you might be the next victim of "Netflix guilt.") An additional benefit of these recommendation systems is that while they impose some order on a massive number of options, they don't remove any options, so experts who want something that isn't on the computer's list of suggestions can still find it on their own.

Categorizing options can also ease the burden of choosing. Reduce your choice set into a manageable number of categories, and within any category include a manageable number of alternatives. In doing so, it turns out that you might not even feel as though you're limiting yourself. To see this in action, I, along with two research assistants, Cassie Mogilner and Tamar Rudnick, staked out the magazine aisle in several Wegman's supermarkets and found that shoppers actually felt that they had more choices if there were fewer options overall but more categories. Arranging a smaller selection of magazines under a wide range of subheadings, like "Health & Fitness" or "Home & Garden," created a structure that made choosing more efficient and more enjoyable. This ends up being a win-win because customers are happier with fewer options and magazine publishers save money on the cost of producing the extra options.

Categories can be as simple as a department store dividing its goods into, well, departments, or as in-depth as sorting a single type of product into different categories based on attributes that would otherwise be difficult for most consumers to recognize, like the flavor categories at Best Cellars. The crowd-driven form of categorization is perhaps best demonstrated by the use of keywords and "tags" on media-sharing Internet sites like YouTube and Flickr, which are added by users to describe their massive amounts of content. Tagging a picture of a dog with "dog" is easy to do, but it transforms the task of finding dog-related pictures from the nigh-impossible one of sorting through every image on the site to merely typing a word into a search box. Whatever form it takes, categorization allows novices to reproduce experts' abilities to ignore the irrelevant options and focus their attention on the most promising ones.

Recommendations and categorization are both useful features to seek out when trying to make a difficult decision, because they can benefit our choices in two ways. They make the decision in question easier by allowing us to borrow the knowledge of experts or crowds, and they also help us to develop our own expertise more rapidly than we would if we chose without assistance. Learning what others consider good and relevant provides us with a general overview of a given field, catalyzing our understanding of it and the development of our preferences within it. Becoming an expert in every domain of choice is impossible, but we can become experts in the *process* of choosing, learning how to use the expertise of others to improve our choices and our knowledge of choice.

Just as we can learn from others, we can also learn from ourselves. When making decisions based on multiple attributes, the way we approach the decision can significantly impact how well we can handle large numbers of options. Along with my colleague Jonathan Levav, Mark Heitmann of Christian Albrecht University in Kiel, Germany, and Andreas Herrmann of the University of St. Gallen in Switzerland, I conducted an experiment with a major German car manufacturer that allowed car buyers to build their new cars to order, choosing everything from the engine to the rearview mirror from a list of options.

We compared two groups of people who were purchasing the same model of car online. One group first made their choices for the dimensions with the most options: interior and exterior color, which had 56 and 26 different options, respectively. From there they chose in descending order by number of options, ending with interior decor style and gearshift style, which had only four options apiece. The second group encountered the same choices in the opposite order, starting with the ones with the fewest options and ending with the most. Although both groups ended up eventually seeing 144 total options across eight categories, the people who started high and ended low had a significantly harder time choosing. They started off carefully considering each option, but quickly became tired and went with the default option. In the end, they wound up less satisfied with their final cars.

This study shows that people can learn to choose from more options, but they're less likely to drown if they start off in the shallows and then slowly move toward the deep, all the while building their skills and their nerve. A large choice pool of 56 paint colors isn't as overwhelming when it occurs near the end of the choosing process, by which point we have a much clearer vision of the whole car. If we generally know what kind of car we want to buy—sporty, sophisticated, family-friendly—this provides additional structure that simplifies the choosing task by eliminating some options and highlighting others. We should, therefore, focus first on the dimensions that are easiest to choose from, whether because they offer fewer options or because we already know what we want, and let these choices guide us through the more difficult dimensions.

Henri Poincaré, a celebrated French mathematician and philosopher of science, said, "Invention consists in avoiding the constructing of useless combinations and in constructing the useful combinations which are in infinite minority. To invent is to discern, to choose." I'd like to invert the second sentence and propose a corollary: To choose is to invent. What I mean by this is that choosing is a creative process, one through which we construct our environment, our lives, our selves. If we ask for more and more material for the construction, i.e., more and more choice, we're likely to end up with a lot of combinations that don't do much for us or are far more complex than they need to be.

We've worked very hard for choice, and with good reason. But we've become so accustomed to producing it and demanding it and producing even more of it, that we sometimes forget to assess when and why it is useful. Managing our expectations is perhaps the most difficult challenge of choice, but one way to do so is to look to those who have shown how constraints create their own beauty and freedom. Inventors and artists and musicians have long known the value of putting constraints on choice. They work within forms and strictures and rules, many of which they break only to establish new boundaries, sometimes even tighter ones. There is more than one story to tell about choice, and there should be more than one way to read and write choice in our culture. In her essay "The Rejection of Closure," poet Lyn Hejinian considers "[t]he relationship of form … to the materials of the [written] work":

Can form make the primary chaos (the raw material, the unorganized impulse and information, the uncertainty, incompleteness, vastness) articulate without depriving it of its capacious vitality, its generative power? Can form go even further than that and actually generate that potency, opening uncertainty to curiosity, incompleteness to speculation, and turning vastness into plenitude? In my opinion, the answer is yes; that is, in fact, the function of form in art. Form is not a fixture but an activity.

If form can accomplish all this in art, might it not do something similar for the way we make choices in life? It is worth our while, I believe, to experiment with a structured approach to choosing, one that encourages us to pay close attention to the choosing process and to connect the power of choice not to what it is but to how we practice it. If choice is indeed something we *make*, as we *make* art and *make* music, then surely we can look to those creative disciplines for guidance. The key, however, is to recognize—to return to the words of de Tocqueville—that in order to "hold fast" to something, one must allow oneself to *be held to* something. That commitment may be one of the hardest things to practice in a world of so much choice.

In a conversation with the master jazz musician and Pulitzer Prize–winning composer Wynton Marsalis, he told me, "You need to have some restrictions in jazz. Anyone can improvise with no restrictions, but that's not jazz. Jazz always has some restrictions. Otherwise it might sound like noise." The ability to improvise, he said, comes from fundamental knowledge, and this knowledge "limits the choices you can make and will make. Knowledge is always important where there's a choice." The resulting action is based on informed intuition, or as he calls it, "superthought." In jazz, superthought goes beyond determining the "right" answer: It allows one to see new possibilities where others see only more of the same, and to construct the rare "useful combination." Perhaps we can superthink our way through choice by learning the fundamentals of its composition, and then using this knowledge to create music where there might otherwise be only noise. Insisting on more when one already has a great deal is usually considered a sign of greed. In the case of choice, it is also a sign of the failure of the imagination, which we must avoid or overcome if we wish to solve our multiple choice problem.

CHAPTER SEVEN

And Then There Were None

I. A PIECE OF CAKE

The British comedian Eddie Izzard is well known for his "Cake or Death" routine, in which he imagines the Spanish Inquisition as overseen by the Church of England. Where the original tribunal might have offered a choice between being tortured or sending others to be tortured, the Church of England simply asks, "Cake or death?" Each "victim," one after the other, responds, "Uh, cake please," and the Church of England obliges: "Very well, give him cake!" This is funny for many reasons, not least because we know choosing is never supposed to be this easy, even when there are only two options. On the one hand, we have the spongy goodness of cake, and on the other, the grim finality of death. We have known difficult choices, and this, sir, is no difficult choice: We'll have the cake every time. When the hapless inquisitors run out of cake—"We only had three bits, and we didn't expect such a rush!"—they end up allowing the would-be victims to make their own requests for other alternatives to death, such as chicken. A clear right answer *and* the opportunity to change the options? This is the chooser's dream.

In this dream, all the usual clichés and dramatic tropes about life-and-death choices are called to mind and then dismissed. There is no test of will and character, no scarred and rotten-to-the-core villain. There is nothing to stand for, nothing to oppose. The hero's journey, which usually requires overcoming great odds and obstacles, suddenly becomes…a piece of cake. Izzard, biting and coy at the same time, gives us a dream that is so delicious because it reverses all our worst expectations while playfully swiping at the religion and culture that established those expectations in the first place.

As tempting as this is, every dream must come to an end. Making decisions in waking life is almost always more complex and anxiety inducing. It's highly unlikely that you'll ever face an English Inquisition and its absurd threat of baked goods, but one day you may very well find yourself having to choose between cake and cake. Chocolate fudge or red velvet? Carrot or cheese? The stakes may be only *social* victory or death—those potluck partygoers take their cake very seriously—but this decision is still more difficult to make than the one between cake and death. Now imagine that the Spanish Inquisitors have taken over again, since their English counterparts *just don't get it*, and they've reimplemented their policy that victims choose between torture for themselves and torture for others. This cake or that cake required some thought, but this torture or that torture? No one is laughing anymore.

Choosing between two flavors of cake and between two victims of torture may seem like completely different dilemmas because the possible outcomes—cake and death—are too far apart. But the psychological *process* of choosing in these two situations may be more similar than we think, and it is certainly more reflective of choice as we experience it in real life. All humor aside, we're often called upon to make decisions for which there are no clear "right" or "best" choices. What are we to do when we're not able to act, or all the answers are wrong, or the question itself is too terrible to contemplate?

II. THE JULIE DILEMMA

Julie is your premature baby, born after only 27 weeks of gestation and weighing less than two pounds. She's critically ill from having suffered a brain hemorrhage. For these reasons, she is being treated in the neonatal intensive care unit (NICU) of a renowned academic hospital, her life sustained by a machine that helps her breathe. After three weeks of this treatment, Julie's overall health has not improved. The doctors explain to you that her critical condition implies severe neurological impairments that would confine her to bed, unable to speak, walk, or interact with others. After much deliberation, they have decided that it's in Julie's best interest that they withdraw treatment—by turning off the ventilation machine—and let her die.

Take a little time to reflect on what has just happened and then answer the following questions:

1) Please rate the extent to which you feel each of these emotions, with 1 indicating *not at all* and 7 indicating *extremely*.

    a) Overwhelmed   1   2   3   4   5   6   7

    b) Upset   1   2   3   4   5   6   7

2) How confident are you that the best decision was made?

    1   2   3   4   5   6   7

3) To what degree would you have preferred to make this decision yourself?

    1   2   3   4   5   6   7

In the above scenario, the doctors didn't provide you with much information, and they made the final decision. This approach may seem surprising, even unfair, but it's how things were done for much of Western medical history. The Greek physician Hippocrates revolutionized the practice of medicine in the fifth century B.C.E. by positing that illness was caused by environmental factors, not by divine punishment, which meant it could be treated with physical remedies instead of spiritual ones. For this and other contributions, such as developing the ethical code known as the Hippocratic Oath, he came to be considered the Father of Medicine. While doctors no longer swear allegiance to the original oath, it has served as a model for similar pledges still in use today. Hippocrates deserves the title of "father" not only because of his guiding influence but because he saw the relationship between doctor and patient as similar to the one between parent and child. For him, doctors possessed knowledge, experience, and sound judgment, while patients were ignorant of their own best interests and reduced to mental passivity by illness. It seemed only right, therefore, that all medical decisions should rest in the capable hands of these wise and conscientious doctors. The prevailing logic held that allowing patients to participate in medical decisions would degrade the quality of treatment and be tantamount to negligence. Had you been a doctor then, you'd likely have hidden the diagnosis from the patient himself, heeding Hippocrates' advice of "concealing most things from the patient while you are attending him," "revealing nothing of the patient's future or present condition," and focusing instead on comforting and distracting him. Had you been Julie's parent, you might not even have been told about her impairments or the withdrawal of treatment, only that she had died.

Hippocrates advocated a paternalistic paradigm, and the Roman Empire—and later the European and Arab civilizations of the medieval period—had such high regard for his works that they made little attempt to challenge his outlook. The doctor's position as the unquestioned authority remained the norm, and it was further

strengthened by the religious fervor of medieval times. The belief
that a doctor's authority was bestowed by God rendered disobedience not just foolish and disrespectful but almost blasphemous. Even
the rational revolution of the eighteenth century, the Enlightenment,
failed to propose alternative models. After all, the people thought, if
a patient were as knowledgeable as his doctor, he would inevitably
agree with whatever treatment the doctor had already prescribed.
Wasn't it simply sensible and efficient, then, to proceed without
informing the patient, let alone consulting him? In 1847, the American Medical Association certainly thought so, as is shown by its first
set of ethical guidelines, which bore a striking resemblance to the
teachings of Hippocrates: Doctors were instructed to unite "conde-
scension with authority, [so] as to inspire the minds of their patients
with gratitude, respect, and confidence," while granting "reasonable indulgence" to the "mental imbecility and caprices of the sick."
Physicians were urged to "not be forward to make gloomy prognostications," only giving "notice of danger" to patients "if absolutely
necessary." In fact, doctors were advised to avoid this duty if at all
possible, leaving the delivery of bad news to "another person of sufficient judgment and delicacy."

Before, when the doctors made the decision for Julie and gave
you little information, they were following the paternalistic model.
Let's return to Julie, but this time, imagine a slightly different
scenario.

Julie is your premature baby, born after only 27 weeks of gestation
and weighing less than two pounds. She's critically ill from having
suffered a brain hemorrhage. For these reasons, she is being treated
in the neonatal intensive care unit of a renowned academic hospital,
her life sustained by a machine that helps her breathe. After three
weeks of this treatment, Julie's overall health has not improved.

The doctors inform you of the two possible courses of action:
Continue the treatment, or withdraw the treatment by turning off
the ventilation machine. They also explain the consequences of each

action. If the treatment is withdrawn, Julie will die. If the treatment is continued, there's about a 40 percent chance that Julie will die and about a 60 percent chance that she will survive with severe neurological impairments that would confine her to bed, unable to speak, walk, or interact with others. Because of Julie's critical condition, the doctors have decided it's in her best interest that they withdraw treatment and let her die.

Now take a little time to reflect on what has just happened and then answer the following questions:

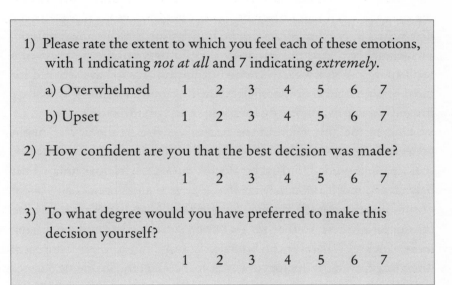

1) Please rate the extent to which you feel each of these emotions, with 1 indicating *not at all* and 7 indicating *extremely*.

   a) Overwhelmed   1   2   3   4   5   6   7

   b) Upset   1   2   3   4   5   6   7

2) How confident are you that the best decision was made?

                       1   2   3   4   5   6   7

3) To what degree would you have preferred to make this decision yourself?

                       1   2   3   4   5   6   7

Were your responses any different this time around? The doctors still made the decision and Julie still died. However, the fact that they went over the possible courses of action and their respective consequences with you probably made it easier to accept their decision, both increasing your confidence that it was the right one and reducing the emotional stress associated with it. While this approach might seem natural today, it was not until the twentieth century that the medical profession began to revise its previous position and recognize that patients and family members could benefit from being kept in the loop about their health. Why did it take so long, and what prompted this radical change in perspective?

Hippocrates' disciples subscribed not only to his views on the doctor-patient relationship but also to his belief that disease resulted from an imbalance of the four bodily "humors" (blood, phlegm, yellow bile, and black bile). Patients were subjected to therapies such as bloodletting, induced vomiting, and even more disagreeable purges in an attempt to restore the ever-elusive balance. Having escaped leech and knife, the patient might have been placed on a diet suited to his temperament, be it sanguine, phlegmatic, choleric, or melancholic. Although a doctor could unwittingly have cured a food allergy in this way, the remedy was unlikely to have worked for most other maladies. Nonetheless, the four humors theory of disease proved tenacious, surviving for more than two millennia.

During the long reign of the humors, a visit to the doctor might often have done more harm than good, which meant, paradoxically, that a patient needed to trust his doctor *more* than he does today. That naive trust, much as we may scoff at it now, is an essential component of the "placebo effect": Patients *believe* they'll get better by following the doctor's orders, so they *do* get better, suffering less and recovering more quickly. Whatever the limitations and flaws of their theoretical knowledge, even the doctors of yesteryear could rely on practical experience to improve their decisions and hone their intuition. Without experience of their own and with little understanding of the arcane discipline of medicine, what else could patients do in the face of rampant and frequently fatal disease except put their faith in the doctors?

It was not until the mid-nineteenth century that a paradigm shift began to take place. As part of a broader movement that emphasized scientific discovery and testing, the practice of informed consent gradually replaced the practice of medical paternalism. Treatments were not as mysterious and haphazard as they had been. Their mechanics and risks were better understood, and consequently, their application was more systematic and effective. The changes were not easy to accept, however, and doctors were still reluctant to change their attitudes toward patients. They often continued to act as sole decision makers, withholding information and treating patients without their knowledge.

In one shocking case from 1905, a Dr. Pratt told a female patient he could cure her epilepsy by performing a minor unspecified surgery, but while she was under anesthesia, he removed her uterus and ovaries to stabilize her hormone levels and thereby reduce her seizures. He was sued for this gross violation of trust and found liable, but his disregard for the patient's opinions and for her rights over her own body was not unusual for his time. Even in the post–World War II era, doctors continued to take liberties in a manner considered unconscionable today. In his book *The Silent World of Doctor and Patient*, Jay Katz recounts his conversation with a respected French doctor who, when consulted by a rural man dying of kidney failure, told him there was nothing to be done. He intentionally didn't inform the man that his life could be saved by dialysis; in order to receive this treatment, the man would have had to move to the city, but "[p]easants do not adjust well to a permanent move to a large city," the doctor explained, so that was that.

Eventually, the lessons of the past and growing confidence in the scientific method combined with increasingly accessible information to undermine the rationale behind medical paternalism. If treatments and procedures were logical and scientifically valid, why couldn't and shouldn't they be explained to patients? Transparency also led to greater accountability, which was difficult to argue against. In the 1950s and 1960s, a series of court cases formalized these attitudes by establishing the doctrine of "informed consent," meaning that doctors were obligated (1) to inform patients of the different treatment options and of the risks and benefits of each one, and (2) to obtain patient permission before treatment.

Medical schools trained their students in the importance of informed consent, and the threat of malpractice suits compelled doctors to respect the new law, with sweeping results. Only 10 percent of doctors surveyed in 1961 reported that they would tell a patient he had been diagnosed with cancer, but by 1971—in a complete reversal of numbers—over 90 percent were prepared to tell the patient. And as the millennia-long tradition of keeping patients in the dark about their own health met its demise, another significant change was on the horizon as well, one that we can observe in the third and final Julie scenario.

Once again, Julie is your premature baby, born after only 27 weeks of gestation and weighing less than two pounds. She's critically ill from having suffered a brain hemorrhage. For these reasons, she is being treated in the neonatal intensive care unit of a renowned academic hospital, her life sustained by a machine that helps her breathe. After three weeks of this treatment, Julie's overall health has not improved.

The doctors offer *you* a choice: Continue the treatment, or withdraw the treatment by turning off the ventilation machine. The doctors also explain the consequences of each decision. If the treatment is withdrawn, Julie will die. If the treatment is continued, there's about a 40 percent chance that Julie will die and about a 60 percent chance that she will survive, but with severe neurological impairments that would confine her to bed, unable to speak, walk, or interact with others.

What do you do?

Once more, take a little time to make your decision, reflect on what has just happened, and then answer the questions that appear on the following page:

1) Which option did you choose for Julie?

2) Please rate the extent to which you feel each of these emotions, with 1 indicating *not at all* and 7 indicating *extremely*.

   a) Overwhelmed   1   2   3   4   5   6   7

   b) Upset   1   2   3   4   5   6   7

3) How confident are you that the best decision was made?

                    1   2   3   4   5   6   7

4) To what degree would you have preferred to have the doctors make this decision?

                    1   2   3   4   5   6   7

This time, the choice lay in your hands. Not only did the doctors provide you with the necessary information, they allowed you to act. You didn't have to sift through a large number of options, and you made the final decision. How do your responses compare to the ones you gave twice before? It's an important question, because this Julie scenario is the one that real people in similar situations increasingly face.

The '60s and '70s saw not only the decline of paternalism in medicine but also a rise in the value placed on independence and personal choice in American culture as a whole. The shift toward a more autonomous approach to medical decision making was supported by several famous studies that demonstrated the benefits of choice in medical contexts. For example, as we saw in chapter 1, elderly patients in a nursing home who were given even trivial choices—whether and where to place a plant in their room, what night to watch a movie—were not only happier but healthier and less likely to die than patients for whom the staff made such decisions, as was the norm at that time. If a trivial choice could bolster happiness and health, more serious choices were assumed to have even more powerful benefits. It was a small jump from requiring patient consent for a proposed treatment to giving patients all the options and encouraging them to choose for themselves.

We no longer say, "Doctor knows best," and our own judgment takes center stage when an important medical decision must be made. Perhaps this is as it should be. In the case of Dr. Pratt, the issue wasn't whether hysterectomy was a legitimate treatment for epilepsy but rather who should determine whether it was the right treatment for that particular patient. Pratt's error, and by extension that of the paternalistic paradigm as a whole, was in failing to recognize that the right treatment wasn't just a matter of symptoms and prognoses; it was also a matter of the patient's life circumstances and preferences, such as whether she wanted to have children in the future. While the paternalistic paradigm treated the disease, the new and autonomous one treats the person. The doctor inarguably has specialized knowledge and a more complete understanding of the medical risks and benefits associated with a specific treatment. But as the patient, you're a specialist of a rarer sort: Only you can know how the procedure is likely to affect your life outside the hospital or doctor's office. Since only you will experience the actual consequences of the choice, shouldn't you be the one to ultimately make it?

Chances are you replied, "Yes," and our medical system tends to agree. So you and I and those parents unlucky enough to find their babies in the NICU should be glad that in America, unlike in many other countries, paternalistic medicine has been on its way out for some time now. But as we'll see next, most of us don't feel happier and healthier and grateful when we're offered a choice between continuing Julie's treatment and withdrawing it. And parents who make this choice in real life are often worse off than parents whose doctors make the call.

III. SUSAN'S CHOICE

Susan and Daniel Mitchell were expecting their first child. Though they had not been in their new home for long, they had already finished fixing up the nursery. They even had a name picked out: Barbara, in honor of the baby's grandmother. Susan hadn't experienced any problems during the pregnancy, so when her water broke at three o'clock one morning, she and Daniel weren't overly anxious. As they drove to the medical center of a well-known academic hospital in the Midwest, the thought that they were soon to become parents helped Susan through her increasingly rapid contractions. However, as she was being prepped for delivery and a much-needed epidural, she heard through the fog of pain and medication that the baby's heart had stopped, and she was subsequently rushed to the operating room for an emergency cesarean. She felt the pressure of a cut on her abdomen, and then she drifted into unconsciousness.

When Susan opened her eyes in the recovery room, she saw her husband but not her daughter. She remembered hearing the words "code blue," but was still in a haze and did not know what had happened. The doctor came in to explain the situation to her and Daniel, and she learned that the child she had been carrying for nine months and had expected now to be cradling in her arms was on a ventilator in the NICU. Barbara had suffered severe cerebral anoxia, a shortage of oxygen that had left her with life-threatening brain damage. It was impossible to predict the exact effects of the damage, but there was very little good news. For now, unable to even breathe on her own, she was being sustained by a ventilator and a feeding tube. She was likely to survive for a long while if this life support continued, but it was almost impossible that her higher brain functions would ever return. She would remain in a persistent vegetative state, unaware of her surroundings and unable to interact with others.

The doctor said this and more, and Susan listened and nodded and cried, but still she held on to the hope that her baby would be fine. Hoping that a look at Barbara would prove her right, Susan asked to be taken to the NICU. She was weak and couldn't walk yet, so she cajoled the staff into putting her in a wheelchair and pushing her there. But what she saw did not comfort her. Surrounded by medical equipment, Barbara appeared small and frail. Though Susan had known that her baby was on a ventilator, she was unprepared for the sight of that white tube snaking down her throat. The beep of the heart monitor announced that Barbara was alive, but it also served as a persistent reminder of her critical condition. Susan and Daniel held their daughter's hand and spoke to her for 15 minutes before they had to leave. The reality of the situation finally hit them: Only a miracle would allow Barbara to lead any semblance of a normal life. They had never imagined that this would be their first—perhaps last—major decision as Barbara's parents.

After speaking at length with the doctors, who laid out the consequences of each course of action and answered all their questions but respectfully avoided making a suggestion, the Mitchells had to choose whether to continue their daughter's life-sustaining treatment or not. A couple of days later, they decided to discontinue treatment, and Barbara died within hours. Susan, still healing from the surgery, stayed a little while longer. She saw other babies when she walked by the nursery on her floor, but it wasn't until she left the hospital without *her* baby that she fully and deeply felt the loss. The months that followed were very difficult for the Mitchells, and regardless of whether or not we've walked in their shoes, we can understand why their grief was so profound.

Bioethicists Kristina Orfali and Elisa Gordon conducted interviews with Susan and Daniel and other parents—American and French—all of whom had been through the ordeal of the death of an infant child. In every case, the severely ill child had died after the withdrawal of life-sustaining medical treatment. But in America, parents must make the decision to withdraw treatment, while in France doctors make the decision, unless explicitly challenged by the parents. This means that there was a crucial difference between the choosing experiences of the two sets of parents. I teamed up with Simona Botti, a marketing professor at the London Business School, and Kristina Orfali to examine the repercussions of this difference, and to ask a critical question: After several months had passed, were American and French parents equally distressed by what they had suffered?

Both groups were still grieving, of course, but one seemed to be coping better than the other. Many of the French parents expressed a belief in the inevitability of the outcome, and so in telling their stories, they focused less on how things might have been or should have been than the American parents did. They were able to speak, without much confusion or anger, about what had actually happened, and some of them even highlighted the few but very precious positive moments they had shared with their babies. Nora, a French mother, said, "We lost Noah, but he brought us so many things. Not happiness, far from that, but while he was here, we loved him as our son. And beyond that, he brought us, maybe, a certain philosophy of life." She also mentioned that through him, she and his father had developed friendships with some of the nurses. "It is sad," she said, "but if he's dead, it's because he had to die." Neither she nor the other French parents blamed themselves or the doctors. Some of them did wish they had been more involved in choosing whether to discontinue treatment, but they also felt that such a choice might have been too unpleasant and demanding. Pierre, who lost his daughter Alice, explained it in this way: "[The doctors] make the decision and then they discuss it with the parents. Since we are parents, if we had to help with a decision like that, I think it'd be impossible. I don't know that I could say to stop the machine. It's already difficult as it is, without adding extra stress."

That extra stress may account for the persistent guilt, doubt, and resentment of the American parents. Bridget, mother of Eliot, felt that the nurses and doctors had rushed her, and now, she said,

"I walk around thinking, 'What if, what if, what if?'" She thought she should have been even more involved in making treatment decisions, yet she was upset at being the one to "pull the plug": "They were purposely torturing me. How did they get me to do that? Now I live with having made the decision." Sharon, whose son Charlie died, expressed a similar sentiment, saying, "I felt I played a part in an execution. I shouldn't have done that." These statements, chilling and anguished, sound significantly different from those of the French parents. They could almost have come from the mouth of Sophie Zawistowska, the titular character of William Styron's novel *Sophie's Choice*.

As a survivor of the WWII Nazi concentration camps, Sophie remembers many horrifying experiences. The title of the novel refers to the worst of these, a forced decision that haunts and ultimately destroys her. Near the end of the book, we finally learn about the choice that Sophie can neither forgive nor forget. When she and her two children, son Jan and daughter Eva, arrived at Auschwitz, they stood on the ramp, waiting to be sent to either a labor camp or the gas chamber. The man in charge of the selection was an SS doctor. After a panicked and desperate Sophie blurted out that she and her children were Polish and Catholic, not Jewish, he told her that since she was "a Polack, not a Yid," she had the "privilege" of choice: She could keep one child, and the other would be sent to the chamber. "'Don't make me choose,' she heard herself plead in a whisper, 'I can't choose,'" but if she didn't, both children would be killed. "'Take the baby!' she called out. 'Take my little girl!'" And with that, both Eva's and Sophie's fates were sealed. Many years later, Sophie finds it "'still so terrible to wake up these many mornings with a memory of that, having to live with it.'" Her heart, she says, "'has been hurt so much, it has turned to stone.'"

"Torture" and "execution" are terms that we would expect far more to hear from Sophie than from Bridget and Sharon. Even the possibility that the American parents' reactions could resemble hers may seem shocking. After all, the circumstances of the American parents seem much more similar to those of the French parents, and we expect similar circumstances to lead to similar reactions. Of course, there are cultural variations that could lead to some differences, but wouldn't the reaction to such a tragic life-or-death situation be so visceral and fundamental as to be shared by all who experienced it? But perhaps there's another force at work here, and the burden borne by the American parents and Sophie—that of making the choice—had a greater influence than everything else that the two groups of parents had in common. Could you be pushed to the limit in terms of your grief not by the events themselves, but by being the primary actor, the one who makes the decision? What are the costs exacted by the choice itself?

IV. THE COSTS OF COMPARISON

You read three different vignettes about Julie and you answered questions for each one. In the first of these, the doctors didn't talk about other options and they made the decision to withdraw treatment (the uninformed-no-choice condition). In the second, they explained the two possible courses of action and their consequences before announcing that they had chosen to withdraw treatment (the informed-no-choice condition). In the third, you were provided with the information and asked to make the decision yourself (the informed-choice condition). In 2008, we conducted a study at Columbia University in which we presented participants with these same Julie vignettes. The participants imagined themselves as Julie's parents and filled out questionnaires, just as you did, but whereas you saw and responded to all of the scenarios, each of the study participants was randomly assigned to only one of the three conditions. By comparing their responses, we established that the informed nonchoosers (equivalent to the French parents) expressed less negative emotion than the choosers (equivalent to the American parents).

Informed nonchoosers were also better off than the *un*informed nonchoosers, who were just as unhappy as the informed choosers. This suggests that telling people about different treatment options can help to reduce the negative impact of the situation, even when their doctors serve as the final decision makers.

We also learned that choosers were more confident than nonchoosers that withdrawing treatment was the right thing to do. That is to say, the choosers felt worse in spite of believing more strongly in the final decision. To further explore this result, we modified the no-choice vignettes so that the doctors decided to *continue* treatment. In this case, the nonchoosers and the choosers who continued treatment were equally confident, but once again, the choosers felt worse. The extent of negative emotion seems, then, to depend less on the confidence in the actual decision to withdraw or continue treatment and more on the perception that one is the causal agent, the person directly responsible for the child's death or suffering.

The importance of perceived causality was confirmed by another variation of the study, one that examined the effects of framing the withdrawal of treatment as the professionally recommended option. Two groups, choosers and nonchoosers, read the corresponding Julie vignettes with the following sentence inserted into the doctors' comments: "In our opinion, there's nothing else to do but withdraw treatment." In contrast to the results of the previous studies, when the doctors framed treatment withdrawal as the medically superior option—rather than just one of the possible alternatives—choosers felt no worse than nonchoosers! This variation erased the significant difference in negative emotion between the two groups, suggesting that doctors, by clearly stating their own preferences, may be able to alleviate the burden of personal responsibility for people making tough medical decisions. And along with the other Julie studies, it demonstrates just how heavily difficult choices weigh on the heart and the conscience when we hold ourselves solely—or even primarily—accountable.

On the one hand, just as we saw in previous chapters, we're reluctant to give up choice in any situation because we believe it enables us to change and shape our lives for the better; on the other hand, we recognize from experience and perhaps from intuition that some choices, no matter which option we choose and what the outcome, will always diminish our happiness. This is true when a choice is unavoidable and offers us only undesirable options, and it is particularly true when we must think about what we cherish not in terms of *worth* but in terms of *value*. I borrow this distinction from Lewis Hyde, who writes in his book *The Gift*: "I mean 'worth' to refer to those things we prize and yet say 'you can't put a price on it.' We derive value, on the other hand, from the comparison of one thing with another." The life of a child has worth, but when parents like the Mitchells are asked to make decisions about treatment, they must compare options, and in order to compare, they must determine value. What amount of suffering is equal to death? That is, when you add up your and your child's present suffering and anticipated future suffering, what must the total be before you'll deem your child's death preferable? Or how much hope, calculated as probability of survival or likelihood of recovery, must you have before deciding to continue treatment? Do you measure and consider emotional stress and financial pressures and the effects on your other children when making your choice, or do you put this child's life ahead of everything else? What happens when we try to fix a value on that which is priceless?

Let me consult Hyde once again:

> If a thing is to have market value, it must be detachable or alienable so that it can be put on the scale and compared. I mean this in a particular sense: we who do the valuation must be able to stand apart from the thing we are pricing. We have to be able to conceive of separating ourselves from it.... We feel it inappropriate, even rude, to be asked to evaluate in

certain situations. Consider the old ethics-class dilemma in which you are in a lifeboat with your spouse and child and grandmother and you must choose who is to be thrown over-board to keep the craft afloat—it's a dilemma because you are forced to evaluate in a context, the family, which we are nor-mally unwilling to stand apart from and reckon as we would reckon commodities. We are sometimes forced into such judg-ments, to be sure, but they are stressful precisely because we tend not to assign comparative values to those things to which we are emotionally connected.

Sophie and the American parents faced choices that demanded that they assign value to their children. To do so, they needed to detach from the children, but because they could not, they were pulled apart. It is as though they were tied to the rack and stretched until their structures snapped. For the American parents, this led to unrelenting guilt, anger, and in some cases, depression. For Sophie, who also suffered in many other ways during the war, it ends in suicide. When we read the scene in which the SS doctor asks her to choose, we understand at once that he is intentionally torturing her, but in our own lives, we sometimes have difficulty acknowledging the tragic costs of certain choices.

We all hope that we'll never have to make such a choice. The stark truth, however, is that there's a high probability each one of us will be faced with a decision almost as agonizing at some point over the course of our lives. There are now 4.5 million people liv-ing with Alzheimer's disease in the United States, and this number is expected to increase to a staggering 11 to 16 million by 2050. The American Cancer Society has estimated that a person's chances of developing an invasive cancer over their life span may be as high as 1 in 2 for men and 1 in 3 for women. Each year, nearly 60,000 new cases of Parkinson's disease are diagnosed. I don't mean to depress you, but the point is that none of us are truly sheltered from dealing with such circumstances. The quality of health care continues to improve, and people are living longer, but these developments mean that we're likely to eventually find ourselves in a situation in which we're forced to make difficult choices about our parents, other loved ones, or even ourselves that ultimately boil down to calculations of worth and value.

These decisions can be even more difficult than in the Julie scenario; instead of one heartbreaking choice, you're wrestling with all the minutiae of day-to-day things that are so easily taken for granted. One is forced to assign value to degrees of a loved one's very quality of life—should we err on the side of safety and hide the car keys, or give in to Mom's wishes to lead as much of an independent life as is still possible? How do you keep Grandpa from wandering outside and getting lost in a neighborhood he once knew like the back of his hand? If Dad can no longer feed himself, is it better to put him in a nursing home where he can receive constant care, or to seek alternatives, like a private caretaker, to keep him in familiar surroundings with some measure of autonomy?

It's more of a balancing act than a yes or no dilemma; certainly, health and safety are significant factors in the calculation, but shouldn't we also allow people to retain as much freedom and independence as possible? It is no easy task to constantly weigh protection and dignity against each other on a scale of values, and to continually reevaluate these judgments in accordance with the sufferer's current condition. It certainly doesn't help matters that even as the mind and body deteriorate, the instinct to stay in control remains—at times sufferers will resist the help of others, hoping to defend what liberties they have left. Again and again, family members cite the process of deciding when and how to take away a loved one's choice as the most difficult part of an already agonizing experience.

As we learned from the Julie study, when doctors presented the option to remove Julie from life support as the medically superior option, the choosers felt better about their decision than when the

doctors merely presented the options without voicing their preferences. We frequently look to sources of authority and expertise to
alleviate the burden of a difficult decision—finding someone who
tells us that we went the right way in a tough bind can go a long way
toward making us feel better about it, even if the actual outcome
remains unchanged. In a culture where our conception of choice is so
tied up with virtues of dignity and independence, the reluctance to
deny someone—even if they are suffering from a degenerative brain
disease—the right to choose can be so strong that it overrides even
the concern for physical well-being. One coping strategy available
is to defer the touchiest aspects of care to medical authorities; when
a son or daughter or spouse doesn't have the heart to hide the keys,
a doctor's prescription to stay off the road can provide the needed
impetus to retire Grandma's license. When it comes to these difficult
decisions, it seems that choosing is a right we'd prefer to exercise
with some outside help.

Infancy and very old age may render a human being totally
dependent on others for protection and care, but only old age transforms former independence into utter reliance. When we become
caregivers, it means taking on the mental burdens of making choices
for another person in addition to oneself. Though we always want
the best for our loved ones, the dizzying array of qualitative choices
is enough to drive a person crazy. One female colleague told me that
she experienced immense relief after a particular epiphany: "After
years of agonizing over treatment options, I realized one day that
my mother was going to die regardless of what I did or didn't do.
It sounds grim, but it was so important for me to understand that
I couldn't fix her, that I couldn't give her back her independence.
I was able to focus instead on giving both of us a quality of life in
our last years together that wasn't possible when I was still obsessed
with being the perfect caregiver." Maybe we all need to focus less on
perfection and more on the joys of simply spending time with the
people we love.

V. BETWEEN A ROCK AND A HARD CHOICE

Given the dubious practices and quackery of doctors and healers throughout medical history, our aversion to paternalistic medicine makes a lot of sense. But the shift to patient autonomy comes with new questions and consequences. There are, to be sure, powerful psychological benefits to participating in the decision-making process, even when one chooses no differently from the doctor or from other patients. However, as we've seen, choice can also be punishing and destructive. And though we'd like to believe otherwise, one of the main concerns in the previous era of medicine—that we'd choose poorly if given the opportunity—was not unfounded. For instance, physician and medical decision-making scholar Peter Ubel points out in his book *Free Market Madness* that many parents in the 1970s resisted vaccinating their children for polio because of the risk of contracting the disease from the vaccine itself. Since the chance of this happening was only 1 in 2.4 million (far lower than the chance of an unvaccinated person contracting polio), any medical professional would have encouraged vaccination. But probability is cold comfort when that 1 in 2.4 million is your child; some parents must have been so afraid of making their children ill by *choosing* to vaccinate, thereby becoming causal agents, that they preferred the far riskier option of doing nothing. This is just one example of how our well-known tendency to give more weight to the potential harms of action than to those of inaction can get us into trouble.

We are also led astray sometimes by our suspicion or fear of complications. In a recent study, also by Peter Ubel and colleagues, participants were asked to imagine that they had been diagnosed with colon cancer, which they could treat with one of two different surgeries. The first surgery offered the following: 80 percent chance of a complete cure, 16 percent chance of death, and 4 percent chance of a cure accompanied by one very unpleasant side effect (colostomy, chronic diarrhea, intermittent bowel obstruction, or wound infection); the second surgery's odds: 80 percent chance of a complete cure and 20 percent chance of death. Which of these surgeries would you choose? Do you think it would be better to live with a side effect or to die?

Over 90 percent of the participants said beforehand that living with any of the possible side effects was preferable to death. Based on their *own* preferences, most of them should have picked Surgery 1, but about half of them picked Surgery 2! Though we may *know* that the surgery with complications is better than the surgery without complications, we might *feel* that the latter is a better option. Perhaps we can see ourselves struggling with painful and embarrassing side effects but we can't conceive of dying, and so the complications seem real in a way one's own death never does. Thus we are often inconsistent and biased, even when—or maybe because—our lives are at stake.

Where does this leave us? We certainly don't yearn for the days when patients were wheeled out of surgery with more missing than they had expected. We don't want to be told what to do, but we also don't want to make choices detrimental to our health and happiness. We'd like to minimize the suffering of people facing illness and death, whether their own or a loved one's, but we're loath to do so by restricting choice. Given what you know now, would you more readily relinquish choice in the kinds of scenarios presented so far? If yes, whom would you trust and how frequently would you allow them to choose for you? If not, why? Is it because you have uncommon insight into your own anxieties, motivations, and behaviors, and are thus less prone to error? Are you able to make objective evaluations when others' emotions run high? Or maybe you're worried it's only a couple of short steps from forgoing a few choices to becoming automatons in an Orwellian dystopia; you give an inch, they take a mile.

That's why we don't bother to mull over the tough questions until we're caught between a rock and a hard place, and by that time, we're in no shape to give the answers most beneficial to us. My urging you to think about onerous choices may seem pushy and, as Hyde puts it, rude. And some people might believe that to contemplate such choices is to invite them into your life. I won't deny that it's all a bit morbid, but we take out life insurance policies and write wills, both of which require us to acknowledge our mortality. Death knocks on the door but once, and the tax man once a year, but unpleasant dilemmas can force themselves upon us at any time. Though they appear more often in the form of pesky neighbors than SS tormentors, we do ourselves no favors by ignoring or trivializing their accreting effects when we have the ability to prepare ourselves for the inevitability of choosing between unattractive options.

To examine how we react to these unpleasant everyday choices, I teamed up with Simona Botti for another set of studies. The participants, students at the University of Chicago, thought they were doing taste tests for consumer research purposes. We whipped up a variety of flavored yogurts and asked some of the students to rate, on a scale of 1 to 9, how much they thought they would like or dislike each flavor. Based on their ratings, we selected four more appetizing flavors (brown sugar, cinnamon, cocoa powder, mint) and four less appetizing ones (celery seed, tarragon, chili powder, sage). Other students now walked in to find four cups of yogurt—either the more appetizing group or the less appetizing group—arranged on a table. The yogurts were in labeled, uncovered, transparent cups, allowing students to easily see and smell them. Half of the participants got to choose a flavor to sample; the other half drew from a hat and sampled whichever flavor the slip indicated. Actually, we had rigged the hat so that whoever pulled from it ended up with the same flavor that the previous taster had freely chosen. Everyone ate as much of the sample as they wanted, and then they filled out surveys on how much they enjoyed the taste and at what price the company supposedly running the study should sell an eight-ounce cup of the yogurt in stores.

For the appetizing yogurts, people who chose the flavor ate more than those who were assigned the flavor. Also, choosers priced an

8-ounce cup $1 higher than nonchoosers did. But when the yogurts were less palatable, *nonchoosers* ate 50 percent more and priced the cup $1.50 higher than choosers did. The results for the better flavors need no explanation, but why are they reversed for the other flavors? Why should something unappealing taste any better to someone who did not choose what to eat for themselves than for someone who did? The surveys and our discussions with the participants shed some light on this. Each chooser had selected a yogurt by weighing the pros and cons, and as she tasted her sample, she couldn't help but continue the process of evaluation: Just how bad was it and why? With every spoonful, she was reminded that she had made the choice, but had she really picked the least objectionable one? In contrast, a nonchooser had no reason to dwell on how her sample stacked up against the others, and since she hadn't chosen it, she was less invested in the taste outcome; to her, it was just an experiment, not a measure of personal success or failure. It seems that even when we have very little to lose, choosing between disagreeable options leaves a bad taste in our mouth.

We are not, of course, stuck in a bizarro world where we're forced to eat disgusting flavors of yogurt because BadYogurt Corp is running the show. If the tasting booth at our local supermarket has nothing enticing to offer, we move along. But "none of the above" is not always an option, or sometimes it's the worst option. Say your spouse has a penchant for Uwe Boll movies. On date night, do you submit to *BloodRayne* or *House of the Dead*, or do you break your sweetie's heart by imposing an indefinite ban on all things Uwe? When the holidays come around, do you spend them with the in-laws and upset the parents, or visit the parents and upset the in-laws, or stay home and upset everyone? Do you give the family heirloom, which has mostly sentimental value, to this daughter or to that one, or do you sell it for a pittance and split the money? Individually, these decisions are far from life altering, but if each one disturbs your happiness, how long before the sum total exacts a significant toll? Perhaps it's time to challenge some of our strongly held beliefs about choice, and to consider what we may gain by letting go.

VI. THE RED BUTTON SYNDROME

Welcome to Paradise Park! We're so glad you're here, and we hope you'll stay with us for as long as possible. Eat well, make merry, do whatever you want! That's right: There are no rules in Paradise and you're in charge (and don't touch the button). Grab a map, explore, enjoy. The weather is always perfect. What's that? The button? Ah, yes, just don't press it and everything will be fine. But if you do, well, we can't be responsible for the consequences. Look, just stay away from the big round button (imagine it a bright red one) at the bottom of the page, okay?

If you're like me, you're wondering what that button does. You have plenty to keep you occupied, but your thoughts keep returning to the button. Surely it can't be that bad. They're just trying to keep something from you. And if you don't press it, someone else will. No, you probably shouldn't risk it, but would it hurt to take a closer look? Why did they tell you about the button, anyway? Maybe they *want* you to press it. Then again, it might be a government setup. Only one way to find out…

We learn very early in life that some things are simply not allowed, and we don't take this lying down. In our terrible twos,

we throw tantrums and juice boxes; in our teens, we slam doors and sneak out windows. The characters in many of our most compelling and enduring stories try—and often fail—to resist the lure of the forbidden. Eat any fruit but the one on this tree? Love anyone but the son of the enemy? We know how that turns out. Call it disobedience, defiance, or rebellion. In the 1960s, psychologist Jack Brehm called it "reactance" and explained it as follows:

> [W]hen a person believes himself free to engage in a given behavior, he will experience psychological reactance if that freedom is eliminated or threatened with elimination. Psychological reactance is defined as a motivational state directed toward the re-establishment of the threatened or eliminated freedom, and should manifest itself in increased desire to engage in the relevant behavior....

Surely you have personally found yourself grabbing for exactly those choices you didn't already have. But as we've seen, people don't always make the "best" choices for themselves. A possible solution to this problem is to take away the choices that have harmful potential and turn them over to those who are trustworthy and more qualified and/or objective. But this is easier said than done. Even if we could reach a consensus on what is "harmful" and who is "qualified," removing choice would very likely provoke reactance. It's one thing to have never had a choice at all, quite another to have it and then lose it. In the Julie studies and the yogurt experiment, choosers indicated on their questionnaires that they would not have wanted to switch to the no-choice condition. Nonchoosers, on the other hand, would have liked to switch and give choosing a try. Most people thought it was better—or at least good—to be a chooser, even though nonchoosers were actually more satisfied overall than choosers were.

Perhaps because these scenarios were either hypothetical or everyday, the stakes were too low to prompt participants to question their commitment to choice. But that doesn't explain why the American parents who made real, critical decisions about treatment for their babies, and who expressed anger and resentment at being put in that position, also balked at the idea of relinquishing choice. They understood that choice can be a liability in circumstances like theirs, so if given the opportunity, why not let doctors make the call? Furthermore, though the French parents benefited from a culture in which medical decisions aren't seen as matters of personal choice, even they had mixed feelings about not being able to choose.

In earlier chapters, I proposed that choice is a basic necessity for human well-being and is inextricably linked to the "unalienable Rights" of life, liberty, and the pursuit of happiness. As such, choice has worth rather than value. It requires that we assign value to the options under consideration, but choice itself resists such evaluation, demanding steadfast love and loyalty. When Choice as principle competes against choice as practice, we are torn: Should we claim and exercise our Right, or should we do whatever is right for us in the situation at hand? If lack of choice is the status quo, this question might never come up. But if others have choice when we don't, or if a choice we currently have is threatened with elimination, our hackles are sure to rise. Then the balance usually tips in the favor of Choice as principle, and regardless of the consequences, we insist on our Right to choose. This means that trying to spare people from difficult choices by removing them may produce adverse effects.

In 1972, the inhabitants of Miami, Florida, began to stockpile a substance that was about to be banned. In the short time between the announcement of the ban and its implementation, Miamians rushed to the stores, grabbing as many of the soon-to-disappear boxes as they could. Once the ban was in place, some of them persisted by smuggling in the product from counties where it was still legal. What was so precious to these Miami residents that they simply couldn't do without? Turns out, it was laundry detergent...but not just any laundry detergent. Their city was one of the first in the country to ban the sale and use of detergents containing phosphates, chemicals that increased cleaning power by softening the water in washing machines. Unfortunately, the phosphates were also effective fertilizers. When drained into the water supply, they could lead to rampant growth of algae, which clogs bodies of water, suffocates plants and animals, and in some cases produces neurotoxins harmful to humans. Yes, but how white those whites were! What's strange, though, is that even at the time of the ban, phosphates weren't the only option for making a detergent more powerful, and manufacturers were already introducing new formulations with carbonates and other replacements. Why break the law for clean clothes, especially when they'll get just as clean with environmentally safe, *legal* detergents? It was "like Prohibition, but with soap," says a colleague of mine, and it's just one example of the considerable impact of reactance on our attitudes and behaviors.

As a psychological phenomenon, reactance doesn't depend on the facts of a situation but on our perception of it. If we believe choice has been taken away, it may not matter that we're wrong. One of the areas in which we greatly desire choice is health care, and we dislike having restrictions imposed. Quick, when I say health maintenance organization (HMO), what's your first thought? I doubt it's a positive one, since you've probably heard your share of HMO horror stories. A poll in 2000 recorded a 29 percent public approval rating for HMOs, just 1 percent higher than the rating for tobacco companies. HMOs have become the health care that everyone loves to hate, but do they truly deserve our ire?

Whereas traditional health insurance plans pay some or all of your medical expenses no matter who treats you, an HMO covers only care received from within its network of providers, which varies from plan to plan. If you want your visit to a specialist to be covered, you need approval from a primary care physician in the network. This system allows the HMO to negotiate better rates with in-network doctors and pass the savings along to customers in the form of lower premiums. It's true, people like savings, but perhaps not as much as they like choice. They feel constricted by HMOs, and they consistently report receiving worse care from them. But wait— some of these reports come from people who don't even belong to HMOs. For one study, researchers analyzed survey data from more than 18,000 respondents and found that nearly 25 percent of them were mistaken about their coverage, believing they were in an HMO when they actually had traditional insurance, or vice versa. The respondents who thought they had traditional coverage were more satisfied than those who thought they had HMO coverage; the plan they *actually* had turned out to have less of an effect on their sat-isfaction than the plan they *believed* they had. HMOs do, indeed, offer fewer choices, but does that necessarily lead to inferior health care? We seem to think it does, but our assessment may be skewed by our aversion to restrictions on choice. If reactance is compromis-ing our judgment, can't we do something about it?

VII. GOVERNING REACTANCE

A truly democratic society must, to a certain extent, encourage reac-tance. When people aren't motivated to challenge threats to freedom, what's to stop them from acquiescing to totalitarianism? So I'm not suggesting that we initiate a top secret project to suppress reactance. We can design and adopt strategies that bypass, manipulate, or take advantage of reactance in such a way that they serve our interests without endangering our rights. For instance, how about reverse psychology, that old standby of parents everywhere? It worked well for Brer Rabbit when he was trapped by his nemesis, Brer Fox. As his captor considered how exactly to punish him—roasting, hang-ing, drowning—Brer Rabbit begged, "Please don't throw me into the briar patch! Do anything else you want, but please don't throw me into the briar patch!" So what did Brer Fox do? He threw him into the briar patch, of course, and Brer Rabbit, who had grown up in the patch, escaped with ease. One of my colleagues applied the same principle in order to spark his young son's interest in Shakespeare. Those, he said, were "Daddy's books," and kids weren't allowed to read them. He hid them behind other books on the shelf and in the cabinet underneath the bathroom sink, as if they were issues of *Playboy* or *Penthouse*, but he always left a small corner visible. It didn't take long for his son to find the illicit texts and study them in private. Gradually, the boy developed a deep interest in the classics, and my colleague was very pleased with himself.

There are better solutions, though. Remember Mark Lepper, my adviser from Stanford University? In the 1970s, he conducted a series of now-classic studies with psychologists Mark Zanna and Robert Abelson. On an otherwise normal day, the children in a kindergarten class in California got a "special treat." One at a time, they were whisked away from their regular classroom activities and taken to another room. Here, an experimenter in a white lab coat showed the children six toys: a train, a Slinky, a bulldozer, a wind-up donkey, an Etch A Sketch, and a battery-powered robot named Robbie (one of the hot toys that year). He asked the children to rate the toys from favorite to least favorite, and Robbie turned out to be the overall winner. Next, he told them he was going to leave the room, and while he was gone, they could play with any of the toys *except* Robbie. He strongly warned some of the children against playing with Robbie by saying, "I will be very upset and very angry with you, and I'll have to do something about it." To the other children, he said only, "I will be a bit annoyed with you." While the experimenter was away, the children who had been threatened with anger gazed at Robbie but didn't go near him. The children who had received a milder threat also obeyed the experimenter, but they got much closer to Robbie. They focused intently on him and reached out to touch him, pulling back only at the last second. A week later, another experimenter asked these same children to once again rate the six toys. The mildly threatened children, who had found it so difficult to resist Robbie, weren't as interested in him as they had been before. But the other children, who had been threatened more severely, wanted more than ever to play with Robbie.

All of the children were subject to the same restriction, but the mild threat to choice provoked less reactance *in the long run* than the strong threat did. Fearing anger and other reprimands, the strongly threatened children kept their distance from Robbie, but they began to suffer from something similar to "red-button syndrome," the condition we endure when a red CAUTION button stares us in the face. We can imagine these children thinking, "Robbie must be really amazing if that guy doesn't want me to play with him!" and "Why do I have to listen to him? He's not the boss of me!" The mildly threatened children almost gave in to their urges, but their hesitation itself indicates that they believed they had a choice. Their thoughts went more like this: "I can play with Robbie if I really want to because the man said he would be only a *bit* annoyed, and that's not a big deal because Dad gets annoyed all the time, but maybe I don't really want to play with Robbie, anyway."

When the children were asked about the toys one week later, they recalled the earlier event and rated Robbie accordingly. To the strongly threatened children, it was clear they had been forced to give up Robbie and they hadn't had any choice at all. So now they displayed reactance by giving Robbie even higher ratings. For the other children, however, matters were a little more complicated. They had said they wanted very much to play with Robbie, but then they didn't play with him. Since the consequences of disobedience were mild, they had a choice, so why didn't they choose the toy they most wanted?

One possible explanation is that doing so would have produced cognitive dissonance, bringing their stated desires and actual behaviors into unpleasant conflict. Since the action was in the past and couldn't be changed, the only way to avoid the dissonance was to reinterpret the desire: "I guess Robbie's not that special. I thought it would be a lot of fun to play with him, but it wouldn't really." By asking the children not to play with Robbie, but still allowing them some wiggle room, the experimenter was able to minimize reactance and render Robbie less attractive. Since the children believed they had independently concluded that Robbie wasn't so great, their new attitude would persist.

Insurance companies were quick to learn from studies like the one above. They recognized the benefits of restrictions that don't *feel* like restrictions, and applied their newfound insight to the problem of low public confidence in HMOs. They didn't tell plan members about reactance or try to convince them it was all in their heads. Instead, they developed a new plan called the preferred provider organization (PPO). Like an HMO, a PPO offers a network of approved providers and primary care physicians who act as gatekeepers to specialist care. The key difference is that PPOs *do* cover out-of-network care, albeit at a significant extra cost relative to in-network care. The incentives to stay within the network are strong, so people usually do, but they still feel that they have other choices. Thus, they benefit from the low premiums of PPOs but avoid the dissatisfaction aroused by the strict limitations of HMOs.

Laws often employ similar means to influence our choices. "Sin taxes," which lower our consumption of alcohol and tobacco, are restrictive but not prohibitive, so we're willing to live with them. Such taxes are introduced or raised for a variety of reasons: for example, to reduce societal costs such as missed work, health-care expenses, and alcohol-related accidents. Studies have found that a 10 percent increase in alcohol tax results in an average 3 to 4 percent drop in consumption. That's quite impressive considering that the alcohol tax is generally quite low—only pennies on the gallon for beer in some states. In the case of cigarettes, for which the tax can exceed $2 per pack, a 10 percent tax increase could produce a consumption drop of up to 8 percent, according to an analysis by Nobel laureate Gary Becker and his colleagues. What's more, these effects are heightened in groups that have more to lose from smoking and drinking, such as teenagers and pregnant women. And the percentage decrease in consumption is usually lower than the percentage increase in tax, resulting in more tax dollars overall for the government to spend as it sees fit. But how do the consumers footing the bill feel about these taxes?

A recent study found that people at high risk for smoking were happy when the cigarette tax was raised! Are smokers mathematically challenged? Do they have money to burn? No, they do realize that a higher tax means more expensive smokes, and they don't want to pay extra. So what's going on? Well, smokers and potential smokers *know* they shouldn't smoke. In both medical and financial terms, it's a poor choice. The incentives to *not* smoke, however, aren't compelling enough to them. Maybe it's peer pressure or the cool factor; maybe they're already addicted. Whatever the reason, smoking is still pretty attractive. But when cigarette prices rise, the incentives rise, and that's a good thing. At some point, people decide they simply can't afford the habit. If they don't smoke yet, they might never pick it up; if they do smoke, they'll try to cut down. And those attempting to quit may find it just a little bit easier: The same cigarette is less tempting when it costs more.

Sounds like a win-win! But before we go tax crazy, let's get some perspective. Taxes may be less restrictive than outright bans, but they can still induce reactance if raised very high. What happens when people want a product but it's too expensive? Canada discovered the answer the hard way when it steadily increased the cigarette tax during the 1980s and early 1990s. Smoking fell by 40 percent over that period, but by 1994, there was a thriving black market: Thirty percent of the cigarettes sold were contraband brought across the U.S. border by organized criminals. In addition to the crime, the Canadian government also had to contend with the decrease in revenues as fewer people paid taxes on the cigarettes they were buying. By 1997, the government relented and lowered the tax, and Canada's current levels of both smoking and cigarette tax are similar to those of the U.S.

There's an art to subtraction. Too little is ineffective, while too much is counterproductive. Finding the sweet spot at all is difficult, and for taxes and other decisions that affect many people, no single solution will work for everyone. If only there were a way for each person to determine the perfect level of influence for himself.

VIII. LASHING OURSELVES TO THE MAST

The Greek epic *The Odyssey* recounts the story of the trickster hero Odysseus as he sails home after helping the Greeks achieve victory in the hard-fought decade-long Trojan War. Due to a series of misadventures, his journey took another ten years, giving the word *odyssey* its meaning of a long and adventurous voyage. Odysseus battled monsters and lost many men, and though the winds blew his ship every which way but home, he persevered. Thanks to the advice of the sorceress Circe, he survived even the enchanting but deadly Sirens. The "high, thrilling song" of these bird women was so irresistible that countless sailors had wrecked their ships on the rocky coast or jumped overboard and drowned, all in an attempt to get closer to that otherworldly sound. Odysseus told his men that when they drew near to the island of the Sirens, they should plug their ears with beeswax. But he himself wanted to hear the song, so he gave the following order to the crew:

> [Y]ou must bind me with tight chafing ropes
> so I cannot move a muscle, bound to the spot,
> erect at the mast-block, lashed by ropes to the mast.
> And if I plead, commanding you to set me free,
> then lash me faster, rope on pressing rope.

Under the influence of the Sirens, he did plead, but his loyal shipmates only tied him tighter and rowed harder until they were clear of danger. From there, Odysseus and company went on to sail between Scylla, a six-headed monster with an appetite for sailors, and Charybdis, who could create whirlpools that might capsize the whole ship. Our fearless hero was forced to choose between two terrible options, but you know by now how that goes.

It was well known even in ancient Greece that we act against our better judgment with disturbing regularity, a condition the Greeks called *akrasia* (literally, "lacking command" over oneself). Though not every instance of *akrasia* will lead to a watery grave, we are constantly confronted by dilemmas of temptation, and when we give in to our cravings for a double quarter-pounder with cheese and extra-large fries or our urge to procrastinate on responsible actions like saving more and exercising regularly, the cumulative effects can take a harmful toll. In chapter 4, I mentioned that one of the best ways to resist such temptations was to avoid them in the first place, but this works only up to a point. We can put that cake back in the fridge rather than leaving it in plain sight on the counter to tantalize us, for example, but we can't completely escape. If we're bound and determined to go for seconds (or more), the only way to resist giving in is to be bound by a power beyond ourselves. We, too, should consider lashing ourselves to the mast.

We know Odysseus made a wise decision by making it impossible for himself to do anything but remain on the boat. His choice—stay on board or jump into the water—was transformed into his crew's choice: Keep Odysseus bound or let him leap to his death. Since the men couldn't be tempted by the Sirens, they made the right choice where Odysseus would have made the wrong—and fatal—one. We can similarly *choose* to relinquish our difficult choices to others, which neatly avoids having to decide between the distress or harm that would result from choosing for ourselves and the diminished autonomy that would result from others' restricting our choices without our approval. We aren't reducing the total amount of choice in our lives so much as redistributing it, making an additional choice now to remove or alter one in the future. All we need is a helpful crew and some rope.

Quite a few services and devices can aid us in these endeavors, by enabling us to *precommit* when our wills are strong to avoid making the wrong choice when they are weak. For example, casinos use sophisticated databases and facial-recognition technology to prevent cheaters, card counters, and other blacklisted individuals from entering their establishments. Compulsive gamblers can voluntarily add their personal information to these blacklists, directly through the major chains or through free services like BanCop, and thereby keep themselves from squandering their hard-earned money. Even if we can't make it physically impossible to succumb to *akrasia*, we can impose penalties on our poor choices. The SnūzNLūz alarm clock is a nifty little gadget if you're a chronic oversleeper. Every time you hit the snooze button, the clock automatically connects to your bank account through the Internet and donates $10 or more of your money to a preselected charity. Its creators recommend that for maximum effect you choose an organization you despise (an "anti-charity"): Try the NRA if you favor strong gun control laws, or PETA if you have a closet full of fur coats.

Another entry into the precommitment field is stickK.com, a website that Dean Karlan, assistant professor of economics at Yale University, started with a couple of colleagues. As a PhD student, Karlan lost 38 pounds by agreeing to pay a friend half of his annual income if he didn't shed the weight. Years later, he had the idea to create a "commitment store" that would make the process fun and convenient, and so stickK.com was born. StickK tells you to "put a contract out on yourself!" You can't modify the contract, and if you don't fulfill it, you forfeit a prearranged amount of money to a person, a charity, or an anti-charity. StickK also allows you to recruit other people as referees, or shipmates, if you prefer, in case you're tempted to lie about a costly failure. The site launched in January 2008, and it had 10,000 users by March of the same year. Its members are committing to a wide variety of goals, some of them common (lose weight, quit smoking) and some of them less so (use rechargeable batteries, avoid burping in public). The amount of money on the line might be paltry (flossing: $1 a week for four months) or awesome. One teenager was willing to put up $150 a week for a year to control his Internet addiction, an impressive contract made even more impressive by the fact that he had to go online to report his progress.

Of course, if our goals involve money to begin with, a stickK contract will either be extremely effective or else cruel and unusual punishment. After all, the last thing anyone who's already having trouble making ends meet needs is to lose even more money if they fail to pay off their credit card debt. Indeed, while there were many commitments to saving money on the site, they were all purely symbolic. If users are unwilling or unable to wager money on their commitments, stickK is no more effective than a New Year's resolution. Fortunately, there are some programs designed to make saving for the future a less painful experience. For example, we can turn to Save More Tomorrow, or SMarT, a program designed by professors Richard Thaler and Shlomo Benartzi to increase retirement savings by having people precommit to increasing their contribution rates. SMarT takes into account the factors that most often thwart our savings goals—aversion to smaller paychecks, focusing on the present, inertia—and cleverly circumvents them or turns them to our advantage.

SMarT can be seen in action among the employees of one company who met with a financial adviser to calculate whether they were saving enough for retirement. The adviser discovered they were far off their targets, saving only 4 percent of their salaries, and now they needed to gradually bump up that number to 15 percent. He suggested they start by contributing an extra 5 percent to their 401(k) plans. For those who thought this was too big a jump, he presented SMarT as an alternative. The SMarT users didn't increase their contributions when they signed up. Instead, every time a SMarT-er received a raise, her contribution automatically went up by 3 percent, an amount just shy of the typical raise of 3.5 percent. So she never saw the number on her paycheck decrease, which made it less painful to commit to saving more. SMarT-ers were free to cancel at any time, but few bothered to do so, and within five years of their enrollment, they were saving an average of 13 percent. In fact, they were saving more than the group that had followed the adviser's first recommendation; those people were stuck at 9 percent because they hadn't added to their initial 5 percent increase.

Though the above techniques and programs are highly unlikely to backfire, we may still hesitate to adopt them because of a seemingly natural aversion to ceding any control. Yet, there are other ways in which many of us regularly and willingly give up choice. When restrictions on choice are spotlighted, we find the glare unbearable, but if the same restrictions are more softly illuminated, we might see a certain beauty in them. For instance, the majority of Americans follow a religious code of conduct that prescribes some behaviors and proscribes others. Ignoring these rules comes with a price, a different kind of sin tax, one could say. But like the smokers I mentioned earlier, believers often embrace the strictures. They offer their choices in exchange for a sense of belonging and moral rectitude; they make a deal with their community and their god. Indeed, faith of any sort, religious or not, depends at least in part on trusting others to make choices for us. "You decide," we say. "I trust you."

To adapt from *Hamlet*, when "to choose or not to choose" is the question, the "heart-ache and the thousand natural shocks / That flesh is heir to" cannot all be escaped. Life is perpetually testing us not only by administering these "thousand natural shocks" but by making us choose among them. Rarely is the answer as easy and obvious as "cake." In the most challenging predicaments, perceived causality for an undesirable outcome, even if there was no clearer or better choice, can be a debilitating burden. We frequently pay a mental and emotional tax for freedom of choice.

The scenarios of choice covered in this chapter range from the fictional to the all too real, from the humorous to the tragic. Ending up with inadequate yogurt may not seem even remotely like ending up with inadequate health care, but remember that every choice, whether life altering or not, has the potential to leave us anxious or regretful. However, the cumulative results of the diverse array of studies in this chapter tell us that we have the power to reduce the exhausting effects of choice, not by expanding our options but by delegating parts of a decision to others or by limiting ourselves in ways that positively affect the choosing process. Specific examples of these strategies include consulting experts when we're too emotionally tied to a situation to make a sound judgment, and using programs like SMarT to encourage the actions and behaviors that we know to be beneficial. These methods cannot erase difficult choices, but they *can* better prepare us for the vicissitudes of life. There is, in fact, no way to completely avoid choice: No matter how you answer the question "To choose or not to choose?," you always make a choice. But that choice need not leave you feeling tortured. Now, won't you pass the cake, please?

Epilogue

We shall not cease from exploration
And the end of all our exploring
Will be to arrive where we started
And know the place for the first time.

—T. S. Eliot

Here I am, finally, seated on a divan in an airy room, feeling somewhat airy myself—perhaps from anticipation, perhaps uncertainty—awaiting the attentions of the famous S. K. Jain. Above me, ceiling fans turn languidly, not so much to cool visitors, I think, as to disperse the incense that has been lit somewhere in this antechamber. I arrived through a long corridor, a passage from the ordinary world into a quieter, more mysterious one, and was met at the door by two women who asked me to please remove my shoes. The floor is smooth and cold, seeming to my exposed feet the perfect foundation for a new experience.

One of the women gets things started by asking for the date and precise time of birth for me, my son, and my husband. She needs to know the exact minute of each in order to print our charts, which will reveal the locations of the stars and planets when we were born. Before she leaves to enter the information into the computer in an adjoining room, she instructs me to pray to Lord Vishnu to take away my sorrows and shortcomings and replace them with bliss and joy. This involves chanting the following mantra one hundred times: "Hare Krishna, Hare Krishna, Krishna Krishna, Hare Hare / Hare Rama, Hare Rama, Rama Rama, Hare Hare." To help me keep count, she hands over a string of one hundred beads; with each repetition, I should slide my forefinger and thumb from one bead to the next. The other woman, who has been waiting patiently, now sits beside me to monitor my progress and come to my aid if I stumble over the words. Not wanting to disturb the hush that seems native to this place, I proceed in a whisper, my voice barely audible even to myself.

Upon reaching the last bead, I return, as if from a trance, to the fans and the fragrance of the waiting room. The time has come to meet Dr. Jain, one of India's most famous astrologers, thanks to his popular show on Udaya TV and his high-profile consultations with prominent government officials. My visit, shortly after New Year's 2009, has been prompted not by any resolutions but by an interest in the relationship between prediction and choice. Over the years, I have seen how the diverse group of my Indian friends and acquaintances has used astrology to make a variety of decisions. Marriages, for example, have been sealed, scheduled, or broken. The path to my own marriage was lit by the stars, if you will. When my husband and I decided to marry, our families were not entirely pleased. He, an Iyengar, member of a South Indian Brahmin caste, was expected to marry another Iyengar. Not only was I not an Iyengar, we didn't even share the same religion; as far as our relatives were concerned, the match was inappropriate and most likely doomed. My soon-to-be mother-in-law hastened to a trusted astrologer. As soon as she walked in, even before she was able to ask her question, the woman told her, "They've been married for the past seven lives and will be married for seven more!" All that was left was to make it official in this life: We were married—in a traditional Iyengar wedding, no less.

In India, astrologers are frequently solicited for advice on personal affairs, but their influence also extends to the public sphere. The politicians and officials who consult Dr. Jain might be asking him about the outcome of an election or looking for guidance on a matter of state business. How are they able to put so much faith in one man? What is it that gives astrology such sway over them? I'm here as an observer, a seeker, a skeptic. I want to know why people allow their choices to be directed by this arcane art. However, in the atmosphere and ceremony of this unusual "office," I'm finding it a little difficult to keep my researcher's hat from slipping. Chanting complete, I am led into the inner sanctum and seated at a desk, across from the man himself, whom I imagine as a slight but impressive figure dressed all in white. After examining the charts, paper skies rustling at his touch, Dr. Jain tells me in a gentle voice that my marriage was destined—now the second time I've heard that. He also says that my son was born under a lucky star and will live a long and fulfilling life. We spend an hour talking about my life, my work, the ways in which I could be a better guide to my family. To conclude our session, I'm allowed to ask one specific question.

"Anything you like," he says.

I think for a moment. "The book I'm working on," I say. "How will that turn out?"

He needs a little while to mull it over. A little distance, too. He shuffles off to another room, leaving me to wonder what he might be doing in there. Perhaps meditating upon a statue of Krishna and then ringing a bell to summon the answer? Maybe he's poring over a book containing the wisdom of the ancients or reciting his own special mantra. Whatever his method, he does come back with an answer, one he delivers with confidence and benevolence: "Madam, this book will far exceed your expectations."

———

To choose means to turn ourselves to the future. It means to try to catch a glimpse of the next hour, the next year, or further still, and make a decision based on what we see. In that sense, we are all amateur foretellers, though our predictions are usually based on factors closer to home than Mars or Venus or the Big Dipper. Professional foretellers do what we do, but bigger and better. They are masters at "revealing" the future through a mix of common sense, psychological insight, and theatrics. Oddly enough, they seem at once mystical and objective; though we cannot fathom their techniques, their reliance on the physical and the observable (except in the case of psychics) creates the illusion that their prognostications are evidence-based.

Before I visited Dr. Jain, I had my own ideas about how well this book might or might not do. I hoped to write, as all authors do, a book that people would want to read, that they would connect to, engage with, learn from. But when the voice of Dr. Jain, commanded by the planets and stars, made its pronouncement, I confess that my own assessment went right out the window for a few fleeting moments. "Far exceed" sounded good, very good! This man was an expert, after all, and who was I to argue with the heavens?

Of course, my rational self knows that he didn't perform any miracles. His predictions were vague, and some of them can't even be disproved. Creative interpretation—or misinterpretation—could make any outcome seem to be in accordance with Dr. Jain's words. Because I recognize this, I've tried to actively ignore the forecast. Yet I cannot deny that my foray into that quiet, reverent, incense-filled world was both intoxicating and comforting. The ritual of it and most especially the conviction, the sense that real answers could be coaxed from celestial bodies, from bodies other than our own—this is why the experience was so seductive.

The process of choosing, as we saw in the later chapters, can be confusing and exhausting. There is so much to consider, so much to bear responsibility for, it's no surprise we sometimes long for an easier path. Choice draws power from its promise of almost infinite possibility, but what is possible is also what is unknown. We can use choice to shape our lives, but we still face great uncertainty. Indeed, choice has power precisely because there is uncertainty; if the future were predetermined, choice wouldn't be worth much. But to face that future equipped only with the complicated tool of choice scares us as much as it excites us. Every so often, it might be a relief to get advance news of how a decision might turn out.

If you read *Choose Your Own Adventure* books as a child, you probably recall what a thrill it was to play the protagonist and influence the narrative through your choices. And part of the fun was the cheating. When you had to pick from three options to continue the story, occasionally you'd take a peek at the consequences of each one before making a choice. It was great to control your actions, but you didn't want to end up in a dragon's belly because of them. A few wrong turns were fine—you could always go back—but the final goal was to make it all the way, to win! As adults, we write our lives through choice, we have more control than ever before, but we still have a desire to win. Sometimes we'd like to be readers rather than writers, to cheat by turning to later pages, to read ahead in the story of our lives.

Astrology and other methods of divination offer a way to do just that. However, in order to view fuzzy excerpts of the future, we must relinquish some choice. The more we want to see, the more choice we must surrender. Some people are willing to make a substantial exchange, some less, some none at all. Thus, we each develop a personal equation to account for the trajectory of life: x amount of choice, y of chance, z of destiny. Perhaps some of us have found more variables. I cannot say what your equation ought to be, but even after experiencing the charms of astrology, I believe that choice—though it can be finicky, unwieldy, and demanding—is ultimately the most powerful determinant of where we go and how we get there. Still, facing a future of ever-expanding choice, you may very well wish for a map of some sort, at least a few signposts along the way, and you wouldn't be the only one.

———

Rachel, the 28-year-old daughter of a friend I've known for years, had dreamt for much of her life of becoming a lawyer. She excelled at mock trials in high school. In college, her favorite professor remarked on her nimble legal mind. Rachel worked hard and gained acceptance to a prestigious law school. Her grandmother had dreamt of becoming a librarian while she worked in a factory, and her mother had dreamt of becoming a professor while she worked as a nurse; Rachel would be the first woman in her family to fulfill her professional dreams.

While she was in law school, Rachel married a fellow law student. After graduation, she was often asked whether they wanted children, and she said yes…someday. For now, she intended to focus fully on her career. But to her surprise, Rachel found she was pregnant only a few months into her new job as a first-year associate. Now she had to decide whether or not to continue the pregnancy. She had made many choices in her life, but this one was accompanied by the biggest, reddest CHOICE sign she had ever seen. This was due less to her personal feelings than to the fact that the word "choice," at least in America, has come to be so strongly associated with the abortion debate. It was as if, being a woman, she should consider this choice to be the most significant of her life. For her, however, though the choice *was* important, it didn't precipitate a crisis of conscience. She was concerned first and foremost with the practical questions.

How would having a child now rather than later affect her career? In what ways would her life and her relationship with her husband change? Was she physically, emotionally, and financially prepared to be a parent? Not only would her set of choices be considerably altered by having a child, particularly so early in her career, she would have to take responsibility for that child's choices, too. Becoming a lawyer had not been easy, but she had been able to proceed step by step on a straight and solid path. Becoming a parent seemed far more complicated.

On one level, Rachel's dilemma was that of any prospective parent. Who wouldn't have doubts in such a situation? But Rachel recognized that there was a dimension to the problem that was specific to women. Her husband was also a young, ambitious lawyer, but he didn't have quite as many concerns about how a child would affect his professional life. The two of them had always had an equal partnership, one in which traditional gender roles didn't matter much. She knew he would do his share, if not more, of the chores and the parenting. Yet, though a child would change both their lives, it was unlikely that his commitment to work would be questioned as a result. She could easily imagine that his boss and colleagues would slap his back and propose a celebratory drink upon hearing the news. At her job, people would be far more likely to wonder how long she planned to stick around if she was already pregnant. Her husband would be seen as the lawyer who happened also to be having a child; she would be seen as the mother playing at law, unserious and intellectually compromised, as though her former self had been replaced by a simpler clone. It would be very difficult to hold on to the identity that she had constructed with great effort, and maybe it was this, more than anything else, that made the choice so daunting.

In comparison to her mother and grandmother, Rachel enjoyed greater freedom at work and at home. Doors that had been firmly shut to women of earlier generations were open to her. That said, she did not feel particularly welcome to walk through every one of those doors. Though she was *free from* certain social restrictions, she was not *free to* take full advantage of the new opportunities, at least not without substantial cost. In spite of having the same education and abilities as her husband, she knew she could not make the same choices as he did and expect the same results. In certain domains, her choices would always be more complicated and more fraught. That she had these choices at all was certainly an improvement, but at this particular point in her life, she realized it was not enough, not nearly.

Then again, beneath the trepidation, she had discovered a strong current of joy; the pregnancy was a surprise but not an unwelcome one. Though she could ignore this emotion in favor of a strictly reasoned approach, she felt that would be no better than choosing motherhood only because it was expected of her. She knew women who had been in a similar position, and some had chosen to become mothers, some had not. As far as she could tell, whatever their decisions, the ones who had ended up most happy had given consideration to both their instinctive and their calculated responses. For Rachel, this meant acknowledging all the ways, positive and negative, in which having a child would affect her. She had to be clear-eyed about the unfair constraints that would most likely be imposed on her and the extra sacrifices she would have to make. With all this in mind, did she still want a child right now? She decided yes, she did, and then she braced herself for the challenges ahead.

Rachel's story is the story of every woman whose choices are limited without good reason. More broadly, it is also the story of anyone who has found that after the most visible obstacles to choice are removed, a lot of other things still get in the way. At its best, choice is a means by which we can resist the people and the systems that seek to exert control over us. But choice itself can become oppressive when we insist that it is equally available to all. It can become an excuse for ignoring inequities that stem from gender or class or ethnic differences, for example, because one can blithely say, "Oh, but they had a choice! We all have choices." When we begin to use choice as a strategy for evading the problem rather than finding the best solution, we know we've gone wrong.

There's no quick fix for the imbalances of power that frequently place practical limitations on choice, but one step in the right direction would be to encourage more public conversation about those limitations. It is tempting to promote choice as the great equalizer—after all, that's what so many dreams, including the American one, are built on. As we saw in the very first chapter, the promise of choice, the language of choice, and even the mere illusion of choice have the power to motivate and uplift us. We should not, however, take this to mean that faith, hope, and rhetoric alone are sufficient. Like the swimming rats in Richter's experiment, we can survive for only so long without solid ground beneath our feet; if the choices aren't real, sooner or later we will go under. It's important, therefore, that we examine our assumptions about choice and that we openly discuss how, when, and why it falls short. Only then can we begin to realize the full potential of choice. Such a conversation is also likely to raise questions about what choice is and whether we're willing to defend it to the very end.

Jane Aiken Hodge, daughter of Pulitzer Prize–winning poet Conrad Aiken, had spent most of her 91 years living in the United Kingdom. Though diagnosed with mild forms of leukemia and hypertension, she was in good health for her age. She had written more than 40 books over the course of her 60-year career. Hodge specialized in historical-romance novels—she called them "my silly books"—but also wrote literary biography and published a title on Jane Austen, whose work she had studied while a student at Oxford. In addition to her success as a writer, she had enjoyed a long second marriage and a close relationship with her daughters and their families. All told, Hodge had achieved in her personal and professional lives what many of us only dream of.

When she died at her home in Sussex on June 17, 2009, it was a shock to her family and friends. During the weeks that followed, and as details about her death emerged, it became clear that Hodge had arranged a neat exit. She was discovered, for instance, with a DNR card in her pocket; had previously left instructions with her physician that she was not to be resuscitated under any circumstances;

and had even written a letter, found beside her body, explaining that she had planned and committed the suicide entirely on her own. In the note she also revealed that she had been hoarding pills for years for this very purpose. Her patient, methodical preparations suggest that she knew full well what she was doing, that impulsiveness was not to blame. It seems she carefully and reflectively *chose* to die.

Yet one hesitates to speak of suicide as a choice because one usually conceives of it as an act of desperation, somehow forced rather than freely chosen. In his essay "The Myth of Sisyphus" Albert Camus writes, "Judging whether life is or is not worth living amounts to answering the fundamental question of philosophy." Hodge's suicide was her answer: Life is no longer worth living. But is this an answer we can accept as a choice rather than a cognitive glitch? (I should clarify that when I say "accept," I don't mean that it's up to us to approve or reject her actions on moral grounds. From my perspective, we have no business labeling the suicide "right" or "wrong." Rather, I'm wondering where and how we draw a line between choice and not-choice.)

One could argue that life inherently has worth since you cannot put a price on it (unless you work in the insurance industry). So when someone weighs reasons to live against reasons not to live, she is actually trying to decide how much *value* life has. It is this assigning of value that can seem like an error in the brain. According to Camus:

> Living, naturally, is never easy. You continue making the gestures commanded by existence for many reasons, the first of which is habit. Dying voluntarily implies that you have recognized, even instinctively, the ridiculous character of that habit, the absence of any profound reason for living, the insane character of that daily agitation, and the uselessness of suffering.

Whether or not you can ever see suicide as a choice depends on how you feel about the *recognition* that Camus describes. If you can imagine this recognition as a deep emotional, intellectual, perhaps spiritual realization, then it may seem truly possible to choose death. If, on the other hand, the recognition appears to you to be the result of depression or some other mental illness, then you might argue that one cannot be of sound mind *and* choose to die.

As we saw in chapter 7, we do make life-or-death decisions for other people. When the decision is viewed as a choice rather than a matter of fate, it is often agonizing. Maybe the reason some of us balk at the idea of choosing death is that it's simply too painful to think of as a choice. Maybe we would rather believe that such things are beyond our control and comprehension. For others, however, the thought of choosing death might be comforting, a logical extension to making choices throughout life. The year before she died, in an interview for the local newspaper, Hodge said, "At 90, I still enjoy and run my life with some help from family and friends. However, I would be much happier if I knew I had a reliable exit strategy planned for the dubious future." She wanted to exercise control over her life *and* her death, to be as prepared as possible to face whatever came her way. Having written a novel about terminal care, she must have been acutely aware of the problems one confronts near the end of life and of the ways in which one's choices gradually decrease and then disappear. As a writer, she may have considered it particularly important to end her story on her own terms; if choice is a way of writing our lives, it can also be a way of writing the end of our lives. Perhaps it is said best by her father's poetry. Conrad Aiken's poem "When You Are Not Surprised" concludes with the suggestion that when the world ceases to surprise you, "then welcome death and be by death benignly welcomed / and join again in the ceaseless know-nothing / from which you awoke to the first surprise." If one sees death as a return to where one came from, perhaps it becomes much easier to accept it as the final choice.

––––––

We tell stories about choice for many reasons. We want to learn or teach; we want to know others or have them know us; we want to understand how we got from there to here. We take the choices that for some reason or other have lit up like stars across our memory, and we chart our journey by them. This is why I won the race. This is how I survived. This is when everything changed. Through these stories we assert that what we do matters. By speaking choice, we find a way to navigate the strange waters of life, maybe even appreciate their unpredictable movement.

Consider how Camus presents the myth of Sisyphus, whose punishment in the underworld is to repeat the action of rolling a rock up a mountain, watching it roll down, and then rolling it up again. Sisyphus, a man who loved life, seems condemned to spend eternity engaged in a futile task, but when he walks back down after reaching the top, he has time to reflect. His situation is absurd, but "his fate belongs to him. His rock is his thing.... At that subtle moment when man glances back over his life, Sisyphus returning toward his rock, in that slight pivoting he contemplates that series of unrelated actions which becomes his fate, created by him, combined under his memory's eye and soon sealed by death." In our brief labor in *this* world, we can move the rock by, and with the aid of, choice. If, as Camus claims, "[o]ne must imagine Sisyphus happy" because "[t]he struggle itself towards the heights is enough to fill a man's heart," we can either sulk at the bottom of the mountain or reach for the heights and for happiness through choice.

In other words, choosing helps us create our lives. We make choices and are in turn made by them. Science can assist us in becoming more skillful choosers, but at its core, choice remains an art. To gain the most from it, we must embrace uncertainty and contradiction. It does not look the same to all eyes, nor can everyone agree on its purpose. Sometimes choice pulls us to itself, other times it repels us. We use it without exhausting it, and the more we uncover, the more we find still hidden. We cannot take full measure of it. Therein lies its power, its mystery, and its singular beauty.

Acknowledgments

During the nerve-racking period of my career leading up to my review for tenure, my friend and colleague Eric Abrahamson sought to allay my fears of failure with the following allegory.

"What do you want with tenure, anyway?" he asked me. "Being an academic is kind of like being a rat, stuck in a cage, pedaling away on a stationary bicycle. You pedal harder and faster all the time, not moving an inch, until eventually you're pedaling so furiously that you're absolutely convinced that you're about to die. If you're lucky, someone notices your pedaling and likes the way you make those wheels spin, so they open your cage door in the nick of time, just as you're about to collapse. Miracle upon miracles, you can now breathe. And not only that, but you're allowed to dismount from your bicycle, step outside of your cage, take a deep breath of fresh air, and have a good look at the outside world, which you haven't done in years. This is what getting tenure is like. But after some time you turn around, go back into your cage, and return to your bicycle, the only difference now being that you can pedal at a much more leisurely and thoughtful pace."

So when I ventured out of the cage and looked with bewilderment at the many possible paths that lay before me, I had the good fortune to run into Malcolm Gladwell. "What should I do next?" I asked him. "Write a book," he advised. It was as simple—and as staggeringly difficult—as that. This book is in part a result of my desire to linger awhile more outside the "cage" and to use what I learned within the "bars" to illuminate the world that lies beyond them. Thank you to my colleagues at the Columbia Business School for showing infinite support, patience, and encouragement over the course of this endeavor, and graciously allowing me the time to concentrate outside of the "cage."

In writing this book, I discovered that despite having spent more than a decade studying how people choose, I knew very little indeed. This book proved a far greater challenge than my dissertation or any of the various papers and grants I have worked on, and I learned more than I ever anticipated along the way.

I hope that you, the reader, have enjoyed the results of my efforts, and that this book has indeed managed to shed some light on many of the choices you make in your life. This matters because the story of choice belongs not only to those who study it but to all of us, and I was amazingly fortunate in the quantity and quality of fellow choosers who so generously lent me their wisdom, experience, and opinion. They wrote this book, too.

First, I owe a debt of gratitude to the numerous experts I consulted along the way, who helped to fill in the gaps where my own knowledge was lacking.

Kristen Jule, Lisa Leaver, Lauren Leotti, and Martin Seligman helped me to better understand the research on the nature of choice.

Although I had heard about my parents' wedding in bits and pieces over the years, my aunt Rani Chadha generously provided a detailed description of my parents' wedding and Sikh traditions more generally.

A number of scholars offered insights on the history of freedom and choice throughout the globe, including: Alex Cummings, Dennis Dalton, Eric Foner, Jon Hanson, William Leach, Orlando Patterson, Peter Stearns, and Jude Webre.

I was fortunate to meet with a number of political scientists, sociologists, and economists in Eastern Europe and China, who helped to inform my understanding of the way communism influenced people's reality and views about what constitutes fair choice. So many people were incredibly helpful. Special thanks to: Olga Kuznia, Carsten Sprenger, and Sergey Yakovlev in Russia; Svitlana Chernyshova, Mykhajlo Kolisnyk, Dmitry Krakovich, Victor Oksenyuk, Volodimir Paniotto, Yehven Pentsak, Pavlo Sheremeta, Inna Volosevych, and Dmytro Yablonovskyy in Ukraine; Maria Dabrowska, Ewa Gucwa-Lesny, Dominika Maison, and Joanna Sokotowska in Poland; and Kai-Fu Lee and Ningyu Tang in China. In addition, Elena Reutskaja deserves particular acknowledgment for her help in coordinating and conducting much of this research with me.

Quite a number of people in the fashion industry allowed me a sneak peek into what they do and how we end up knowing what to wear. Many thanks to David Wolfe, Ana Lucia Bernal, Pat Tunksy, Abby Doneger, and the rest of the Doneger Group; all the folks at the Color Association of America, particularly Leslie Harrington and Margaret Walch; Rachel Crumbley; Sherri Donghia; Steven Kolb and the Council of Fashion Designers of America; Michael Macko; Jerry Scupp; The Trybus Group, especially Larry Drew and Sal Cesarani; and everyone at Faith Popcorn. Thanks also to Snowden Wright and Aaron Levine for accompanying me at the various presentations and meetings, offering their observations, and conducting background research on the consumer retail sector. In addition, I'm grateful to Henri-Lee Stalk for contributing much of the background research on a variety of topics, and for raising the questions that led to my study of the fashion industry.

In an unexpected turn, I learned a great deal about the art of choosing through the study of jazz. Much credit is due to my colleague Paul Ingram, for challenging me to give a talk on jazz and the multiple choice problem at Columbia's Center for Jazz Studies.

Baffled by this task, I spoke with a number of experts, including George Lewis and Wynton Marsalis, and found that this foray changed my understanding of the way choice can work in our lives. I owe a great deal to them, as well as to Carolyn Appel and Jude Webre, for providing further lessons on jazz.

I am also grateful to Atul Gawande, Kristina Orfali, and Peter Ubel for expanding my knowledge on medical decision making.

Second, there are a number of people I must thank for getting me started on the journey of studying choice. A special thanks first and foremost to Judy Kurpis, my high school Commission for the Blind counselor, for encouraging me to go to college, and to Wharton in particular. I wouldn't have done it if not for her.

When I was an undergraduate and struggling to figure out my future, it was John Sabini who first introduced me to the idea that a blind person could run experiments. I still remember nervously asking him if I could participate in his psychology lab in some capacity, and fearing that his silence would go on forever, until he suddenly pounded his desk and said he had it: I would run experiments on whether people would be equally embarrassed after performing a silly task in front of a sighted person as they would in the presence of a blind person. That was the beginning.

Martin Seligman gave me the chance to design and run my own study as an undergraduate, and as such, made clear to me what I was going to do with the rest of my life. He also decided that I needed to go to Stanford for graduate school, to study with Mark Lepper and Amos Tversky. And so I did.

I am indebted to Mark Lepper, who became my doctoral adviser, for all his dedication to mentoring me. Under his tutelage, I formally began my study of choice. He taught me how to think, and how to ask questions. I can never express enough gratitude for all that he did.

Amos Tversky also deserves special mention. Though he died before I finished my doctorate, his research and ideas have influenced my thinking tremendously over the years. In addition, I am enormously grateful to Danny Kahneman for all the time he spent offering insights on the research he did with Tversky, in order to help me understand my own thoughts on choice.

There are so many people who through their work and conversations shaped my thinking over the years. I could easily write a whole book about all of the great scholars in the field. Let me at least offer a special thanks to the following people: Dan Ariely, John Bargh, Jon Baron, Max Bazerman, Roland Benabou, Shlomo Benartzi, Jonah Berger, Colin Camerer, Andrew Caplin, Robert Cialdini, John Dayton, Mark Dean, David Dunning, Carol Dweck, Craig Fox, Dan Gilbert, Tom Gilovich, Chip Heath, Robin Hogarth, Chris Hsee, Shinobu Kitayama, Rakesh Kurana, David Laibson, Jennifer Lerner, Jonathan Levav, Hazel Markus, Barbara Millers, Walter Mischel, Olivia Mitchell, Read Montague, Richard Nisbett, Wolfgang Pessendorfer, Lee Ross, Andrew Schotter, Barry Schwartz, Cass Sunstein, Phil Tetlock, and Richard Thaler.

So much of my thinking was also influenced by my numerous research collaborators over the years, many of whom appear throughout the text in this book. Thank you for putting up with me.

I thank also my first audiences, all of the readers who donated their invaluable time and commentary in serving as sounding boards for the book through countless generations of drafts: Jon Baron, Simona Botti, Dana Carney, Roy Chua, Sanford DeVoe, Sumit Halder, Akhila Iyengar, Radhika Iyengar, Jonah Lehrer, Kristina Orfali, John Payne, Tamar Rudnick, Barry Schwartz, Bill Duggan, Bill Scott, Joanna Scutts, Karen Siegel, and Peter Ubel all saved me from myriad missteps while providing valuable suggestions that pointed me in the right direction.

I may have been the visionary behind this book, but in the end, it is the product of a remarkable collaboration. My assistants were truly invaluable, and I learned so much from all of them. Each brought unique talents into the mix, and together they made a fabulous and powerful combination. Kanika Agrawal played the role of sage adviser, constantly asking the most difficult questions, which also turned out to be the most necessary. When she deemed something interesting, I knew that I had made a real accomplishment. Kate McPike was the great mediator, always able to delve into the heart of the matter and offer the perfect solution to the conundrum of the hour. So many times, she kept the wheels rolling when a stall seemed imminent. Lani Akiko Oshima lent the word wizardry and added countless creative touches that have made the material come alive in ways I never could have imagined. And from beginning 'til end and all over the globe, it was John Remarek who showed truly tireless dedication and devotion to the logic of our arguments and the breadth and depth of our research.

However, I would have had nothing to show for all these contributions were it not for the two people who performed a feat of alchemy by shaping these raw materials into a real, physical book. It was a tremendous honor to work with Jon Karp, my editor at Twelve Publishing; his reputation for being the best in the business precedes him but doesn't even begin to do him justice. His team at Twelve Books has been a great privilege and pleasure to work with. And I have nothing but immense wonder and gratitude for the skills of my agent, Tina Bennett, and for her invaluable guidance, constant encouragement, and tireless work to bring this book to its highest potential. Tina, how can an agent as brilliant and driven as you still manage to be one of the nicest people I've ever met? Amazing.

And above all, to my family—for being there before, during, and after the writing of this book. My father-in-law, N. G. R. Iyengar, in true Dad-like fashion, checked on my progress throughout and constantly reminded me to keep prioritizing. My mother-in-law, Leela Iyengar, provided wonderful and continuous reassurance that everything would turn out the way I hoped. I'm deeply grateful to you both. Thanks also to Tsewang Chodon: It was such an incredible relief to know that I could trust my son and my home to your care while I focused on writing. My sister, Jasmin Sethi, was always available to bounce ideas off of and give comments along the way. Through it all, my mom, Kuldeep Sethi, went above and beyond the call of duty, doing anything and everything she could to smooth the way and offer encouragement. Mom, thanks for always being there.

To my husband, Garud, you deserve a medal for your unflagging patience and support. You put up with so much, including the transformation of our apartment into a book-writing factory and all the time I spent away. I couldn't have done it without you. And finally, to our most important joint creative project—our son, Ishaan. You were the invaluable "youth consultant" who asked every night "What story did you write today?" and listened patiently as I explained. In my efforts to make the stories clear and engaging for you, I inevitably discovered new and better ways to tell them to everyone else. More important, I could always rely on you to dispel all discouragement with a single hug. I love you both more than words can say.

Notes

*In some of the personal stories in which I discuss family and friends, a few names and details have been changed. In the epilogue, Rachel is a composite character.

CHAPTER 1. THE CALL OF THE WILD

The full description of the swimming rats can be found in Richter (1957), which considers its links to humans who die suddenly and of no apparent cause after violating a cultural taboo. For more on this phenomenon, see also Sternberg, E., "Walter B. Cannon and 'Voodoo Death': A Perspective from 60 Years On," *American Journal of Public Health* 92 (10) (2002): 1564–1566. The study of learned helplessness in dogs can be found in Seligman and Maier (1967).

The description of the brain systems involved in choice draws on Berridge and Kringelbach (2008), Bjork and Hommer (2007), Delgado (2007), Ochsner and Gross (2005), and Tricomi et al. (2004). The importance of the striatum and basal ganglia more generally for motivating us to choose can be further seen by the fact that damage to these areas can lead to a condition called "athymhormia," in which individuals retain their intelligence and ability to respond to others but lose the desire to initiate voluntary action of any sort, up to and including self-preservation. For examples, see Verstichel, P., and Larrouy, P., "Drowning Mr. M.," *Scientific American Mind* (2005), http://www.scientificamerican.com/article.cfm?id=drowning-mr-m. The importance of the prefrontal cortex for long-term planning can similarly be seen in the famous story of Phineas Gage, who survived having the frontal lobe of his brain penetrated by an iron rod. In the words of the physician who treated him:

The equilibrium...between his intellectual faculties and animal propensities seems to have been destroyed. He is fitful, irreverent, indulging at times in the grossest profanity (which was not previously his custom), manifesting but little deference for his fellows, impatient of restraint or advice when it conflicts with his desires, at times pertinaciously obstinate, yet capricious and vacillating, devising many plans of future operations, which are no sooner arranged than they are abandoned in turn for others appearing more feasible....In this regard his mind was radically changed, so decidedly that his friends and acquaintances said he was "no longer Gage" [Harlow, J. M., "Recovery from the Passage of an Iron Bar through the Head," *Publications of the Massachusetts Medical Society* 2 (1868): 327–347].

The information on how children's decision-making abilities mature over time comes from Bahn (1986) and Kokis et al. (2002), and the development of the prefrontal cortex is described in Sowell et al. (2001).

The studies on the preference for choice in animals can be found in Catania (1975), Suzuki (1999), and Voss and Homzie (1970), and the corresponding human studies are described in Bown et al. (2003) and Lewis et al. (1990).

The accounts of animals' attempted zoo escapes can be found in Marshall (2007), as well as "Berlin bear's breakout bid fails" (2004) and "Orangutan escapes pen at US zoo" (2008) from BBC News. The harmful effects of captivity for animals is drawn from Clubb and Mason (2003), Clubb et al. (2008), Kalueff et al. (2007), Kifner (1994), and Wilson (2006). For more on the unfortunately large body of research into how confinement can be used to intentionally induce stress in animals (e.g., as a prelude to testing anti-ulcer medications), see Pare, W. P., and Glavin, G. B., "Restraint Stress in Biomedical Research: A Review," *Neuroscience and Biobehavioral Reviews* 10 (3) (1986): 339–370, and its 1994 update in the same source (18 [2], 223–249).

The details of the stress response and its potentially harmful effects for humans can be found in the classic Selye (1946), and a complete listing of publications based on data from the second phase of the Whitehall studies is maintained by the University College London Department of Epidemiology and Public Health, available online at http://www.ucl.

ac.uk/whitehallII/publications/index.htm. The findings on the connection between well-being and control at work have been summarized in
the booklet "Work, Stress, and Health," edited by Dr. Jane E. Ferrie and
published on behalf of the UK Council of Civil Service Unions and the
Cabinet Office, which is also available online at http://www.ucl.ac.uk/
whitehallII/findings/Whitehallbooklet.pdf. The fact that other minor but
pervasive stressors can have a cumulative impact comparable to larger but
less frequent ones is demonstrated by DeLongis et al. (1988) and Ames et
al. (2001).

Evidence for how perceptions of control impact health on the general
level can be found in Friedman and Booth-Kewley (1987). Recent research
has found that perceiving control activates the ventral medial prefrontal
cortex, inhibiting the body's response to stress, as seen in Maier, S., Amat,
J., Baratta, M., Paul, E., and Watkins, L., "Behavioral control, the medial
prefrontal cortex, and resilience," *Dialogues in Clinical Neuroscience* 8 (4)
(2006): 353–374.

The study of nursing home patients is described in Langer and Rodin
(1976). One important caveat to the Langer and Rodin findings is addressed
in Schultz, R., and Hanusa, B., "Long-term effects of control and predict-
ability-enhancing interventions: Findings and ethical issues," *Journal of
Personality and Social Psychology* 36 (11) (1978): 1194–1201. The researchers
tracked the participants of a similar retirement home study over the course
of several years and found that in the long run, perceiving additional control
and then having it taken away (once the study had concluded and their daily
routines returned to the status quo) was worse than never having perceived
that control at all. Also, the technique of improving well-being through the
provision of relatively minor choices has a parallel in the animal welfare
practice of "environmental enrichment." Zoos increasingly attempt to not
only replicate animals' physical environment, but also to give them opportunities to exercise their instincts (e.g., freezing apples in a block of ice or putting
food in a simple puzzle box so that animals actively obtain their meals rather
than passively receiving them, providing toys to satisfy their curiosity and
hunting instincts, and allowing them to interact with others of their kind).

For an overview of the research on how perceiving control over one's
life benefits men with HIV and AIDS, see Taylor et al. (2002). The Royal
Marsden Hospital study is described in Watson et al. (1999), but unlike the

generally consistent findings for HIV/AIDS, the extent to which maintaining hope materially benefits cancer patients can vary quite dramatically from study to study; see Turner-Cobb (2002) for details, including the consequences of stress and depression, which are linked to feeling powerless. The specific control beliefs of breast cancer patients and their positive psychological effects are drawn from Taylor et al. (1984).

CHAPTER II. A STRANGER IN STRANGE LANDS

The figures on Unitarian Universalists are from "Engaging Our Theological Diversity," by the Unitarian Universalist Association Commission on Appraisal (2005), available online at http://www25.uua.org/coa/TheoDiversity/. My study on religion and happiness was published under my maiden name, as Sethi and Seligman (1993). Other studies have supported the positive association between religiousness and happiness, e.g., Witter, R. A., Stock, W. A., Okun, M., and Haring, M., "Religion and subjective well-being in adulthood: A quantitative synthesis," *Review of Religious Research* 26 (4) (1985): 332–342. Interestingly, the association was stronger for frequency of religious attendance than strength of religious belief, which raises the possibility that the majority of these benefits don't come from a belief in a God or gods per se, but rather from the increased social support, assistance in exercising self-control, and guidance in life that membership in a religious group typically provides. For a lighthearted look at disentangling the two, see Jacobs, A. J., *The Year of Living Biblically: One Man's Humble Quest to Follow the Bible as Literally as Possible,* Simon & Schuster (2007). Many anecdotal reports also indicate that fully secular but highly structured environments, such as military service, can have positive "character-building" effects on individuals as well.

Descartes' iconic quote originally appeared in French (*je pense donc je suis*) in his *Discourse on Method* (1637), and in its more famous Latin form (*cogito ergo sum*) in his *Principles of Philosophy* (1644). Mill's quote comes from his essay *On Liberty* (1859). A representative overview of early communist philosophies can be found in Marx and Engels (1972).

The connection between individualism and democracy, and between collectivism and communism, is seen by many as evidence that the value for freedom is uniquely a product of Western individualistic culture, while collectivistic cultures are tolerant of authoritarianism and oppression. I would argue that this is a gross oversimplification of the issue, and that while the status of freedom as the *primary* social value is a Western invention, the value for freedom itself is cross-cultural. For further reading see Patterson, O., *Freedom, Volume I: Freedom in the Making of Western Culture*, Basic Books (1992), as well as Sen, A., *Development as Freedom*, Anchor (2000), pp. 223–240. Section VII of this chapter also addresses the ways in which the concept of freedom can vary across cultures, which can easily be perceived as a lack of freedom by outsiders.

The studies that ranked countries by level of individualism (and other dimensions) are described in Hofstede (1980), but the specific values given are drawn from Hofstede's most current data, available online at http://www.geert-hofstede.com/hofstede_dimensions.php. This pattern is supported by the studies described in Triandis (1995), and both Hofstede and Triandis provide information on the factors that influence individuals' and cultures' tendencies toward individualism or collectivism. For those interested in learning where they personally stand on the continuum from individualism to collectivism, a scale can be found in the index of Triandis's book.

When discussing marriage, it is important to distinguish between, arranged marriage and forced marriage, defined as one or both spouses' being married without their consent (which includes marriages involving minor children). Forced marriage was common historically but is almost universally outlawed today as a violation of human rights, though it still occurs in regions where enforcement is lax. All forced marriages are, by definition, arranged by a third party of some sort, but the majority of arranged marriages are not forced.

The story of Mumtaz Mahal and the monument built in her honor is described in Koch, E., *The Complete Taj Mahal: And the Riverfront Gardens of Agra*, Thames & Hudson Ltd. (2006). The Sumerian poem referred to is "A balbale to Inana and Dumuzid," translated as part of the Electronic Text Corpus of Sumerian Literature at Oxford University, and is available online at http://www-etcsl.orient.ox.ac.uk/section4/tr40802.htm. The two biblical references are to Deuteronomy 25:5–10 and the Song of Songs 4:9 respectively, and the quote for the second comes from the New International Version.

Capellanus's quote can be found in Capellanus (1969), and a further example of the disconnect between love and marriage can be seen in the following quote from Michel de Montaigne's "Upon Some Verses of Virgil," in his *Essays* (1580): "A good marriage, if such there be, rejects the company and conditions of love. It tries to reproduce those of friendship." The story of the change in social attitudes toward marriage is drawn from Coontz (2005).

The comparison of love and arranged matches in India is described in Gupta and Singh (1982). Shaw's quote on marriage can be found in Shaw (1911), and some neurological findings that support it are described in Aron, A., Fisher, H., Mashek, D., Strong, G., Haifang, L., and Brown, L., "Reward, motivation, and emotion systems associated with early-stage intense romantic love," *Journal of Neurophysiology* 94 (2005): 327–337. Aron and Fisher's most recent work, finding that 10 percent of couples (dubbed "swans" by the researchers) can maintain these feelings toward one another for decades, has yet to be published but is described in Harlow and Montague (2009). Fortunately for the other 90 percent, passion isn't necessarily replaced by apathy when it fades, but may instead develop into a calmer but more enduring form of "companionate love." For more on all the different meanings "I love you" can have, see Sternberg, R. J., "A triangular theory of love," *Psychological Review* 93 (2) (1986): 119–135. The statistic on the prevalence of arranged marriages in India is from Bumiller (1990), and the statistics on college students' willingness to marry without love are from Slater (2006).

My studies with the children were published in Iyengar and Lepper (1999). Interestingly, a corresponding pattern of results was later independently discovered in brain activity by Zhu, Y., Zhang, L., Fan, J., and Hana, S., "Neural basis of cultural influence on self-representation," *NeuroImage* 34 (2007): 1310–1316. American students displayed activation in the medial prefrontal cortex and anterior cingulated cortex only when making self-relevant judgments, while Chinese participants also showed activity in these brain areas when making judgments about their mothers, but not about strangers.

The culture clash at Sealed Air is shown in Smith (1994). Further information about the challenges faced by the company and their response can be found in Katzenbach, J., and Smith, D., *The Wisdom of Teams: Creating the High-Performance Organization*, Harper Business (1994).

The fish study is described in Masuda and Nisbett (2001), and the image is reproduced with the permission of the American Psychological Association and Richard Nisbett.

The quote "God helps those who help themselves" is in fact by Algernon Sydney, from his *Discourses Concerning Government* (1698), although the theme can be traced as far back as Sophocles' "Heaven ne'er helps the men who will not act," from *Fragment* 288 (as translated by Edward Hayes Plumptre), demonstrating the long history of this idea in Western culture. The Bhagavad Gita quote is from book 2 verse 47, and is an amalgam of several translations.

The study on control attributions by Olympic athletes is Kitayama et al. (1997), and the study of news coverage is Menon et al. (1999), while differences in perceived control more generally can be found in Mahler et al. (1981) and Parsons and Schneider (1974). For information on how these differing beliefs affect people's responses to events in their lives, see Weisz, J., Rothbaum, M., and Blackburn, C., "Standing out and standing in: The psychology of control in America and Japan," *American Psychologist* 39 (9) (1984): 955–969.

Some of the findings from my study with Citibank employees are reported in DeVoe and Iyengar (2004), while the rest come from the currently unpublished manuscript "Rethinking autonomy as an incentive: The persistent influence of culture within a multinational organization," also with Sanford DeVoe.

Jennings's reaction to the fall of the Berlin wall is from Shales (1989), while the public's quotes are from the article "Freedom!" in *Time* magazine (1989). The poll revealing current nostalgia for the wall is described in Connolly (2007).

Another famous analysis of freedom as a bipartite value can be found in Isaiah Berlin's essay "Two Concepts of Liberty," published in Berlin, I., *Four Essays on Liberty*, Oxford University Press (1969). Whereas Fromm ultimately argues for a synthesis of the two elements, Berlin is more critical of the abuses that may occur under the guise of curtailing people's negative liberties (synonymous with "freedom from") in order to promote their positive liberties ("freedom to").

The statistics on differences in economic policy between the U.S. and Europe are drawn from Alesina et al. (2001). Regarding outcomes, the GDP and Gini index figures (as of June 2009) are from the CIA World Factbook.

The current numbers are available online at https://www.cia.gov/library/publications/the-world-factbook/rankorder/2004rank.html and https://www.cia.gov/library/publications/the-world-factbook/fields/2172.html. The relative number of billionaires in the U.S. was calculated based on Kroll et al. (2009). The findings on income mobility in the U.S. relative to Sweden and Germany are from Björklund and Jäntti (1997) and Couch and Dunn (1997) respectively. The projections of American ancestry in 2042 are from Bernstein and Edwards (2008), and Huntington's thesis on the clash of civilizations is described in Huntington (1996).

CHAPTER III. SONG OF MYSELF

The increase in average marriage age can be found in the Census Bureau's *Statistical Abstracts of the United States: 1997,* and the characterization of twixters is from Grossman (2005).

The analysis of Franklin's principles can be found in Weber (1905), while the principles themselves are from Franklin (2007). The caveats attached to Ford's $5 wage are described in Peterson (1988), while the story of Schmidt is quoted in a condensed form from Taylor (1911), pages 23–25. The full version is considerably longer and more demeaning, which Taylor justifies by noting that such an approach is effective on the "mentally sluggish type." Emerson's various quotes throughout this chapter are all drawn from his essay "On Self-Reliance," in Emerson (1847). The praise for his works comes from Oliver Wendell Holmes, as related in Cheever (2006). Carol's excoriation of small-town life is from page 265 of Lewis (1921).

For more information on the cultural transition centered on the 1950s, see Anderson (1995), Marchand (1986), Steigerwald (2008), and Susman (1984), in particular pages 271–285, the essay "Personality and the Making of Twentieth-Century Culture." The statistics on mobility are from Tarver (1992), while those on religion come from the Pew Forum on Religion & Public Life, available online at http://pewforum.org/docs/?DocID=409. Nicholas Rose's quote is from page 87 of *Powers of Freedom.*

The tendency for people to find supposedly personalized but actually general descriptions highly accurate is known as either the Barnum effect, due to its frequent use by showman P. T. Barnum, or the Forer effect, in reference to the rather bluntly titled Forer, B. R., "The fallacy of personal validation: A classroom demonstration of gullibility," *Journal of Abnormal and Social Psychology* 44 (1) (1949): 118–123. The first study using the dot estimator paradigm is described in Leonardelli and Brewer (2001), and the second in Leonardelli (1998). Further information on the better-than-average effect can be found in Alicke and Govorun (2005); the source of the Lake Wobegon moniker is Keillor's long-running radio program *A Prairie Home Companion*. For further reading, see Kruger, J., "Lake Wobegon be gone! The 'below-average effect' and the egocentric nature of comparative ability judgments," *Journal of Personality and Social Psychology* 77 (1999): 221–223.

The finding that people see themselves as more independent than average is from Pronin et al. (2007), and the comic illustrating this point is entitled "Sheeple," from the online comic series *XKCD* by Randall Munroe, available online at http://xkcd.com/610/. The related finding that people see themselves as less similar to others than they see others as similar to them is from Srull and Gaelick (1983).

My studies on optimal uniqueness in names and clothing are published in Iyengar and Ames (2005). For a broader illustration of a preference for moderate uniqueness in names, see Madrigal, A., "Why your baby's name will sound like everyone else's," *Wired Science* (2009), http://www.wired.com/wiredscience/2009/05/babynames. Another interesting example is the Hit Song Science service, which claims to be able to predict a song's popularity by how similar it is to past hits on a number of underlying musical parameters. The program's accuracy hasn't been scientifically tested to my knowledge, but it has received favorable attention from members of the music industry and reportedly predicted the success of contemporary jazz artist Norah Jones, who has won nine Grammy Awards and sold 16 million albums to date. More information is available on the company's website, http://uplaya.com/.

Donne's famous quote comes from "Meditation XVII," in *Devotions Upon Emergent Occasions* (1624), also the source of "never send to know for whom the bell tolls; it tolls for thee."

The Bennington study and its follow-ups are described in detail in Alwin et al. (1991), while the students' quotes are taken from Newcomb (1958). The classic work on cognitive dissonance is Festinger (1957), and for further reading I recommend Cooper, J., *Cognitive Dissonance: 50 Years of a Classic Theory*, Sage (2007). Elliot and Devine (1994) is a relatively recent example of the numerous counterattitudinal essay studies. Not all instances of conformity will lead to dissonance and attitude shift toward the options in question. Asch's famous group influence studies are examples in which participants knew the answer to be obviously incorrect but conformed due to implicit group pressure, as described in Asch, S. E., "Effects of group pressure upon the modification and distortion of judgment," in Guetzkow, H., ed., *Groups, Leadership and Men*, Carnegie Press (1951). External influences are more likely to be internalized when the correct answer is uncertain; for a classic example in perception, see Sherif, M., "A study of some social factors in perception," *Archives of Psychology* 27 (187) (1935): 23–46.

Colbert's roast of Bush is discussed in Sternbergh (2006). His performance has been posted in its entirety to the video-sharing site YouTube: http://www.youtube.com/view_play_list?p=8E181BDAEE8B275B.

My study of recent graduates' priorities is described in Wells and Iyengar (2005), and the study of group ordering behavior is described in Ariely and Levav (2000). The inverse relationship between utility and identity significance is from Berger and Heath (2007), while the bracelet study is from Berger and Heath (2008). Chip Heath and his brother Dan also deserve credit for the melody-tapping exercise described in this section, which is from their book *Made to Stick: Why Some Ideas Survive and Others Die* (Random House, 2007).

See Kenny and DePaulo (1993) for a review of our generally poor abilities to perceive what others think of us, and Krueger (2003) for more on the processes underlying them. On the bright side, recent research has found that people are aware they show different facets of themselves to different classes of people (e.g., parents vs. friends), and do a good job of predicting the resulting differences in how they are perceived, as described in Carlson, E., and Furr, M., "Evidence of differential meta-accuracy: People understand the different impressions they make," *Psychological Science* 20 (8) (2009): 1033–1039. The facts on perceiving romantic attraction and humor come from a series of studies I conducted with participants in speed-dating sessions. These specific findings are drawn from "Through the looking-glass self: The effects of trait observability and consensuality on self-knowledge," an unpublished manuscript being prepared in collaboration with Alexandra Suppes, but other findings from this investigation have been published in Fisman, R., Iyengar, S. S., Kamenica, E., and Simonson, I., "Gender differences in mate selection: Evidence from a speed dating experiment," *Quarterly Journal of Economics* 121 (2) (2006): 673–697, and in Fisman, R., Iyengar, S. S., Kamenica, E., and Simonson, I., "Racial preferences in dating: Evidence from a speed dating experiment," *Review of Economic Studies* 75 (1) (2008): 117–132.

The numbers on the prevalence of multirater feedback come from Edwards and Ewen (1996). The finding that self-enhancement can backfire at work is described in Anderson et al. (2008), and Swann et al. (2003) provides a review of the many studies showing we personally prefer others to see us similarly to how we see ourselves.

Putnam acknowledges that social capital may not be disappearing, merely changing forms, but these new forms may have problems of their own, as observed by Cass Sunstein in his book *Republic.com*, Princeton University Press (2001). Thanks to the connecting power of the Internet, our interests, hobbies, and beliefs can be tailored to a more specific level than previously possible. However, the ability to self-select the information we're exposed to may lead to an "echo chamber" effect in which groups with different attitudes become ever more extreme and isolated from one another as they seek out information that confirms their current beliefs and avoid that which challenges them. A relatively mild example of this effect can be seen in a survey by the Program on International Policy Attitudes that found 80 percent of FOX News viewers held at least one misconception about the Iraq war (e.g., that clear ties between Saddam Hussein and the al Qaeda terrorist network had been found, compared to just 23 percent of PBS/NPR viewers). The PIPA report is available online at http://www. worldpublicopinion.org/pipa/pdf/oct03/IraqMedia_Oct03_rpt.pdf.

CHAPTER IV. SENSES AND SENSIBILITY

Dr. Seuss is the pen name of Theodor Geisel, and *Oh, the Places You'll Go!* was the last book he published before his death in 1991. Its continued popularity is reported in Blais et al. (2007).

While I discuss the automatic and reflective systems primarily in terms of judgment and choice, they are equally important in controlling action. Engaging in a philosophical debate while walking down the street requires both systems, the automatic to keep from tripping over our own feet and the reflective to keep our arguments from doing the same. What's more, an initially reflective activity like driving a car can become largely automatic with sufficient practice. The terminology of "automatic" and "reflective," also used in Thaler and Sunstein (2008), is from Dennett (1997). These systems are also referred to by a variety of other names in the scientific literature, including the "hot" and "cool" systems, "heuristic" and "analytic" processing, and the no-frills "System 1" and "System 2." For further reading on these systems, see Stanovich, K. E., *What Intelligence Tests Miss: The Psychology of Rational Thought*, Yale University Press (2009).

The statistics on infidelity are from Guerrero et al. (2007), those on procrastination are from Gallagher et al. (1992), and those on saving are from Helman et al. (2004).

The study on how immediate rewards activate additional areas of the brain is described in McClure et al. (2004a). Mischel's original delay of gratification studies are described in Mischel et al. (1972), and their connections to adjustment and success in adolescence comes from Shoda et al. (1990). The findings that these patterns persist into adulthood have yet to be published and are therefore based on "'Willpower': Decomposing Impulse Control," a PowerPoint and verbal presentation that Walter Mischel gave at Columbia University on October 13, 2009. For more on making the avoidance of temptation automatic, see Reyna, V., and Farley, F., "Is the teen brain too rational?" *Scientific American Reports: Special Edition on Child Development* (2007): 61–67.

The heuristics and biases described in the second section are only the tip of the iceberg when it comes to the forces that affect our decisions. The seminal article on biases is Tversky and Kahneman (1974). Kahneman was awarded the Nobel Prize in Economics in 2002 for his work with Tversky on prospect theory, a description of how people's understanding of risk and probability affects their choices. For more on prospect theory, see Kahneman, D., and Tversky, A., "Prospect Theory: An Analysis of Decision under Risk," *Econometrica* XLVII (1979), 263–291. A broader overview of biases can be found in Plous (1993), and their applications to business contexts are discussed in Bazerman, M., *Judgment in Managerial Decision Making*, Wiley (2005).

For examples of how credit cards increase spending, see Feinberg (1986) and Prelec and Simester (2001). The practice of casinos' using chips instead of cash may also be partially explained by the decreased vividness of spending that it produces. This, along with other tricks like the bells and whistles on slot machines (triggering those automatic positive evaluations that are the basis for our decisions in early childhood but never completely disappear even as adults) and the random nature of payoffs (technically known as a variable reinforcement schedule, which a large body of research has shown to be more motivating than a fixed schedule) help explain why gambling is such a popular pastime despite our aversion to losses.

The story of Goizueta is adapted from Tichy and Cohen (1997), page 27. The study on how gain vs. loss framings affected medical decisions is described in McNeil et al. (1988). For more on how framing is used to deliberately influence behavior, see "The Framing Wars" by Matt Bai, *New York Times*, July 17, 2005, available online at http://www.nytimes.com/2005/07/17/magazine/17DEMOCRATS.html.

The statistics on day trading can be found in "Report of the Day Trading Project Group" (1999) and Surowiecki (1999). The study on home buyers' predictions is from Schiller (2008); it's interesting to note that he and Case found an almost identical pattern of responses during a previous and less dramatic housing bubble, as described in Schiller, R. J., and Case, K., "The behavior of home buyers in boom and post-boom markets," *New England Economic Review*, November–December 1988: 29–46. Finally, one aspect of how the damage of the subprime mortgage crisis was compounded because of a similar error in pattern detection by the financial industry can be seen in Salmon, F., "Recipe for disaster: The formula that killed Wall Street," *Wired Magazine*, February 23, 2009, http://www.wired.com/techbiz/it/magazine/17–03/wp_quant?currentPage=all.

The low effectiveness of interviews at predicting job performance can be found in Hunter and Hunter (1984) and McDaniel et al. (1994), while their continued popularity despite this fact comes from Ahlburg (1992). See Snyder and Swann (1978) for more on how we seek to confirm our expectations in social situations. The pundit study is described in Tetlock (2003), and more details can be found in his book, *Expert Political Judgment: How Good Is It? How Can We Know?* (Princeton University Press, 2005). For similar results with ordinary individuals who aren't publicly on record as supporting a particular worldview, see Lord, C., Ross, L., and Lepper, M., "Biased assimilation and attitude polarization: The effects of prior theories on subsequently considered evidence," *Journal of Personality and Social Psychology* 37 (11) (1979): 2098–2109.

The description of Ekman's lie-detecting abilities is described in Ekman (2001) and supplemented by material from several talks of his that I've attended at conferences and academic institutions over the years. Einstein's quote is from Murphy (1933), and Simon's is from Simon (1992). Especially good examples of how, given sufficient expertise, the automatic system can detect and analyze facts that we remain consciously unaware of can be seen in "The Statue that Didn't Look Right," the introduction to Gladwell (2005), and the Silkworm missile incident in "The Predictions of Dopamine," chapter 2 of Lehrer (2009). The abilities of sports players and airport security officers are described in "Gut Feelings," chapter 1 of Gigerenzer (2007). The level of practice necessary to develop world-class levels of expertise comes from Ericsson et al. (1993).

Franklin's description of moral algebra is quoted from Franklin (1833). A similar version of the Raiffa story, which is most likely apocryphal and has been circulating the halls of academia for decades, is reported in Bazerman, M., *Smart Money Decisions: Why You Do What You Do with Money (and How to Change for the Better)*, Wiley (2001).

The findings on salary and satisfaction from my job search study are from Iyengar et al. (2006). Kahneman's research on happiness is described in Kahneman et al. (2006), and is also referred to later in the section when discussing how we overestimate the strength of our feelings by failing to consider the context in which events occur. Kahneman also includes data on happiness by income bracket from the GSS; the complete data set of all waves, including the ability to conduct analyses online, is available at http://www.norc.org/GSS+Website/. More on the link (or lack of it) between money and happiness, as well as on the difficulties we face in predicting our future happiness, can be found in Gilbert (2007).

Wilson's poster study is described in Wilson et al. (1993), and his dating study is described in Wilson et al. (1984). For further reading on how overthinking a choice can reduce its objective quality relative to experts' judgments, see Wilson, T. D., and Schooler, J. W., "Thinking too much: Introspection can reduce the quality of preferences and decisions," *Journal of Personality and Social Psychology* 60 (1991): 181–192. His research finding that people misremember the intensity of their feelings is described in

Wilson et al. (2003). For further reading on the nature and consequences of our two mental systems I recommend Wilson's book, *Strangers to Ourselves: Discovering the Adaptive Unconscious* (Belknap Press, 2002).

The love on a suspension bridge study is described in Dutton and Aron (1974), while the adrenaline study is described in Schachter and Singer (1962).

CHAPTER V. I, ROBOT?

More information about the Doneger Group and the Color Association of America can be found on their websites, at http://www.doneger.com/web/231.htm and http://www.colorassociation.com/site/History.pdf. Another facet of the fashion industry can be seen in Gavenas, M. L., *Color Stories: Behind the Scenes of America's Billion-Dollar Beauty Industry*, Simon & Schuster (2007). For further reading on how marketers and designers co-opt styles and their identity connotations, see Frank, T., *The Conquest of Cool: Business Culture, Counterculture, and the Rise of Hip Consumerism*, University of Chicago Press (1998).

The description of the Gehry Building is quoted from Ourousoff (2007). *The Devil Wears Prada* quote is from the film version, which is based on the book by Lauren Weisberger (2003), loosely based on her time as an assistant to Anna Wintour, the editor of *Vogue*.

Penn & Teller's bottled water trick is from episode 7 of the first season. The results of their taste test are far from unique; a taste test conducted by *Good Morning America* in 2001 similarly found NYC tap water to be the clear winner with 45 percent of the votes, nearly twice as many as the most popular bottled water, as described at http://abcnews.go.com/GMA/story?id=126984&page=1. The wine pricing study is Plassmann et al. (2008), and the study also includes an fMRI component similar to the Coke one described later.

The percent of bottled water consumers expressing concerns about safety is from the "Consumer Attitude Survey on Water Quality Issues" (1993) survey by the American Water Works Association Research Foundation, and the figures on bottled water consumption are from the first chapter of Royte (2008). The relative quality of tap and bottled water, and the percent of bottled waters that begin life as tap water, are from the report "Bottled Water: Pure Drink or Pure Hype?" by the Natural Resources

Defense Council. Poland Spring's liberal interpretation of "spring" resulted in a class-action lawsuit in 2003, which it settled the same year for $10 million without admitting wrongdoing, as reported on NPR (Brooks, 2003).

More details on puffery, including a list of unappetizing cosmetic gimmick ingredients like "chick embryo extract, horse blood serum, and pigskin extracts," can be found in Foulke (1995). The similarities between Lancôme and Maybelline foundations is one of several examples from Begoun (2006). In the section inspired by *The Matrix* (1999), the mysterious man's dialogue is composed of direct quotes from the character Morpheus in the film.

The fMRI study of soft drink preferences is described in McClure et al. (2004b). One prominent case in which blind taste tests have revealed a difference between Coke and Pepsi is the Pepsi Challenge, a series of commercials run by Pepsi in the 1970s and 1980s claiming that a majority of die-hard Coke drinkers preferred Pepsi when drinking from cups labeled with arbitrary letters instead of logos. The Pepsi Challenge provided the impetus for the disastrous introduction of New Coke, Goizueta's biggest misstep during his leadership of the company. The reformulated New Coke outperformed Pepsi in blind taste tests but possessed none of the original's feel-good associations in the minds of the public, and was quickly removed from the market amid flagging sales, boycotts, and even letter-writing campaigns to bring back the original formula.

In his book *Blink,* Malcolm Gladwell attributes the results of the Pepsi Challenge to the "sip test" format of the event, which gave the slightly sweeter Pepsi an advantage. Another possible explanation is that tasters had been influenced by priming of a different sort: The Pepsi cups had been accidentally or deliberately assigned letters with more positive connotations… at least according to Coke. As described in Hughes, M., *Buzzmarketing: Getting People to Talk about Your Stuff*, Portfolio (2005), ads produced by Coca-Cola had a psychologist declare that "M [Pepsi] stands for words like mellow and mild. And Q [Coke] stands for queer," and later, "L [Pepsi] stands for lovely, and light…and you know what S [Coke] stands for." (Hint: It's a word Penn Jillette is quite fond of.) Coke later ran ads comparing the Pepsi Challenge to asking which of two tennis balls was fuzzier, implicitly acknowledging that the two products were effectively identical.

Bargh's study on how priming can affect walking speed is described in Bargh et al. (1996), and his quote on automaticity is from Bargh (1997). The effect of subliminal messages on hunger is described in Byrne (1959). The most famous example of subliminal advertising is a study that claimed briefly flashing the messages "Drink Coca-Cola" and "Hungry? Eat popcorn" on the screen of a movie theater dramatically increased sales of those items. This study, which led to a public outcry against the practice and its banning by media networks, was later revealed to have been based on fabricated data. For more details, see the article "Subliminal Advertising" on Snopes.com, available online at http://www.snopes.com/business/hidden/popcorn.asp.

Marketers and other opinion shapers do not rely solely on priming but take full advantage of other cognitive biases as well, including the ones described in the previous chapter. The store that offers a "discount for paying in cash" rather than a "credit card surcharge" is using framing, and the infamous HeadOn ads use repetition to increase the product's availability in consumers' minds.

The effects of voting in a school are described in Berger at al. (2008), the effects of height on earnings can be found in Judge and Cable (2004) and Persico et al. (2004), and the predictive power of split-second competence judgments is described in Ballew and Todorov (2007). The rest of the various ways we can be led astray by appearances even when making highly consequential decisions are reviewed in Cialdini (1998). For more information, see chapter 3 of *Blink*, "The Warren Harding Error: Why We Fall for Tall, Dark, and Handsome Men." The effects of ballot order in the 2000 elections are described in Krosnick et al. (2004).

CHAPTER VI. LORD OF THE THINGS

At the time I began collecting data for the child studies that would eventually become Iyengar and Lepper (1999), the dominant paradigm for comparing choice and no-choice conditions was based on Zuckerman, M., Porac, J., Lathin, D., Smith, R., and Deci, E. L., "On the importance of self-determination for intrinsically motivated behavior," *Personality and Social Psychology Bulletin* 4 (1978): 443–446, which either allowed participants to choose which of six puzzles to complete or assigned puzzles by an experimenter. For further reading on the theories linking choice and motivation, see DeCharms, R., *Personal Causation: The Internal*

Affective Determinants of Behavior, Academic Press (1968), and Deci, E. L., and Ryan, R. M., *Intrinsic Motivation and Self-Determination in Human Behavior,* Plenum (1985). The various examples of limits on our information-processing abilities are all drawn from Miller (1956). The fact that the choice set used in Zuckerman et al. falls just under the magical number 7 might have contributed to its success but was almost certainly unintentional.

My study in Draeger's is from Iyengar and Lepper (2000). Another study from that paper found similar results in a laboratory setting that gave participants a choice between 6 or 30 pieces of Godiva chocolate. Subsequent research finding that it's possible to have too much choice includes Chernev, A., "When more is less and less is more: The role of ideal point availability and assortment in consumer choice," *Journal of Consumer Research* 30 (2003): 170–183, which also used chocolates; Reutskaja, E., and Hogarth, R., "Satisfaction in choice as a function of the number of alternatives: When goods satiate," *Psychology and Marketing* 26 (3) (2009): 197–203; and Shah, A. M., and Wolford, G., "Buying behavior as a function of parametric variation of number of choices," *Psychological Science* 18 (2007): 369–370.

Statistics on the growth in consumer products (specifically, in products with UPC codes) in the economy as a whole can be found in Weinstein and Broda (2007). The figure for supermarket inventories in 1949 is from *The Supermarket Industry Speaks: 1965,* and the *2005* figure is from a more recent version of the same publication, rebranded in the interim as *The Food Marketing Industry Speaks: 2005.* Walmart inventories are from Zook and Graham (2006), and the number of options available online are taken directly from their respective websites.

The percent of online-only sales is from Anderson (2006), while the description of customers' purchasing habits is from Elberse (2007). These findings, along with research on the benefits of the tail for producers, are further described by Elberse in "Should You Invest in the Long Tail?" from the July–August 2008 issue of the *Harvard Business Review,* with the conclusion that Internet marketing may concentrate success on a smaller number of blockbuster titles, rather than spreading it as the Long Tail theory suggests. Anderson, who maintains a blog on the Long Tail, responded to the article at http://www.longtail.com/the_long_tail/2008/06/excellent-hbr-p.html. The benefits of Procter & Gamble's trimming its product line are reported in Osnos (1997), while Golden Cat's similar success story is from Krum (1994).

The study on chess masters' performance is described in Chase and Simon (1973). Simon's research interests were fantastically diverse, but one contribution relevant to this chapter is his development of the economic concept of "bounded rationality." Classic economic theories typically made the simplifying assumption that people were capable of rationally analyzing the pros and cons of every option in an arbitrarily large choice set to find the one that maximized the benefits to themselves. Simon's influential contribution was the observation that, given the limits on human information processing abilities and the effort involved in comparing options, this process of maximizing could in practice be worse than "satisficing," choosing the first option that met some threshold of quality.

The analysis of 401(k) participation rates and the graph thereof come from Iyengar et al. (2004), and the effects on contribution rates and patterns are from Iyengar and Kamenica (2008). Bush's speech on Medicare reform is given in its entirety in the press release "President Applauds Congress for Passing Historic Medicare Bill" (2003). The volume of discussion and analysis of Plan D is immense; for a brief overview see http://www.medicalnewstoday.com/articles/35664.php. Its benefits in terms of costs and prescription utilization are described in Yin et al. (2008), while the initial enrollment patterns are described in Heiss et al. (2006). Ms. Grant's quote can be found in Pear (2006), and the findings on its perceived simplicity (or lack thereof) more generally are from two Kaiser Family Foundation surveys, "The Public's Health Care Agenda for the New Congress and Presidential Campaign" and "National Surveys of Pharmacists and Physicians, Findings on Medicare Part D," both from 2006.

The door-clicking study was originally described in Shin and Ariely (2004), but is given a more detailed and entertaining treatment in Ariely (2008). The link between food variety and obesity has been demonstrated in Putnam et al. (2002) and Raynor and Epstein (2001), among others. The statistics on Internet time are from Nie and Hillygus (2002), and have almost certainly increased in the meantime, while Shaw's quote comes from Bosman (2006). As much as we like variety, though, we think we like it even more, as seen in Simonson, I., "The effect of purchase quantity and timing on variety-seeking behavior," *Journal of Marketing Research* 27 (1990): 150–162. This study found that when people chose snacks on a day-by-day basis they usually chose their favorite each day, but when required to choose several days' worth in advance they included less preferred items for the sake of variety, failing to realize that any satiation would have time to dissipate in the interval between snacks.

For an in-depth look at the link between increasing choice and regret, including its relationship to maximizing and satisficing as described in the note on Simon above, as well as many of the other challenges faced by modern choosers, I highly recommend Barry Schwartz's *The Paradox of Choice* (Ecco, 2003). De Tocqueville's observation is from page 536 of *Democracy in America*.

The pitfalls of the Swedish pension reform are described in Cronqvist and Thaler (2004). The effects of automatic enrollment on retirement plan participation can be found in Choi et al. (2006), and similarly dramatic results for organ donation can be seen in Johnson, E., and Goldstein, D., "Do defaults save lives?," *Science* 302 (2003): 1338–1339.

My study on magazine assortments is described in Mogilner et al. (2008), and the study on German car buyers is from the working paper "Order in Product Customization Decisions: Evidence from Field Experiments." The interview with Wynton Marsalis took place on July 24, 2008.

CHAPTER VII. AND THEN THERE WERE NONE

The cake or death routine is in the "Church of England Fundamentals" skit from Jordan (1999). The original source of Hippocrates' quote is his *Decorum*, and the information on his theory of humorism and its surprising persistence over time is from Garrison (1966). For those interested in learning more about the placebo effect, its history and an interesting recent development can be found in Silberman, S., "Placebos are getting more effective. Drugmakers are desperate to know why," *Wired Magazine* (August 24, 2009), available online at http://www.wired.com/medtech/drugs/magazine/17–09/ff_placebo_effect?currentPage=all.

The majority of the medical history as it relates to choice, including Hippocrates' concept of the patient-physician relationship more generally, the AMA guidelines, and the cases of Dr. Pratt and the unnamed French physician, are taken from Katz (1984). The percentages of doctors who would inform their patients of a cancer diagnosis are from Schneider (1998).

My study on the effects of choice on real and hypothetical parents' coping is described in Botti et al. (2009). For a broader look at the same data set, see Orfali, K., and Gordon, E., "Autonomy gone awry: A cross-cultural study of parents' experiences in neonatal intensive care units," *Theoretical Medicine and Bioethics* 25 (4) (2004): 329–365. The first quote from Hyde can be found on page 78 of *The Gift*, while the block quote is on page 80.

The Alzheimer's disease forecasts are from Sloane et al. (2002); the cancer figures are from "Probability of Developing Invasive Cancers Over Selected Age Intervals, by Sex, US, 2003–2005," available online at http://www.cancer.org/downloads/stt/CFF2009_ProbDevCancer_7.pdf; and the number of Parkinson's disease cases is from the National Parkinson Foundation's "About Parkinson's Disease" page, available online at http://www.parkinson.org/Page.aspx?pid=225. For a real-life example of the dilemmas these diseases pose, see White, J., "When do families take away the keys? Spokane Woman with Alzheimer's took wrong turn and died," *The Spokesman-Review* October 3, 1999. The study on colostomy complications is described in Amsterlaw et al. (2006), and my study with the yogurts is in Botti and Iyengar (2004).

The button is adapted from a freely available image online at http://www.psdgraphics.com/psd/3d-red-push-button/, and Brehm's description of why you'll want to push it is from Brehm (1966). The case of the forbidden detergent is described in Mazis et al. (1973). The HMO approval ratings are taken from Blendon and Benson (2001), and the study on people's beliefs about their health plans is described in Rechovsky et al. (2002).

The Robbie the Robot study is described in Zanna et al. (1973). The research on how prices affect alcohol and cigarette consumption can be found in Chaloupka et al. (2002) and Becker et al. (1994), respectively. Similar taxes have been proposed for unhealthy foods (sometimes known as the "Twinkie tax"), e.g., in Jacobson, M. F., and Brownell, K. D., "Small taxes on soft drinks and snack foods to promote health," *American Journal of Public Health* 90 (6) (2000): 854–857. The fact that higher taxes can make smokers happier comes from Gruber and Mullainathan (2005), while Canada's problems with excessive taxation are described in Gunby (1994). In an amusing aside, a year later Canada became slightly notorious as the source, rather than the destination, of another smuggled good: full-strength toilets. After a 1995 water-conservation law limited U.S. toilets to only 1.6 gallons per flush, those seeking more powerful plumbing were forced to clandestinely bring it across the Canadian border. These operations were conducted mainly by individual citizens rather than organized criminals, perhaps because no criminal would have wanted the moniker of Commode Kingpin.

Odysseus's command is from page 276 of Robert Fagles's translation of *The Odyssey*. Those wishing to tie themselves to the mast in terms of visiting casinos can do so at http://www.bancop.net/, and anyone wishing to purchase a SnūzNLūz can do so at http://www.thinkgeek.com/stuff/41/snuznluz.shtml. The story behind stickK.com is taken from its "About" page, at http://www.stickk.com/about.php. Save More Tomorrow is described in Thaler and Benartzi (2004), and more information on helping people make good decisions in spite of themselves can be found in Thaler, R., and Sunstein, C., *Nudge: Improving Decisions About Health, Wealth, and Happiness,* Yale University Press (2008). The *Hamlet* quote is from Act 3, Scene 1.

EPILOGUE

The opening quote is from "Little Gidding," and can be found in Eliot (1943). I met with S. K. Jain at his compound in Bangalore on January 5, 2009, at 11 a.m., a date and time with no astrological significance that I am aware of. For more information about his practices, or to get a forecast of your own, you can visit his website at http://www.skjainastro.com/. The information on Jane Aiken Hodge's death is taken from Brown (2009), and her father's poem is included in Aiken (1953).

––––––––

Unless noted otherwise, all Internet-based sources here and in the Bibliography are based on the content available at the given address as of October 15, 2009. If this content has changed or become inaccessible since then, previous versions may be available through the Internet Archive at http://www.archive.org/index.php.

Bibliography

Adams, J. T. *The Epic of America*. Simon Publications (2001).

Ahlburg, D. A. "Predicting the job performance of managers: What do the experts know?" *International Journal of Forecasting* 7 (1992): 467–472.

Aiken, C. *Collected Poems*. Oxford University Press (1953).

Alesina, A., Glaeser, E., and Sacerdote, B. "Why doesn't the US have a European-type welfare state?" *Brookings Papers on Economic Activity* 2 (2001): 187–277.

Alicke, M. D., and Govorun, O. "The better-than-average effect," in Alicke, M. D., Dunning, D. A., and Krueger, J. I. *The Self in Social Judgment*. Psychology Press (2005).

Alwin, D. F., Cohen, R. L., and Newcomb, T. M. *Political Attitudes Over the Life Span: The Bennington Women after Fifty Years*. University of Wisconsin Press (1991).

Ames, S. C., Jones, G. N., Howe, J. T., and Brantley, P. J. "A prospective study of the impact of stress on quality of life: An investigation of low-income individuals with hypertension." *Annals of Behavioral Medicine* 23 (2) (2001): 112–119.

Amsterlaw, J., Zikmund-Fisher, B. J., Fagerlin, A., and Ubel, P. A. "Can avoidance of complications lead to biased healthcare decisions?" *Judgment and Decision Making* 1 (1) (2006): 64–75.

Anderson, C. *The Long Tail*. Hyperion (2006).

Anderson, C., Ames, D., and Gosling, S. "Punishing hubris: The perils of status self-enhancement in teams and organizations." *Personality and Social Psychology Bulletin* 34 (2008): 90–101.

Anderson, T. H. *The Movement and the Sixties*. Oxford University Press (1995).

Ariely, D. *Predictably Irrational*. Harper (2008).

Ariely, D., and Levav, J. "Sequential choice in group settings: Taking the road less traveled and less enjoyed." *Journal of Consumer Research* 27 (3) (2000): 279–290.

Bahn, K. D. "How and when do brand and preferences first form? A cognitive developmental investigation." *The Journal of Consumer Research* 13 (3) (1986): 382–393.

Ballew, C. C., and Todorov, A. "Predicting political elections from rapid and unreflective face judgments." *Proceedings of the National Academy of Sciences* 104 (46) (2008): 17948–17953.

Bargh, J. A. "The Automaticity of Everyday Life," in *The Automaticity of Everyday Life: Advances in Social Cognition,* Volume X. Wyer, R. S., Jr., ed. Lawrence Erlbaum (1997): 1–62.

Bargh, J. A., Chen, M., and Burrows, L. "Automaticity of social behavior: Direct effects of trait construct and stereotype activation on action." *Journal of Personality and Social Psychology* 71 (1996): 230–244.

Becker, G. S., Grossman, M., and Murphy, K. M. "An empirical analysis of cigarette addiction." *The American Economic Review* 84 (3) (1994): 396–418.

Begoun, P. "Best of Beauty 2006." Paula's Choice, Inc. (2006). http://www.cosmeticscop.com/bulletin/BestofBeauty2006.pdf.

Berger, J., and Heath, C. "Where consumers diverge from others: Identity signaling and product domains." *Journal of Consumer Research* 34 (2) (2007): 121–134.

Berger, J., and Heath, C. "Who drives divergence? Identity-signaling, outgroup dissimilarity, and the abandonment of cultural tastes." *Journal of Personality and Social Psychology* 95 (3) (2008): 593–607.

Berger, J., Wheeler, S. C., and Meredith, M. "Contextual priming: Where people vote affects how they vote." *Proceedings of the National Academy of Sciences* 105 (26) (2008): 8846–8849.

"Berlin bear's breakout bid fails." BBC News (August 31, 2004). http://news.bbc.co.uk/2/hi/europe/3612706.stm.

Bernstein, R., and Edwards, T. "An Older and More Diverse Nation by Midcentury." U.S. Census Bureau press release, August 14, 2008.

Berridge, K. C., and Kringelbach, M. L. "Affective neuroscience of pleasure: Reward in humans and animals." *Psychopharmacology (Berl)* 199 (3) (2008): 457–480.

Bjork, J. M., and Hommer, D. W. "Anticipating instrumentally obtained and passively-received rewards: A factorial fMRI investigation." *Behavioral Brain Research* 177 (1) (2007): 165–170.

Björklund, A., and Jäntti, M. "Intergenerational income mobility in Sweden compared to the United States." *The American Economic Review* 87 (5) (1997): 1009–1018.

Blais, J., Memmott, C., and Minzesheimer, B. "Book Buzz: Dave Barry Really Rocks." *USA TODAY* (May 16, 2007). http://www.usatoday.com/life/books/news/2007-05-16-book-buzz_N.htm.

Blendon, R. J., and Benson, J. M. "Americans' views on health policy: A fifty-year historical perspective." *Health Affairs (Project Hope)* 20 (2) (2001): 33–46.

Bosman, J. "The Bright Side of Industry Upheaval." *New York Times* (March 3, 2006).

Botti, S., and Iyengar, S. S. "The psychological pain and pleasure of choosing: When people prefer choosing at the cost of subsequent outcome satisfaction." *Journal of Personality and Social Psychology* 87 (3) (2004): 312–326.

Botti, S., Orfali, K., and Iyengar, S. S. "Tragic choices: Autonomy and emotional response to medical decisions." *Journal of Consumer Research* 36 (2) (2009): 337–353.

"Bottled Water." Penn, Jillette, Teller. *Bullshit!*. Showtime. 2003-03-07. No. 7, season 1.

"Bottled Water: Pure Drink or Pure Hype?" Natural Resources Defense Council (1999). http://www.nrdc.org/water/drinking/bw/bwinx.asp.

Bown, N. J., Read, D., and Summers, B. "The lure of choice." *Journal of Behavioral Decision Making* 16 (4) (2003): 97–308.

Brehm, J. *A Theory of Psychological Reactance*. Academic Press (1966).

Brooks, A. "Poland Spring Settles Class-Action Lawsuit." NPR Morning Edition (September 4, 2003). http://www.npr.org/templates/story/story.php?storyId=1419713.

Brown, D. "Romantic Novelist Plotted Her Death in Secret, and in Fear." *The Times* (July 29, 2009). http://www.timesonline.co.uk/tol/life_and_style/health/article6731176.ece.

Bumiller, E. *May You Be the Mother of a Hundred Sons: A Journey Among the Women of India*. Random House (1990).

Byrne, D. "The effect of a subliminal food stimulus on verbal responses." *Journal of Applied Psychology* 43 (4) (1959): 249–251.

Callahan, S. *Adrift: Seventy-six Days Lost at Sea*. Houghton Mifflin (1986).

Camus, A. *The Myth of Sisyphus*. Justin O'Brien, trans. Vintage/Random House (1955).

Capellanus, A. *The Art of Courtly Love*, John Jay Parry, trans. Columbia University Press (1941). (Reprinted: Norton, 1969).

Catania, A. C. "Freedom and knowledge: An experimental analysis of preference in pigeons." *Journal of the Experimental Analysis of Behavior* 24 (1975): 89–106.

Chaloupka, F. J., Grossman, M., and Saffer, H. "The effects of price on alcohol consumption and alcohol-related problems." *Alcohol Research & Health* 26 (1) (2002): 22–34.

Chaplin, C., dir. *Modern Times*. Chaplin, C., and Goddard, P., perf. United Artists (1936).

Chase, W. G., and Simon, H. A. "Perception in chess." *Cognitive Psychology* 4 (1973): 55–61.

Chaucer, G. *The Canterbury Tales*, Daniel Cook, ed. Doubleday (1961).

Cheever, S. *American Bloomsbury: Louisa May Alcott, Ralph Waldo Emerson, Margaret Fuller, Nathaniel Hawthorne, and Henry David Thoreau; Their Lives, Their Loves, Their Work*. Large print edition. Thorndike Press (2006).

Chernev, A. "When more is less and less is more: The role of ideal point availability and assortment in consumer choice." *Journal of Consumer Research* 30 (2003): 170–183.

Choi, J., Laibson, D., Madrian, B., and Metrick, A. "Saving for Retirement on the Path of Least Resistance," in Ed McCaffrey and Joel Slemrod, eds., *Behavioral Public Finance: Toward a New Agenda*. Russell Sage Foundation (2006), pp. 304–351.

Church of England (1662). *The Book of Common Prayer.* Everyman's Library (1999).

Cialdini, R. B. *Influence: The Psychology of Persuasion,* rev. ed. Collins (1998).

Clubb, R., and Mason, G. "Captivity effects on wide-ranging carnivores." *Nature* 425 (2003): 473–474.

Clubb, R., Rowcliffe, M., Mar, K. J., Lee, P., Moss, C., and Mason, G. J. "Compromised survivorship in zoo elephants." *Science* 322 (2008): 1949.

Confucius. *The Analects.* Lau, D. C., trans. Chinese University Press (1983).

Connolly, K. "Germans Hanker after Barrier." *The Guardian,* November 8, 2007.

Coontz, S. *Marriage, a History: From Obedience to Intimacy, or How Love Conquered Marriage.* Viking Adult (2005).

Couch, K. A., and Dunn, T. A. "Intergenerational correlations in labor market status: A comparison of the United States and Germany." *The Journal of Human Resources* 32 (1) (1997): 210–232.

Cronqvist, H., and Thaler, R. "Design choices in privatized social-security systems: Learning from the Swedish experience." *American Economic Review* 94 (2004): 424–428.

Delgado, M. R. "Reward-related responses in the human striatum." *Annals of the New York Academy of Sciences* 1104 (2007): 70–88.

DeLillo, D. *White Noise.* Penguin Books (1986).

DeLongis, A., Folkman, S., and Lazarus, R. S. "The impact of daily stress on health and mood: Psychological and social resources as mediators." *Journal of Personality and Social Psychology* 54 (3) (1988): 486–495.

Dennett, D. C. *Kinds of Minds: Toward an Understanding of Consciousness.* Basic Books (1997).

De Tocqueville, A. *Democracy in America.* Harper & Row (1969).

DeVoe, S. E., and Iyengar, S. S. "Managers' theories of subordinates: A cross-cultural examination of manager perceptions of motivation and appraisal of performance." *Organizational Behavior and Human Decision Processing* 93 (2004): 47–61.

Didion, J. *The White Album.* Simon & Schuster (1979).

Donne, J. *Devotions Upon Emergent Occasions.* J. Sparrow, ed. Cambridge University Press (1923).

Dr. Seuss. *Oh, the Places You'll Go!* Random House Children's Books (1990).

Dutton, D. G., and Aron, A. P. "Some evidence for heightened sexual attraction under conditions of high anxiety." *Journal of Personality and Social Psychology* 30 (1974): 510–517.

Edwards, M. R., and Ewen, A. J. *360° Feedback: The Powerful New Model for Employee Assessment and Performance Improvement*. AMACOM American Management Association (1996).

Ekman, P. *Telling Lies: Clues to Deceit in the Marketplace, Politics, and Marriage, Third Edition*. W. W. Norton & Co. (2001).

Eliot, T. S. *Four Quartets*. Harcourt, Brace, and Company (1943).

Elliot, A. J., and Devine, P. G. "On the motivational nature of cognitive dissonance: Dissonance as psychological discomfort." *Journal of Personality and Social Psychology* 67 (1994): 382–394.

Emerson, R. W. "Self-Reliance," in *Essays: First Series*. (1847).

Ericsson, K. A., Krampe, R. T., and Tesch-Römer, C. "The role of deliberate practice in the acquisition of expert performance." *Psychological Review* 100 (3) (1993): 363–406.

Feinberg, R. A. "Credit Cards as Spending Facilitating Stimuli: A Conditioning Interpretation," *Journal of Consumer Research* 12 (1986): 384–356.

Festinger, L. *A Theory of Cognitive Dissonance*. Stanford University Press (1957).

Foulke, J. E. "Cosmetic Ingredients: Understanding the Puffery." *FDA Consumer*, Publication No. (FDA) 95-5013 (1995).

Frankel, D., dir. *The Devil Wears Prada*. 20th Century Fox Home Entertainment (2006).

Franklin, B. *Poor Richard's Almanack*. Paul Volcker, ed. Skyhorse Publishing (2007).

Franklin, B. *Private Correspondence of Benjamin Franklin*, Volume 1. Franklin, W. T., ed. R. Bentley (1833), pp. 16–17.

"Freedom!" *Time* (November 20, 1989).

Friedman, H. S., and Booth-Kewley, S. "The 'disease-prone personality': A meta-analytic view of the construct." *American Psychologist* 42 (6) (1987): 539–555.

Fromm, E. *Escape from Freedom*. Farrar & Rinehart (1941).

Frost, R. "The Road Not Taken," in *The Poetry of Robert Frost*. Edward Connery Lathem, ed. Holt, Rinehart and Winston (1969).

Gallagher, R. P., Borg, S., Golin, A., and Kelleher, K. "The personal, career, and learning needs of college students." *Journal of College Student Development* 33 (4) (1992): 301–310.

Garrison, F. H. *An Introduction to the History of Medicine.* W. B. Saunders Company (1966).

Gigerenzer, G. *Gut Feelings: The Intelligence of the Unconscious.* Viking Adult (2007).

Gilbert, D. *Stumbling on Happiness.* Vintage (2007).

Gladwell, M. *Blink: The Power of Thinking Without Thinking.* Little, Brown and Company (2005).

Grossman, L. "They Just Won't Grow Up." *Time* (January 6, 2005).

Gruber, J. H., and Mullainathan, S. "Do cigarette taxes make smokers happier?" *Advances in Economic Analysis and Policy* 5 (1) (2005), article 4.

Guerrero, L. K., Anderson, P. A., and Afifi, W. A. *Close Encounters: Communication in Relationships.* Sage Publications (2007).

Gunby, P. "Canada reduces cigarette tax to fight smuggling." *Journal of the American Medical Association* 271 (9) (1994): 647.

Gupta, U., and Singh, P. "Exploratory study of love and liking and types of marriage." *Indian Journal of Applied Psychology* 19 (1982): 92–97.

Harlow, J., and Montague, B. "Scientists Discover True Love." *The Sunday Times* (January 4, 2009) http://women.timesonline.co.uk/tol/life_ and_style/women/relationships/article5439805.ece.

Heath, C., and Heath, D. *Made to Stick: Why Some Ideas Survive and Others Die.* Random House (2007).

Heiss, F., McFadden, D., and Winter, J. "Who Failed to Enroll in Medicare Part D, and Why? Early Results." Health Affairs Web Exclusive (August 1, 2006): W344-W354 http://content.healthaffairs.org/cgi/content/abstract/hlthaff.25.w344.

Hejinian, L. "The rejection of closure," *Poetics Journal* 4: *Women and Language Issue* (1984): 134–136.

Hofstede, G. *Culture's Consequences: International Differences in Work-Related Values.* Sage Publications (1980).

Homer. *The Odyssey.* Robert Fagles, trans. Penguin Classics (1999).

Hunter, J. E., and Hunter, R. F., "Validity and Utility of Alternative Predictors of Job Performance." *Psychological Bulletin* 96 (1) (1984): 72–98.

Huntington, S. P. *The Clash of Civilizations and the Remaking of World Order*. Simon & Schuster (1996).

Hyde, L. *The Gift: Imagination and the Erotic Life of Property*. Vintage Books (1983).

Iyengar, S. S., and Ames, D. R. "Appraising the unusual: Framing effects and moderators of uniqueness-seeking and social projection." *Journal of Experimental Social Psychology* 41 (3) (2005): 271–282.

Iyengar, S. S., Huberman, G., and Jiang, W. "How Much Choice Is Too Much? Contributions to 401(k) Retirement Plans," in Mitchell, O. S., and Utkus, S., eds. *Pension Design and Structure: New Lessons from Behavioral Finance*. Oxford University Press (2004): 83–95.

Iyengar, S. S., and Kamenica, E. "Choice Proliferation, Simplicity Seeking, and Asset Allocation." Working paper (2008) http://faculty.chicago-booth.edu/emir.kamenica/documents/simplicitySeeking.pdf.

Iyengar, S. S., and Lepper, M. R. "Rethinking the value of choice: A cultural perspective on intrinsic motivation." *Journal of Personality and Social Psychology* 76 (3) (1999): 349–366.

Iyengar, S. S., Wells, R. E., and Schwartz, B. "Doing better but feeling worse: Looking for the 'best' job undermines satisfaction." *Psychological Science* 17 (2) (2006): 143–150.

Jordan, L., dir. *Dress to Kill*. Izzard, E., perf. WEA Corp. (1999).

Judge, T. A., and Cable, D. M. "The Effect of Physical Height on Workplace Success and Income: Preliminary Test of a Theoretical Model." *Journal of Applied Psychology* 89 (2004): 428–441.

Kahneman, D., Kruger, A. B., Schkade, D., Schwartz, N., and Stone, A. A. "Would you be happier if you were richer? A focusing illusion." *Science* 312 (2006): 1908–1910.

Kalueff, A.V., Wheaton, M., and Murphy, D. L. "What's wrong with my mouse model? Advances and strategies in animal modeling of anxiety and depression." *Behavioral Brain Research* 179 (1) (2007): 1–18.

Katz, J. *The Silent World of Doctor and Patient*. Free Press, Collier Macmillan (1984).

Keillor, G. *A Prairie Home Companion*. Minnesota Public Radio (1974–present).

Kenny, D. A., and DePaulo, B. M. "Do people know how others view them?: An empirical and theoretical account." *Psychological Bulletin* 114 (1993): 145–161.

Kifner, J. "Stay-at-Home SWB, 8, Into Fitness, Seeks Thrills." *New York Times* (July 2, 1994). http://www.nytimes.com/1994/07/02/nyregion/about-new-york-stay-at-home-swb-8-into-fitness-seeks-thrills.html.

Kitayama, S., Markus, H. R., Matsumoto, H., and Norasakkunkit, V. "Individual and collective processes in the construction of the self: Self-enhancement in the United States and self-criticism in Japan." *Journal of Personality and Social Psychology* 72 (6) (1997): 1245–1267.

Koch, E. *The Complete Taj Mahal: And the Riverfront Gardens of Agra.* Thames & Hudson Ltd. (2006).

Kokis, J. V., Macpherson, R., Toplak, M. E., West, R. F., and Stanovich, K. E. "Heuristic and analytic processing: Age trends and associations with cognitive ability and cognitive styles." *Journal of Experimental Child Psychology* 83 (2002): 26–52.

Kroll, L., Miller, M., and Serafin, T. "The World's Billionaires (2009)" *Forbes.* http://www.forbes.com/2009/03/11/worlds-richest-people-billionaires-2009-billionaires_land.html.

Krosnick, J. A., Miller, J. M., and Tichy, M. P. "An Unrecognized Need for Ballot Reform: The Effects of Candidate Name Order on Election Outcomes," in Crigler, A. N., Just, M. R., and McCaffery, E. J., eds. *Rethinking the Vote: The Politics and Prospects of American Election Reform.* Oxford University Press (2004).

Krueger, J. "Return of the Ego—Self-Referent Information as a Filter for Social Prediction: Comment on Karniol (2003)." *Psychological Review* 110 (3) (2003): 585–590.

Krum, F. "Quantum leap: Golden Cat Corp.'s success with category management." *Progressive Grocer*, Golden Cat Corp. (1994): 41–43.

Langer, E. J., and Rodin, J. "The effects of choice and enhanced personal responsibility for the aged: A field experiment in an institutional setting." *Journal of Personality and Social Psychology* 34 (2) (1976): 191–198.

Lehrer, J. *How We Decide.* Houghton Mifflin Co. (2009).

Leonardelli, G. J. "The Motivational Underpinnings of Social Discrimination: A Test of the Self-Esteem Hypothesis." Unpublished master's thesis (1998).

Leonardelli, G. J., and Brewer, M. B. "Minority and majority discrimination: When and why." *Journal of Experimental Social Psychology* 37 (2001): 468–485.

Lewis, M., Alessandri, S. M., and Sullivan, M. W. "Violation of expectancy, loss of control, and anger expressions in young infants." *Developmental Psychology* 26 (5) (1990): 745–751.

Lewis, S. *Main Street: The Story of Carol Kennicott.* Harcourt, Brace and Company (1921).

Lindblom, E. *Raising Cigarette Taxes Reduces Smoking, Especially Among Kids (and the Cigarette Companies Know It).* Campaign for Tobacco Free Kids (2005).

Mahler, L, Greenberg, L., and Hayashi, H. "A comparative study of rules of justice: Japanese versus American." *Psychologia* 24 (1981): 1–8.

Marchand, R. *Advertising the American Dream: Making Way for Modernity, 1920–1940.* University of California Press (1986).

Marshall, C. "Tiger Kills 1 After Escaping at San Francisco Zoo," *New York Times* (December 26, 2007). http://www.nytimes.com/2007/12/26/us/26tiger.html?_r=1&scp=5&sq=tatiana%20tiger&st=cse.

Marx, K., and Engels, F. *The Marx-Engels Reader.* Robert C. Tucker, ed. Norton (1972).

Masuda, T., and Nisbett, R. E. "Attending holistically versus analytically: Comparing the context sensitivity of Japanese and Americans." *Journal of Personality and Social Psychology* 81 (2001): 992–934 doi: 10.1037/0022–3514.81.5.922.

Mazis, M. B., Settle, R. B., and Leslie, D. C. "Elimination of phosphate detergents and psychological reactance." *Journal of Marketing Research* 10 (1973): 390–395.

McClure, S. M., Laibson, D. I., Lowenstein, G., and Cohen, J. D. "Separate neural systems value immediate and delayed monetary rewards." *Science* 306 (2004a): 503–507.

McClure, S. M., Li, J., Tomlin, D., Cypert, K. S., Montague, L. M., and Montague, P. R. "Neural correlates of behavioral preference for culturally familiar drinks." *Neuron* 44 (2) (2004b): 379–387.

McDaniel, M. A., Whetzel, D. L., Schmidt, F. L., and Maurer, S. D. "The Validity of Employment Interviews: A Comprehensive Review and Meta-Analysis." *Journal of Applied Psychology* 79 (4) (1994): 599–616.

McNeil, B. J., Pauker, S. G., and Tversky, A. "On the Framing of Medical Decisions," in Bell, D. E., Raiffa, H., and Tversky, A., eds. *Decision Making: Descriptive, Normative, and Prescriptive Interactions.* Cambridge University Press (1988), pp. 562–568.

Menon, T., Morris, M. W., Chiu, C., and Hong, Y. "Culture and the construal of agency: Attribution to individual versus group dispositions." *Journal of Personality and Social Psychology* 76 (1999): 701–717.

Mill, J. S. *On Liberty and Other Writings*. Stefan Collini, ed. Cambridge University Press (1989).

Miller, G. "The magical number seven, plus or minus two: Some limits on our capacity for processing information." *The Psychological Review* 63 (2) (1956): 81–97.

Mischel, W., Ebbesen, E. B., and Raskoff Zeiss, A. "Cognitive and attentional mechanisms in delay of gratification." *Journal of Personality and Social Psychology* 21 (2) (February 1972): 204–218.

Mogilner, C., Rudnick, T., and Iyengar, S. S. "The mere categorization effect: How the presence of categories increases choosers' perceptions of assortment variety and outcome satisfaction." *Journal of Consumer Research* 35 (2) (2008): 202–215.

Murphy, J., trans. Introduction to *Where Is Science Going?* by Max Planck. Allen & Unwin (1933): 7.

Newcomb, T. M. "Attitude Development as a Function of Reference Groups: The Bennington Study," in *Readings In Social Psychology*, 3d ed., Eleanor E. Maccoby, Theodore M. Newcomb, and Eugene L. Hartley, eds. Henry Holt and Co. (1958): 265–275.

Nie, N. H., and Hillygus, D. S. "Where does Internet time come from?: A reconnaissance." *IT & Society* 1 (2) (2002): 1–20.

Ochsner, K. N., and Gross, J. J. "The cognitive control of emotion." *Trends in Cognitive Science* 9 (5) (2005): 242–249.

"Orangutan Escapes Pen at US Zoo." BBC News (May 18, 2008). http://news.bbc.co.uk/2/hi/americas/7407050.stm.

Orwell, G. *1984*. Harcourt Brace Jovanovich (1977).

Osnos, E. "Too Many Choices? Firms Cut Back on New Products." *Philadelphia Inquirer* (September 27, 1997): DI, D7.

Ouroussoff, N. "Gehry's New York Debut: Subdued Tower of Light." *New York Times* (March 22, 2007).

Parsons, O. A., and Schneider, J. M. "Locus of control in university students from Eastern and Western societies." *Journal of Consulting and Clinical Psychology* 42 (1974): 456–461.

Pear, R. "Final Rush to Make Deadline for Drug Coverage." *New York Times* (May 16, 2006).

Persico, N., Postlewaite, A., and Silverman, D. "The Effect of Adolescent Experience on Labor Market Outcomes: The Case of Height." *Journal of Political Economy* 112 (5) (2004): 1019–1053.

Pendergrast, M. *For God, Country and Coca-Cola: The Unauthorized History of the Great American Soft Drink and the Company that Makes It.* Maxwell Macmillan (1993).

Peterson, J. S. *American Automobile Workers, 1900–1933.* State University of New York Press (1988).

Piper, W. *The Little Engine That Could.* Illustrated by George and Doris Hauman. Grosset & Dunlap (1978).

Plassmann, H., O'Doherty, J., Shiv, B., and Rangel, A. "Marketing actions can modulate neural representations of experienced pleasantness." *Proceedings of the National Academy of Sciences* 105 (3) (2008): 1050–1054.

Plous, S. *The Psychology of Judgment and Decision Making.* McGraw-Hill (1993).

Prelec, D., and Simester, D., "Always leave home without it: A further investigation of the credit-card effect on willingness to pay," *Marketing Letters* 12 (1) (2001): 5–12.

Pronin, E., Berger, J., and Moulouki, S. "Alone in a crowd of sheep: Asymmetric perceptions of conformity and their roots in an introspection Illusion." *Journal of Personality and Social Psychology* 92 (2007): 585–591.

Putnam, J., Allshouse, J., and Kantor, L. S. "U.S. per capita food supply trends: More çalories, refined carbohydrates, and fats." *FoodReview* 25 (3) (2002). http://www.ers.usda.gov/publications/FoodReview/DEC2002/frvol25i3a.pdf.

Putnam, R. D. "Bowling alone: America's declining social capital." *Journal of Democracy* 6 (1) (1995): 65–78.

Putnam, R. D. *Bowling Alone: The Collapse and Revival of American Community.* Simon & Schuster (2000).

Raynor, H. A., and Epstein, L. H. "Dietary variety, energy regulation, and obesity." *Psychological Bulletin* 127 (3) (2001): 325–341.

"Report of the Day Trading Project Group." North American Securities Administrators' Association Inc. (1999). http://www.nasaa.org/content/Files/NASAA_Day_Trading_Report.pdf.

Reschovsky, J. D., Hargraves, J. L., and Smith, A. F. "Consumer beliefs and health plan performance: It's not whether you are in an HMO but whether you think you are." *Journal of Health Politics, Policy and Law* 27 (3) (2002): 353–377.

Reutskaja, E., and Hogarth, R. M. "Satisfaction in choice as a function of the number of alternatives: When goods satiate." *Psychology and Marketing* 26 (3) (2009): 197–203.

Richter, C. P. "On the phenomenon of sudden death in animals and man." *Psychosomatic Medicine* 19 (1957): 191–198.

Rilke, R. M. "The Panther," in *The Selected Poetry of Rainer Maria Rilke*, Mitchell, S., ed., trans. Vintage (1989).

Rose, N. *Powers of Freedom.* Cambridge University Press (1999).

Royte, E. *Bottlemania.* Bloomsbury USA (2008).

Schachter, S., and Singer, J. "Cognitive, social, and physiological determinants of emotional state." *Psychological Review* 69 (1962): 379–399.

Schneider, C. E. *The Practice of Autonomy: Patients, Doctors, and Medical Decisions.* Oxford University Press (1998).

Schiller, R. J. *The Subprime Solution: How Today's Global Financial Crisis Happened, and What to Do About It.* Princeton University Press (2008).

Seligman, M. E. P., and Maier, S. F. "Failure to escape traumatic shock." *Journal of Experimental Psychology* 74 (1967): 1–9.

Selye, H. "The general adaptation syndrome and the diseases of adaptation." *Journal of Clinical Endocrinology* 6 (1946): 117–230.

Sethi, S., and Seligman, M. E. P. "Optimism and fundamentalism." *Psychological Science* 4 (1993): 256–259.

Shah, A. M., and Wolford, G. "Buying behavior as a function of parametric variation of number of choices." *Psychological Science* 18 (2007): 369–370.

Shales, T. "The Day the Wall Cracked: Brokaw's Live Broadcast Tops Networks' Berlin Coverage." *Washington Post*, November 10, 1989.

Shaw, G. B. *The Doctor's Dilemma, Getting Married, and The Shewing-up of Blanco Posnet.* Brentano's (1911).

Shin, J., and Ariely, D. "Keeping doors open: The effect of unavailability on incentives to keep options viable." *Management Science* 50 (5) (2004): 575–586.

Shoda, Y., Mischel, W., and Peake, P. K. "Predicting adolescent cognitive and self-regulatory competencies from preschool delay of gratification:

Identifying diagnostic conditions. *Developmental Psychology* 26 (6) (November 1990): 978–986.

Simon, H. A. "What is an explanation of behavior?" *Psychological Science* 3 (1992): 150–161.

Simpson, J. *Touching the Void.* Harper Collins (1988).

Slater, L. "True Love." *National Geographic* (February 2006).

Sloane, P. D., Zimmerman, S., Suchindran, C., Reed, P., Wang, L., Boustani, M., Sudha, S. "The public health impact of Alzheimer's disease, 2000–2050: Potential implication of treatment advances." *Annual Review of Public Health* 23 (2002): 213–231.

Smith, A. *The Wealth of Nations.* Modern Library (2000).

Smith, D. K. *Discipline of Teams: Sealed Air Corp.* Harvard Business Publishing (1994). Prod. #: 6778-VID-ENG.

Snyder, M., and Swann, W. B., Jr. "Hypothesis-testing processes in social interactions." *Journal of Personality and Social Psychology* 36 (11) (1978): 1202–1212.

Sowell, E. R., Thompson, P. M., Tessner, K. D., and Toga, A. W. "Mapping continued brain growth and gray matter density reduction in the dorsal frontal cortex: inverse relationships during postadolescent brain maturation." *The Journal of Neuroscience* 21 (22) (2001): 8819–8829.

Srull, T. K., and Gaelick, L. "General principles and individual differences in the self as a habitual reference point: An examination of self-other judgments of similarity." *Social Cognition* 2 (1983): 108–121.

Stanton, A., dir. *Wall-E.* Walt Disney Home Entertainment (2008).

Statistical Abstracts of the United States: 1997. U.S. Bureau of the Census. Washington, DC (1997).

Steigerwald, D. "Did the Protestant ethic disappear? The virtue of thrift on the cusp of postwar affluence." *Enterprise & Society* 9 (4) (2008): 788–815.

Sternbergh, A. "Stephen Colbert Has America by the Ballots." *New York* (October 16, 2006).

Styron, W. *Sophie's Choice.* Random House (1979).

Surowiecki, J. "Day Trading Is for Suckers." Slate.com (August 3, 1999). http://www.slate.com/id/1003329/.

Susman, W. *Culture as History: The Transformation of American Society in the Twentieth Century.* Pantheon Books (1984).

Suzuki, S. "Selection of forced- and free choice by monkeys (*Macaca fas-cicularis*)." *Perceptual and Motor Skills* 88 (1999): 242–250.

Swann, W. B., Jr., Rentfrow, P. J., and Guinn, J. S. "Self-Verification: The Search for Coherence," in *Handbook of Self and Identity*, Leary, M. R., and Tagney, J. P., eds. Guilford Press (2003): 367–383.

Tarver, J. D. "Lifetime migration to the major cities of the United States, Asia, and Africa." *Genus* 48 (3–4) (1992): 63–71.

Taylor, F. W. *The Principles of Scientific Management* (1911). Kessinger Publishing (2004).

Taylor, S. E., Kemeny, M. E., Reed, G. M., Bower, J. E., and Gruenewald, T. L. "Psychological resources, positive illusions, and health." *American Psychologist* 55 (1) (2000): 99–109.

Taylor, S. E., Lichtman, R. R., and Wood, J. V. "Attributions, beliefs about control, and adjustment to breast cancer." *Journal of Personality and Social Psychology* 46 (1984): 489–502.

Tetlock, P. E. "Correspondence and Coherence: Indicators of Good Judgment in World Politics," in Hardman, D., and Macchi, L., eds. *Thinking: Psychological Perspectives on Reason, Judgment, and Decision Making.* John Wiley & Sons Ltd. (2003).

Thaler, R., and Benartzi, S. "Save more tomorrow: Using behavioral economics to increase employee saving." *Journal of Political Economy* 112 (1) (2004): 164–187.

Thaler, R., and Sunstein, C. *Nudge: Improving Decisions About Health, Wealth, and Happiness.* Yale University Press (2008).

The Food Marketing Industry Speaks: 2005. The Food Marketing Institute, Inc. (2005).

The Supermarket Industry Speaks: 1965. The Super Market Institute, Inc. (1965).

Tichy, N. M., and Cohen, E. B. *The Leadership Engine: How Winning Companies Build Leaders at Every Level.* HarperCollins (1997).

Triandis, H. *Individualism and Collectivism.* Westview Press (1995).

Tricomi, E. M., Delgado, M. R., and Fiez, J. A. "Modulation of caudate activity by action contingency." *Neuron* 41 (2) (2004): 281–292.

Turner-Cobb, J. M. "Psychological and neuroendocrine correlates of disease progression." *International Review of Neurobiology* 52 (2002): 353–381.

Tversky, A., and Kahneman, D. "Judgments under uncertainty: Heuristics and biases." *Science* 185 (1974): 1124–1131.

Ubel, P. *Free Market Madness.* Harvard Press (2009).

Vienna Declaration and Programme of Action. World Conference on Human Rights, Vienna, June 14–25, 1993.

Voss, S. C., and Homzie, M. J. "Choice as a value." *Psychological Reports* 26 (1970): 912–914.

Wachowski, A., and Wachowski, L., dirs. *The Matrix.* Warner Home Video (1999).

Watson, M., Haviland, J. S., Greer, S., Davidson, J., and Bliss, J. M. "Influence of psychological response on survival in breast cancer: a population-based cohort study." *Lancet* 354 (9187) (1999): 1331–1336.

Weber, M. *The Protestant Ethic and the Spirit of Capitalism.* (1905).

Weinstein, D., and Broda, C. "Product Creation and Destruction: Evidence and Price Implications." *NBER Working Paper* #13041 (2007). http://papers.nber.org/papers/w13041.

Weisberger, L. *The Devil Wears Prada: A Novel.* Doubleday (2003).

Wells, R. E., and Iyengar, S.S. "Positive illusions of preference consistency: When remaining eluded by one's preferences yields greater subjective well-being and decision outcomes." *Organizational Behavior and Human Decision Processes* 98 (1) (2005): 66–87.

Whitman, W. *Leaves of Grass.* D. S. Reynolds, ed. Oxford University Press (2005).

Wilson, T. D., Dunn, D. S., Bybee, J. A., Hyman, D. B., and Rotondo, J. A. "Effects of analyzing reasons on attitude-behavior consistency." *Journal of Personality and Social Psychology* 47 (1) (1984): 5–16.

Wilson, T. D., Lisle, D. J., Schooler, J. W., Hodges, S. D., Klaaren, K. J., and LaFleur, S. J. "Introspecting about reasons can reduce post-choice satisfaction." *Personality and Social Psychology Bulletin* 19 (1993): 331–339.

Wilson, T. D., Meyers, J., and Gilbert, D. T. "'How happy was I, anyway?' A retrospective impact bias." *Social Cognition* 21 (2003): 407–432.

Wilson, T. V. "Why is the birth rate so low for giant pandas?" 08 September 2006. *HowStuffWorks.com.* http://animals.howstuffworks.com/mammals/panda-birth-rate.htm.

Yin, W., Basu, A., Zhang, J., Rabbani, A., Meltzer, D. O., and Alexander, G. C. "The effect of the Medicare Part D prescription benefit on drug utilization and expenditures." *Annals of Internal Medicine* 148 (3) (2008): 169–177.

Zajonc, R. "Attitudinal effects of mere exposure." *Journal of Personality and Social Psychology* 9 (1968): 1–27.

Zanna, M. P., Lepper, M. R., and Abelson, R. P. "Attentional mechanisms in children's devaluation of a forbidden activity in a forced-compliance situation." *Journal of Personality and Social Psychology* 28 (3) (1973): 355–359.

Zook, M., and Graham, M. "Wal-Mart Nation: Mapping the Reach of a Retail Colossus," in *Wal-Mart World: The World's Biggest Corporation in the Global Economy*. Brunn, S. D., ed. Routledge (2006), pp. 15–25.

Index